1001 ideas for
better gardening

CREATIVE
HOMEOWNER®

1001 ideas for
better gardening

Pippa Greenwood

MITCHELL BEAZLEY

635
G8160

First published in North America in 2008 by

CRE🏠TIVE
HOMEOWNER®

Creative Homeowner® is a registered trademark of
Federal Marketing Corporation

ISBN 10: 1-58011-180-7
ISBN 13: 978-1-58011-180-5
Library of Congress Control Number: 2003112510

Current printing (last digit)
10 9 8 7 6 5 4 3 2 1

First published as 1001 Ways to be a Better Gardener
by Mitchell Beazley, an imprint of
Octopus Publishing Group Limited,
2–4 Heron Quays, London E14 4JP.
An Hachette Livre UK Company
www.octopusbooks.co.uk
ISBN 978 1 84533 367 6

Commissioning Editor: Helen Griffin
Art Director: Tim Foster
Art Editor: Victoria Burley
Project Editor: Ruth Patrick
Copy Editor: Candida Frith-Macdonald
Special Photography: Torie Chugg
Picture Research: Mel Watson
Picture Research Manager: Giulia Hetherington
Production Manager: Peter Hunt

Printed and bound in China by Toppan Printing company

CREATIVE HOMEOWNER
A Division of Federal Marketing Corp.
24 Park Way
Upper Saddle River, NJ 07458

www.creativehomeowner.com

Contents

Foreword

There is nothing like a garden to bring enjoyment, and to allow you to relax and feel pride and fulfilment in your achievements. The combination of fresh air, beautiful plants, and some gentle or sometimes not-quite-so gentle exercise is enough to bring a smile to your face. Grow some vegetables, fruit, and herbs and enjoy that feeling of satisfaction and happiness that a garden can bring.

Gardening has the potential to be all these wonderful things, but throw in too many hiccups, and the benefits run the risk of being outweighed by the problems. Gardening is like any hobby and passion; it is not always straightforward. Whether you are new to gardening or have gardened for years, there are still things that you can learn. That goes for each and every one of us, including those of us who earn a living by broadcasting, lecturing, and writing about gardening! If you can learn from other people's experiences and know-how, you can get some useful advice on making gardening easier, quicker, and of course, more successful.

In *1001 Ideas for Better Gardening*, I hope you will find plenty to interest and inspire you, and hopefully also to feel the truly infectious nature of gardening. There is nothing like talking to other gardeners about the problems they have taken on, their successes and failures, and the hints and tips they have to offer. This book is packed full of tips I would like to share with you, as other gardeners have passed their observations on to me. Have fun!

Introduction

If you have just started tackling your garden, there are bound to be many questions, problems, and even minor panics that crop up as you go about your gardening.

Even if you are an experienced gardener, there are still likely to be things you are confronting for the first time, or perhaps simply things that you could do more efficiently or more successfully.

1001 Ideas for Better Gardening should prove useful and interesting if you have a love (even if it is still budding) for your garden and you want to take on more and different aspects of gardening. If you are also keen to find easier, quicker, greener, or less expensive ways to perform any aspect of gardening without having to compromise the end result, then this is the book for you.

It is not a chapter and verse tome that contains an encyclopedic-style reference to every aspect of gardening and every plant. But by reading the relevant section in the appropriate chapter you will find suggestions to help you on your way to a better-looking garden, fewer problems, and perhaps most importantly, a garden that really starts to take its hold over you and provides you with more and more fun.

To me, that is what it should be about. While a garden may need some thought and quite a lot of time spent on it, it should also provide you with a perfect surround to your home, and if you wish, a plentiful supply of fresh, home-grown vegetables and fruit. As a bonus, you get a constant

supply of invigorating, muscle-toning exercise that's much better for you than the sweat-filled atmosphere of most gyms and fitness centers!

Each chapter covers either a different aspect of gardening or the garden itself, so it should be easy to find the information you need before you take on any new area of your garden, or any unfamiliar garden task. If you have taken on a new garden and hope to alter it dramatically or construct it from scratch, then there are also some tips and suggestions for making that initial planning and decision-making process a little easier. For those who have only recently been bitten by the gardening bug, there are chapters on just about every aspect of your garden and its contents—including furniture and patios, fresh-grown food, and pumps for your pond.

You will also find Top Ten Style lists of specific plant recommendations to help you select the plants that will do best in your garden's condition. There is no need to regard these as the only plants worth having, but they are my recommendations for each particular situation. Similar lists for specific gardening techniques, such as various propagation techniques, are also included as a guide.

Whatever your knowledge of gardening and whatever the style of your garden (or the garden you aspire to) you will always find parts of it more fun and easier to look after than others. With the aid of this book, you will start to find those less-appealing parts of your plot and your regime less of a challenge and more of a pleasure.

Getting started

Perhaps you have just taken on a new garden, become a garden owner for the first time, or found yourself with a garden that's different in its opportunities and conditions than any you have managed before. Maybe you need some "inside information." Have you finally decided to come to grips with the garden that's been lurking outside your back door for the last few years? You know it well, but sorting it out and getting it into shape is also likely to make you feel as though you need

some support. Whatever your starting point, you can save yourself a lot of time and effort if you take charge from the beginning.

Taming a new garden
A new garden should be something that gives you a lot of pleasure, but it can also be hard work. There may be moments when you wonder who is in charge, and indeed if you will ever manage to take control. With a bit of forward planning and plenty of thought along

the way, you can make your initial efforts meaningful and pave the way for plenty of great things in the future.

Start by getting to know all your garden's advantages, tricky spots, and problem areas. It's like getting to know someone—you need a while to work out what they are like. Next, arm yourself with some great tools. Finally, give yourself lots of time to work and play in the garden, and use it as a place to relax and feel at home. It's all yours!

This chapter shows you how to

❀ Exploit your garden's areas of sun and shade and its level changes.

❀ Find your soil's pH and texture, and discover local plants that will thrive.

❀ Learn how to improve your soil.

❀ Get equipped with the tools you need.

❀ Make some instant transformations.

❀ Assess fences and structures.

Assessing your garden

You need to take a long, hard look at your garden, ideally in all weather conditions and at various times of year. Once you have formed an accurate picture of all it has to offer, you will be much better equipped to make the right choices and decisions later on.

Apparently empty areas may contain dormant bulbs.

Don't rush

❀ The age-old suggestion that when you move into a new garden you should wait for a full year before you do anything makes a lot of sense. A full four seasons allows time for everything hidden to appear; for bulbs and herbaceous plants to emerge, and for the uninspiring shrub in the corner to show you just how great it looks when the time of year is right for its display of blooms, autumn foliage color, or stunning berries.

❀ While you give the garden time to reveal its treasures, make sure that you do keep on top of the weeding—this is something that definitely won't get better if left. Make sure all weeds are cleared, cut back, or dug out before they have a chance to set seed.

Consider any slope

There are advantages and disadvantages to having a garden on a slope. You will get more benefits and fewer problems from a slope if you deal with it carefully, rather than just pretending that it is not there. Try to determine the change in level, and build it in to any rough plans you make.

Shade from buildings and trees

It is essential that you are fully aware of any harder-to-fill areas, and exactly how shady the shaded places are. Shade cast by nearby buildings, high hedges, or trees will influence what grows well and what looks miserable. So check how far the shade is cast and how dense it is—some trees cast very dense shade, others more dappled.

Timber terraces

If you go for timber retaining walls on terraces, choose wood that's certified from a renewable source by the Forestry Stewardship Council (FSC). Check that softwood is pressure-treated to prolong its life.

Changing a slope

Terracing is one traditional way of gardening on a slope, although you will need to do a lot of earth moving and build a series of retaining walls to keep the soil in place on each level. The initial input of time, money, and effort will be high, but terracing should make maintaining the garden a lot quicker and easier later on.

Living with a slope

If you are going to retain a steep slope, access to plants is likely to be difficult and maintaining them very time consuming. Make sure you choose plants that do not need a lot of maintenance. Ground cover plants will also help cover the soil surface rapidly, and so reduce the need for weeding.

Keeping soil in place on a slope

If the soil on a slope has been disturbed, perhaps as a result of extensive weeding or planting activities, it will be easily washed off during heavy rain. Covering the area with plenty of plants will help, but initially laying a woven, weed-suppressing fabric or netting on the soil surface will help to keep the soil where it needs to be, at least until the plants' roots spread. A thick layer of mulch helps to disguise ugly netting, fabric, or mesh, and benefits the plants. (See page 19.)

The damp and often shady conditions at the base of a slope will be perfect for hostas.

Watch the sunshine

Find out which way your garden faces and the approximate amount of sun that each area receives at various times of day and as the seasons change. Make notes, or sketch the sunny and shaded areas on a rough plan of the garden, ideally grading them to indicate the depth of the shade and how long it lasts. This will make it easier to remember what you saw.

Wildflowers need your sunniest spot.

Planting at the foot of a slope

The area at the base of a slope tends to become wet, especially during the autumn and winter months and if a large part of the garden is sloping. You can create a good-looking scheme and help remove some of the water by choosing moisture-loving plants, such as hostas, astilbes, or shrubby dogwoods (*Cornus*) for this area.

Get help with trees

If you're concerned about the health, safety, or even simply the effect a large tree is having on your garden, employ a reputable tree surgeon to look at the tree *in situ* and advise you what the options are. It may be possible to reduce shading by crown reduction (reducing the size of the tree's crown or branch structure), crown lifting (removing some of the lowermost branches), or crown thinning (thinning out the crown or branch structure).

A tree's impact zone

Trees have a big influence on the soil beneath them, often making it very dry, especially during late spring and summer. Mark out the approximate area affected by tree roots—as a rough guide, the roots spread to 3 feet (1m) or so past the outermost spread of the branches.

Understanding your soil

Before you even begin to think about designing new planting schemes, you need to find out what kind of soil you have, as this will determine the plants that will thrive. You need to know your soil's acidity and texture, and then take advantage of what you've got.

Soil pH

The pH of the soil describes its acidity or alkalinity, so it's important that you know what your soil pH is. It will be one of the factors that determines which plants do well, which just about cope, and which look positively miserable.

Be nosy

One good way to work out roughly what sort of soil you have is to take a good look over the neighbors' fences. There may be some local variations in soil conditions, but the soil type should be generally similar, so if you neighbor grows lime-hating plants that all look great, there's a good chance that the soil is acidic. Make a note of what is struggling to survive and what is looking good.

If it grows next door, it will grow for you.

Take advantage of what you have

It is always better to try to work with what is there and improve it than to make dramatic changes. If you have an alkaline soil, for example, acid-loving plants will simply not thrive, often showing severe nutrient deficiency symptoms.

Get tested

❀ It is worth buying an inexpensive soil pH-testing kit so that you can be sure exactly what the pH is, and find any variations within your garden. They are easy to use, so don't be put off at the thought of going scientific.

❀ If you have a large garden, a small, electronic kit may be best. It will allow you to do as many tests as you need, repeating them after treatment if necessary.

Mix the indicator, soil, and water.

❀ Make sure that you test the soil itself, not a mulch or matter that has been dug into the soil. Scrape off the mulch, and check soil from a few inches below the surface.

❀ Do several tests, even in a small garden. There may be localized areas of alkalinity— perhaps due to the liming of a vegetable plot, weathering of concrete and mortar, or buried builders' rubble.

❀ If pH test results are given numerically, remember that pH7 is neutral: lower figures are acidic, and higher figures are alkaline. Remember that the smaller numbers relate to the shorter word (i.e. acid)—hardly scientific, but it works.

The color shows the pH of the soil.

Soil texture

Texture has a huge impact on how soil performs because this determines how well it retains moisture and nutrients. Sandy soils lose both quickly but warm up fast in spring; clay soils are moist and fertile but stay cold for longer over winter.

Handling the soil will tell you a lot about its potential.

Assessing soil texture

Finding the texture of your soil needs no more equipment than your bare hands. When the soil is moist but not wet, take a handful and squeeze it: very sandy soils will not hold together; clay soils will form a solid, sticky lump—often leaving a considerable residue on your hand—and loamy soils will form a ball that crumbles if pressed.

If you really want rhododendrons and don't have acid soil, raised beds may be the only answer.

Raising the soil pH

If your soil is acidic or neutral, then you can often raise the pH significantly by using lime or by mulching with and incorporating alkaline matter, such as mushroom compost.

Reducing the soil pH

❀ Making the soil less alkaline is not easy, but you can try using powdered sulphur. Incorporating and mulching with acidic matter, such as composted ferns, will have some effect, too.

❀ In many cases, the pH will not stay at the desired and adequately low level for lime-hating or acid-loving plants, so it may be better to create a large, raised bed and fill it with imported acidic soil. You should then be able to grow these plants much more successfully and with less effort over the coming years.

Plants that indicate acidic soil

1 *Calluna* (Heather)
2 *Camellia*
3 *Daboecia*
4 *Enkianthus*
5 *Eucryphia*
6 *Fothergilla*
7 *Gaultheria*
8 *Hamamelis* (Witch Hazel)
9 *Kalmia* (Laurel)
10 *Lithodora* (Borage)
11 *Magnolia*
12 *Rhododendron*
13 *Vaccinium* (Blueberry)

Most magnolias do well in slightly acidic soil.

Improving your soil

You want your plants to have the best possible chance to thrive, and the easiest way to help them is through the soil, once you discover what kind of soil you have. There are many ways that you can give your soil a boost.

Organic matter helps to improve the texture of all soils.

Digging in organic matter

Both light and heavy soils will benefit from organic matter. It helps to improve aeration in a heavy, clay-type soil and to improve moisture retention in a light, sandy one. You cannot really add too much, so start digging and see how it helps.

Improving drainage and aeration

Horticultural grit or gravel is extremely useful in heavy soil, helping to improve drainage and aeration. Purchasing grit will be a lot less expensive if you buy in bulk, as opposed to the dinky bags you find in garden centers. Be sure to buy horticultural grade grit; many of the similar materials used by builders contain salts or other contaminants, which can seriously damage plants and soils. To have the desired effect, you need to fork in grit to a depth of at least 12 inches (30cm).

Improve the soil before you plant

It is far easier to incorporate organic matter into an empty piece of ground rather than trying to work it in around plant roots. Adding plenty as a mulch on the soil surface around established plants will also help because earthworms and other creatures will gradually do the work for you. Mulches should always go onto a moist soil; they help to lock moisture in the soil.

Avoid squashing down wet soil

When working in heavy soil, always try to wait until it is not too wet; otherwise you may do more damage by compacting the already heavy, airless texture. If you have to work when conditions are not ideal, lay planks or boards over the soil surface. This provides a surface on which you can stand and helps to spread your weight over a larger area, reducing the risk of compaction.

Old planks are part of the basic toolkit on a clay soil and will help prevent compaction.

Recycle and create compost

Start a compost heap or bin (or two) as soon as possible because garden compost is the perfect soil conditioner. In the meantime, you can use well-rotted farmyard manure, leaf mold, composted bark, grass clippings, or even proprietary bagged compost.

Large, hot compost heaps work fast, but all work eventually.

Beware of woodchips

If material supplied as shredded bark contains too high a level of woodchips then there is a risk that the soil may suffer. Wood or sawdust uses up nitrogen from the soil as it is broken down, and plants may then suffer nitrogen deficiency. Mixing in plenty of nitrogen-rich matter, such as manure, may help to balance this loss.

Spring bulbs push up easily through mulches.

Choosing a manure

If your soil is heavy, choose manures carefully: the stickiest sorts, such as pig manure, tend to make the soil even heavier. Using garden compost or leaf mold in conjunction with a heavier manure will help to counteract the problem.

Slow feeding

While any mulching material keeps the soil moist and suppresses weeds, organic mulches also feed the soil. Garden compost, composted bark, cocoa shells, leaf mold, and manure improve structure and nutrient levels. Mulches are best applied on moist soil in late autumn or early spring.

Using bark

Composted bark can be used to condition soil, but it is essential that it is well composted. Ideally, it should not be used alone, but together with other materials because it may contain levels of tannins that can inhibit healthy plant growth. This is more likely to cause problems with bedding plants than with shrubs and climbers.

Perennial plantings benefit enormously from mulches of almost any kind.

Tools you can trust

Good-quality tools are what you need, whatever the size of your garden, and whatever your level of gardening expertise. It is worth stocking up with fewer, better tools that will do an excellent job over many years rather than a lot of poor quality ones.

Do you really need it?

You don't need a huge number of fancy, complicated tools to get started in your garden. Make a vow not to buy gimmicky tools; there is a lot of junk for sale out there.

Top tools

Fork

Hoe

Pruning Shears

Pronged hand cultivator

Spade

Trowel

Watering can

If possible:

Gardening twine

Hose and outside faucet

Lawnmower

Onion hoe

Spring-tined rake

Wheelbarrow

The essential toolkit is neither bank breaking nor space hungry.

In a larger garden, you will need a decent shed to store your tools.

Test the tools

Always handle garden tools before you buy; they vary immensely. Check that the length of the shaft or handle feels comfortable and that the tool is not too heavy. Also ensure that the handle grip is comfortable—there are various styles available.

Your digging tools can make or break your back.

Forks for clay

If you garden in heavy clay soil, you should use a fork for digging most of the time. This is less likely to exacerbate the poor drainage characteristics of clay than a spade, so make a really good-quality, heavy-duty fork your first priority.

The price is right

With garden tools, you really do get what you pay for, in terms of both their design (and therefore how easy they are to use) and how long they last. If money is short, start with the bare essentials and add to your collection slowly as necessary—but go for quality. The only piece of equipment I would recommend buying from the lower end of the range is a wheelbarrow: the very basic galvanized barrows from builders' supply stores are extremely tough (in fact almost indestructible) and often cost a fraction of what you would pay for a slightly more attractive, up-market model.

Scaled down tools

❀ If you are not very tall or prefer a lighter tool, choose a short-handled border fork or border spade.

❀ If you are smaller still, there are some very good-quality children's tools, the larger ones of which can perfectly well be used by a small adult.

Try each tool till one fits.

Choosing a wheelbarrow

❀ Whatever price you pay for a barrow, it is essential to get one with a pneumatic tire because it'll be so much easier to push than one with solid tires. Although repairing punctures is not my favorite job, at least it can be done and does not take too long.

❀ If you can, try pushing a wheelbarrow before you buy it. Your barrow needs to feel balanced and comfortable on the move, and it must be easy to hold with the stabilizer legs off the ground. Choose carefully.

A sturdy can with a removable rose will give years of useful service.

A seriously useful watering can

❀ When choosing a watering can, make sure you would be happy carrying it full of water. If you are reasonably strong, a standard large can should be fine—in fact, you might find some of the very pretty (but often less functional) types quite infuriating.

❀ Galvanized watering cans are considerably more expensive than plastic types, but they are virtually indestructible and are well worth the money.

❀ Avoid watering cans without removable roses; they are extremely difficult to clean when the rose gets clogged, and only allow you to water in one way. A rose that you can rotate and remove gives two degrees of sprinkling and a solid surge of water.

Make digging easier

If you intend to dig a lot with a spade, look for one with a tread on the head—a small flange running along the length of the top of the head. Small as it is, this tread really helps to prevent your boots from slipping off when you drive the spade into the ground.

Instant transformations

It is well worth indulging in an instant transformation or two—a quick-fix solution that will produce immediate results. It can make your garden look so much better and encourages you to carry on in the bleaker moments, too!

Clematis can cover a multitude of sins in a garden.

Disguise a heap of rubble

If there is the odd pile of rubble in your garden and you are not yet ready to hire a crew to remove it, don't be tempted to bury it because its effect will come to light in the future. In the short-term, plant an inexpensive, fast-growing climber next to it, and allow it to scramble over the heap. Try a clematis or a rose, but make sure you do not plant any acid-loving plants nearby if the rubble includes concrete.

Start by tidying up

It is very easy to accumulate things you do not need or to put off removing dead plants and broken flowerpots. But one hour, or sometimes even just half an hour, spent with two containers—one for junk that is destined for the trash and the other for compostable items—will make a huge difference in how the garden looks for relatively little effort.

Look at the paving

Paving often looks awful as slabs start to crack or the surface becomes discolored. If you are sure you want to keep the paved area, then it is worth spending some time on it. If it is possible to obtain replacement slabs, just lift and replace any damaged ones that are spoiling the area's overall appearance.

You may find you can turn marked slabs over.

Create storage

The idea of a shed that takes up valuable planting space may not appeal at first, but it is worth getting one if you possibly can. It can be used to keep tools and equipment dry and safe and to store seeds and bulbs before planting, and it's the perfect storage place for all those things that are currently stacked and left around looking messy.

A packed shed keeps the garden tidy.

Age replacement paving

Brand new slabs may be of exactly the same type as the original, but because they are unweathered they will look radically different. Use the trick that is often used on new pots, and paint the surface with either liquid manure or plain yogurt. This encourages algae and mosses, and should not make the surface slippery unless you use huge quantities.

Re-lay paving

Sometimes slabs have simply shifted off level. Insert a spade beneath the edge of the slab to lever it up carefully, taking care not to damage the edges. A small amount of crushed stone or dry, sharp sand placed beneath the slab should then allow you to raise or level as necessary.

Protect adjacent plants when cleaning with chemicals or pressure washers.

Renovating graveled areas

If there are a lot of weeds coming up through a graveled surface, it may well be because no landscape fabric was used when the path or graveled area was first constructed. If this is the case, it is best to start from scratch completely. (See page 165.) But do not be tempted to use a solid plastic sheet; rain will not be able to drain away, and waterlogging will soon become a problem.

Clean up paving

Sometimes the surface of a patio or steps may have simply become discolored, and pressure washing or scrubbing using a proprietary cleaner may be sufficient to transform the area. But before you tackle the whole surface, check that the treatment won't cause further damage: pressure washing can damage a slightly loose surface, and some cleaning agents can cause discoloration themselves, so do a test-slab first in a less prominent area.

Topping off gravel

If graveled areas have become thin, try to ensure that any replacement material you buy to top it off matches the original stone. If you cannot achieve this, then make sure you mix in the new stones as evenly as possible over the whole surface. This will give a different but acceptable appearance without starting from scratch.

Gravel should be at least 1 in. (3cm) deep.

Plant in paving gaps

Rather than fix damaged or discolored slabs, you can remove them completely. Dig out the material beneath the slab and replace it with good top soil to a depth of at least 6 inches (15cm) and you'll have a great planting hole for a small plant.

Replace slabs beyond the most-used routes with plants.

Damaged edges

Paved areas, including paths, may have become damaged around the edges, especially if the area has been well used. It is essential to repair them promptly; they'll not only be safer but will also look a lot more attractive. Take out broken bricks, pavers, or slabs, and replace them. If you cannot match them, consider a new edge along the path, or perhaps replace several slabs in a regular pattern so that it looks intentional.

Plants for paving

Precisely what you plant is up to you, but drought-tolerant plants, such as the thymes, sages (*Salvia*), and houseleeks, usually do well. For gaps towards the edge of a paved area, you could always choose a small shrub or perhaps even a climber that will grow to cover an adjacent wall.

Pots of bright flowers can hide or distract from any defects.

Houseleeks will produce offsets and soon fill a planting pocket.

"Pretty up" with pots

Broken or damaged steps or paths that are still perfectly safe will look a lot better if you add a few small pots, prettily planted, at the edges. Change the contents of the pots each season for a year-long display. Make sure that the paths or steps are wide enough to take this reduction in their usable space without becoming cramped.

Tackle the jungle effect

Seriously overgrown climbers could pose a threat to your house foundation, but more likely they are simply obstructing pathways and blocking light. Before you grab the pruning shears or saw, check your plant's needs because pruning methods vary considerably.

Great plants for edging paths and patios

1. *Arenaria*
2. *Armeria maritima* (Sea thrift)
3. *Aubrieta* (Aubrieta)
4. *Dianthus deltoides* (Maiden pink)
5. *Draba*
6. *Erinus alpinus* (Fairy Foxglove)
7. *Helianthemum* (Rock Rose)
8. *Iberis sempervirens* (Candytuft)
9. *Salvia officinalis* (Common Sage)
10. *Saxifraga* (Saxifrage)
11. *Sempervivum* (Houseleek)
12. *Thymus* (Thyme)

Plants creeping over paving edges hide minor unevenness or damage.

Timing pruning

It is always best to avoid pruning a plant toward the end of the summer; this may stimulate new growth, which will not have the chance to toughen or harden up properly before the onset of frosty weather. It is generally best to cut back either when the plant is dormant or earlier in the year, when any new growth produced will be able to harden off.

Take your time

If in doubt about just how far you can go with serious pruning of an overgrown shrub or climber, it is best to err on the side of caution. The work can be spread out over two or maybe even three years.

How to prune overgrown shrubs

❀ Different plants need tackling in different ways, so try to identify exactly what the plant is. But whatever you are renovating, there are basic guidelines that you should always follow, the first job being to prune out dead, diseased, and dying growth.

❀ Look at the plant with a critical eye to decide whether the whole plant needs general thinning out or just the crown needs opening out. Whatever you are pruning out, always ensure your pruners, saw, or loppers are in good condition and very sharp—crushed stems often become infected and show die-back. Choose a vigorous-looking, outward-facing bud or shoot, and cut back to it, creating a sloping cut just above the bud but not right on top of it.

Renovate and feed

It may seem illogical to feed overgrown plants that have had to be cut back, but they do benefit. Feeding an old shrub that has been heavily pruned helps encourage new, productive growth. Feeding does not mean the plant will put on excessive new growth, provided you do not apply excessive quantities of feed.

Most plants do fine if you don't cut back beyond leafy parts.

Boundaries and structures

Your garden will both look and feel better with well-kept boundaries that suit its overall style, giving privacy and security. Screening can also be used within the garden to hide clotheslines, compost bins, or sheds—all of which can be a blot on your landscape.

A clean, uniform boundary gives a feeling of tidiness.

Spruce up fences

A decrepit fence can make a whole garden look unkempt and allow unwanted visitors, such as other people's pets, to get into your garden too easily. Replacing a fence may be a job you want to leave until later; in the meantime, once you have made sure that the fence is basically safe and secure, it will look a lot better if you paint or stain it, using a color that suits your site.

Make sure fences are where they should be

If you've just moved into a new house, make sure that any concerns about boundaries are clarified promptly. Problems like this don't disappear, they tend to get more complicated instead.

Evergreen ivy is perfect for screens.

Hide eyesores

❀ Use fence posts to support a trellis and make a freestanding screen that allows quick and easy access for maintenance, pruning, and so on. While longer-term climbers are getting established, fill in gaps with quick-growing annuals, such as sweet peas (*Lathyrus*).

Plant around fences

Unless the fence is in a seriously bad state, you can plant climbers to cover it. Choose fast-growing plants, such as *Clematis montana*, for a speedy effect. If you intend to remove the fence within a year or two, you can use annual climbers, including sweet peas (*Lathyrus*), cup-and-saucer vine (*Cobaea*), or morning glory (*Ipomoea*), on wire mesh or a temporary frame. Alternatively, tackle the problem from the top down with trailing plants in hanging baskets.

❀ To obscure taller, thinner eyesores, roll up chicken wire to create a column; anchor it firmly to the ground; and grow climbers up it.

❀ If the eyesore has a less-than-desirable odor—like a trash-can corral—include some perfumed plants in your screen or a nearby planter. Jasmine, roses, or honeysuckle (*Lonicera*) not only look good but also act as great natural air fresheners.

Loosestrife and *verbena* are a winning combination.

Shabby sheds

Sometimes a shed can be an eyesore, not because it is ugly in itself, but because it looks decrepit. A coat or two of paint or stain, perhaps in an exciting color, can help to make it look better instantly. Make sure the treatment adheres well by cleaning off all algae, moss, and dirt, and then allowing the wood to dry thoroughly before applying the wood treatment.

Colored stains allow a shed to stand out or fade into the scenery.

Damaged roofs

❀ The roofing on sheds often deteriorates after a few years, leaving the shed without a fully waterproof roof and making it look ugly. Replacing the roofing on a reasonably sound shed will instantly make the whole thing look so much better.

❀ If it doesn't seem worthwhile to reroof a shed, make it look better for what is left of its life by growing a climber up and over its roof. A shed covered with hundreds of flowers of a clematis or honeysuckle can look really beautiful. Doing this may, however, speed up the deterioration of the shed, so it's best reserved for those that are definitely well past their sell-by dates.

Use distractions

If the edges of your garden are still looking lackluster, despite your efforts at tidying them up, then get planting. (See pages 38–39.) In the meantime, make good use of seasonally filled containers to focus attention elsewhere. A good-looking pot or tub or two will help to draw neighbors' eyes away from the less attractive areas of a garden, making the whole place seem more appealing. They also indicate just what the whole garden will look like when you've had time to come to grips with it.

Planting near the house draws the eye away from the edges.

Honeysuckle will smother a shed and remain green for most, or all, of the year.

Instant screening

You don't need permanent planting to make a screen or hedge: beautifully planted containers can be lined up to make an instant screen. This can be of almost any height, depending on what you plant in them, from lavender to laurel.

Flower beds & borders

Unless you want the ultimate minimalist look in your garden, it is likely that you will have at least one flower bed or border, quite possibly several. The size, shape, and number of beds you have will of course be determined by the size and shape of your garden and the emphasis you want to put on flowers and other plants as opposed to the hard landscaping elements. Each may have a similar theme, or they may be quite different in character and content, but whatever their style, flower beds and borders are

an integral part of most gardens, and something that can make or break them.

Creating the perfect design
There is an art to creating beautiful borders and ensuring that they develop as you want and look good for as much of the year as possible. Beds and borders that are devoid of color and interest for all but a fraction of the year are a lost opportunity. It's easy to cobble together a flower bed that looks good for a season or two, but it's

harder to ensure that the space is used to its best effect as time goes on. I would certainly not want to suggest that you should steer clear of herbaceous borders unless you are an experienced and very knowledgeable gardener—far from it—but there is no doubt that this is one of those areas of the garden where a few timely tips can go a long way toward making that dream border a great-looking reality! Whatever your parameters, it is all about ensuring that your flowers really fulfill their potential.

This chapter shows you how to

❀ Make a new border—choose a shape that fits in with your garden design and cut it into an existing lawn.

❀ Choose a variety of plants for a new border, thinking about shape, color, and height.

❀ Plant a new border or bed.

❀ Care for established beds—staking, protecting, feeding, and weeding.

How to make a new border

It is an exciting moment when you sit down to plan a new border, and that planning is vital to the border's long-term success. Take time to choose those really magical ingredients.

Smooth, broad curves are easier to plant and maintain.

Keep it simple

An unusually or intricately shaped border may appeal to you, but it's also likely to be a nightmare to keep in shape, especially if the border is next to a lawn, which has edges that need to be mown. Smooth, flowing outlines are an easier option, and usually end up being changed less frequently as a result—go for the classic, timeless look.

Think ahead

Try to imagine what a new flower bed will look like before you begin creating it. You may not yet know exactly what plants you will have in it, but think about its shape and dimensions and how it will affect or interact with the rest of the garden. Remember that a flower bed or border is likely to be visible from several different places, including the ground floor and upper windows of your house. Make sure that you create your border in a position that can be enjoyed from wherever it is seen.

Marking curves

❀ Get a bit of help with the border edge. Ideally, use a peg and line to help you mark out curves, marking the grass with landscaper's paint in a spray can. If you have only one to do and want to economize, use plenty of dry horticultural sand to mark the edge. You can either drizzle this onto the turf by hand or make a dispenser by cutting the base off a plastic bottle. Tie the end of the line to the bottle, and invert it. Pour the dry sand in, and it will flow out when you remove the lid, allowing you to mark the turf as you move the bottle.

❀ A garden hose laid in the desired shape of the edge of the border will work, but there is a risk of accidentally creating a lopsided or uneven curve.

A lawn barrier edge is a good investment, saving hours of work later.

Keep it neat and easy

Lawn grass will try to grow into the flower bed. Sink a barrier to a depth of 2 inches (5cm) around the edge, protruding above the grass roots, but not so high that you cannot mow right up to the edge. This should prevent the grass from creeping in and hugely reduce the time you spend tidying the edges.

A path in a large bed can be practical and a pleasure.

Size matters

The size of your bed or border depends on what you want and the size of the garden. But consider its future maintenance and any way to make this simpler, quicker, or easier. Bigger borders may look better because they hold more plants, but if they are too deep it may be difficult to reach central areas, especially once it is full of plants. Stepping stones or a path through the middle make access easier.

Recycling turf

❀ Removed turf needs to be lifted with its roots, so that it can be used as patching material for any sparse areas in the rest of the lawn, or to repair broken lawn edges. If you don't need it for this, turf composts brilliantly, so add it to the compost heap.

❀ If there is a lot of turf, you can make your own miniature loam heap. Stack the turf grass-side down in an out-of-the-way spot; as long as it does not become too dry, it will rot down into super loam.

Take care to undercut deeply enough to remove all roots.

Get straight lines straight

A straight-edged border that isn't really straight looks awful. Even when plants are growing in it and partially hiding a wobbly line, the problem is still obvious. Don't try to cut the edge by eye, use either two pegs and a line or a long steel rule or plank, and then make sure you cut precisely along the line.

Cutting the edge

The best tool for cutting the edges of a border in an existing lawn is a half-moon edging iron, which makes it easier to cut accurately and neatly. Alternatively, a good, sharp spade will work pretty well, but it is essential that you keep the blade at a right angle to the lawn as you cut.

A half-moon edger has a completely flat blade.

Cutting out the turf

Once you have created the shape of the edge, you will need to remove all the turf from within the outline. It is much easier (and makes for a much neater end result) if you stand inside the new border area and cut out toward the edge. Cutting inward from the edge is likely to crush that nice, neat vertical cut. It is also best to remove a relatively small ring of turf first; then as you get into the central area of the border you can move more of the turf at a time.

Choosing plants for a new border

Start by deciding when you want the border to look its best. If you are creating a border to look good for as much of the year as possible, you need a wide range of plants whose main performance times or seasons of appeal span many months.

Use a mix of plant types

If you want a border that will be interesting at all levels, use a mix of shrubs and perennials. To achieve a gloriously solid mass of color, you may also want to include annual bedding plants whose flowering times fit in with your specific need. Once you've got your core of permanent plants in place, visit garden centers for seasonal interest plants at the time you need them. These easy-come, easy-go plants give maximum impact in quick time when other plants fade.

You will see your garden differently when sitting or standing: use plant heights to suit both angles.

Mix and match

Considering the heights and spread of the plants is important. Make sure you don't choose plants that are all of a very similar height; you will be able to enjoy more of the display they offer if some are taller than others.

Follow your heart, but use your head

Choosing plants is a very personal business, but remember to check on their fundamental requirements before you take them home. Unless you can provide the right amount of sun or shade, soil texture, moisture levels, and soil pH, they'll find it impossible for plants to thrive.

Illustrated labels are useful to tell you what a plant does when.

Read the label

Plants in small pots always look easy to cope with in the nursery or garden center, but remember that while many herbaceous plants do look rather similar early or very late in the season, they have hugely different potential heights and spreads. The information given on the plant label or the header-board in the garden center is something you really need to note.

Out of reach

When you are choosing plants for an island bed, especially one that is quite large, make sure that the plants in the center are relatively low maintenance because they will be harder to reach, and so maintenance could be difficult.

The center of the border is ideal for low-maintenance evergreens and those spiky plants that you wouldn't want too close to the edge.

Think about shape

Everyone probably has a favorite plant shape—you may love dreaming spires of delphiniums or sprawling mounds of catmint (*Nepeta*)—but one shape repeated endlessly quickly looks dull. Vertical spikes of flowers bring a border of solid, sturdy shapes to life, while cascading plants can soften and knit blocks together. And don't automatically send all the tall plants to the back: some, such as *Verbena bonariensis*, are gauzy enough to put at the front.

Leaf shades and shapes last most of the year.

Look at leaves

There is a lot more to a plant than just its flowers; many herbaceous plants have stunning foliage, too. Make an effort to incorporate some good foliage plants in your design because the leaves offer interest far longer than many of the flowers.

Vertical plants can act like exclamation marks, giving punch to borders of lower, more solid shapes.

When to buy your plants

If you need widely spread seasons of interest, you can still buy the plants you need in the main buying seasons (spring and, to a lesser extent, autumn for herbaceous plants). If you want to ensure you have some seriously showy plants throughout much of the year, make sure you visit a good garden center at regular intervals. You can be sure that the real seasonal show-stoppers with the most flamboyant displays will be in a prominent position each time you visit.

Color harmonies

I'm a great believer that color combinations are a very personal thing and that you should have what you like, not what someone else says. However, if you need a bit of a suggestion to get you started, remember that generally warm colors go better with other warm colors, and cool with cool. You could go for a border with a very limited or even single color theme, or perhaps with a longer border, grade colors from warm to cool.

Buy fresh

If possible, find out when the garden center has its main deliveries and go on that day. You'll get the pick of the plants before they have had a chance to become dry or damaged!

Shades of blue and purple give a soothing, harmonious feel to a garden.

Learn by example

If you find choosing plants that go well together difficult, try visiting plenty of well-planned and beautifully planted gardens. This will not only provide you with a gorgeous day out but also inspire you and provide plenty of great planting ideas.

Safe passage

If the flower bed is next to a path, avoid plants with prickly or spiky foliage and anything known to cause skin reactions, such as the euphorbias or rue (*Ruta*).

Use movement

Plants of various heights add a dimension to a flower border, but your creation will look even more delightful if you can include plants that introduce movement as well. Use tall plants with flexible stems, such as *Verbena bonariensis*, and your border will positively dance in the breeze.

Please yourself

Color combinations can be daunting, especially to those who are not artistically inclined. Remember, you are creating your own beds and borders. You and the others who live in the house and admire the garden are the only people whose opinions really matter!

Be choosy

Avoid garden plant outlets where the plants are not maintained. Dead or drought-stricken plants or a lot of weed growth on the compost are all telltale signs of neglect.

Neat edges

If the border is adjacent to a lawn, make sure that you choose some plants to go around the edges of the border that are not inclined to spread too much and that have a fairly upright habit. Plants that flop over the grass will make mowing difficult and will soon cause the grass that they shade to deteriorate. Plant a little way back from the edge to allow some room to spread.

Planting time

It's easy to get carried away when suddenly you find yourself with a great new planting space, but if you're too hasty you may regret it later. Make sure you prepare the soil for the new border before you start planting.

Reduce weed seeds

If the bed is in an area where there were a lot of annual weeds, remove them. Then, having dug the soil over, leave the bed empty for at least three weeks before you even think about putting in any plants. During these weeks, numerous weed seeds previously lying dormant in the soil will germinate (especially rapidly because the soil has been dug over) and you can regularly hoe off the growth. If you do this throughout the first few weeks following the creation of the bed, you should be able to clear most of the dormant weed seeds before you plant, making future maintenance much easier.

Repeated hoeing to kill weeds as they germinate reduces them dramatically.

Feed the soil

The soil may be undernourished, so incorporate plenty of well-rotted manure or garden compost to improve its texture and fertility. Fork this in well throughout the entire bed.

Remove roots

The new well-fed and manured bed you're about to create is an ideal place for any pernicious weeds, such as dandelions, docks, or bindweed, to survive and thrive. This means you must turn over the area really thoroughly, carefully removing as many intact weeds and their roots as you can. It's crucial that you clear all the roots and other plant fragments because many have the ability to form an entire new plant if they are left in the soil.

Check the pH

If you are unsure about the soil's pH, this is a good time to carry out a pH test to determine what exactly it is before you start to add anything. (See page 16.) Most herbaceous plants perform perfectly well on all but the most extreme soil types, but it is still a good idea to check. If you intend to plant any shrubs in the border, knowing the pH will really help you determine what to grow.

The easiest time to improve the soil is before you put plants in it.

Open up the soil

Soil, especially the soil in an area beneath a well-used lawn, often becomes seriously compacted. Fork over to at least a spade's depth, preferably more, breaking up any hard layers or "pans" that have developed. If the top soil is thin, make sure you do not bring any subsoil to the surface!

Using fertilizer

To make sure that fertility is high, you could use some proprietary fertilizers. If you have very fertile soil or have just incorporated lots of manure or compost, then a general feeding should not be necessary initially. Instead, wait until the plants have started to grow strongly.

How many of each?

❀ If the space you have to plant is very small, then a single plant of each type may be all you need. If you want a bolder effect, restrict yourself to plants that stay small and go for several of each type.

❀ Plant in odd numbers, say three or five of the same plant, rather than even numbers; this will help the border to look more natural.

Odd numbers of plants give the appearance of a more naturally formed border.

Leave each plant in a bucket of water while you dig its planting hole.

Presoaking plants

Once you have got the plants home and just before you start to plant, give them a thorough watering if their soil is at all dry. Standing them in water ensures that the entire root ball is thoroughly moistened when they go into the ground.

Working in clay

If your garden soil is heavy clay, try to do major digging or bed creation when the weather and soil are not too wet, or else the soil will become seriously compacted. (See page 18.) Do as much of the digging as possible with a fork, rather than a spade; a spade is more likely to cause smearing or compaction of the soil at the edges of the bed.

If you have a paper plan, marking it on the ground with sand or landscaper's paint will make things easier.

Prior arrangement

Before you start to plant, arrange the pots of plants in the positions in which you intend to plant them. It is much easier to change your mind at this stage than it will be once they are in the ground. If you have not yet managed to get all the plants you need, use an empty pot to represent each missing plant.

When to plant

❀ I recommend planting in autumn or early spring so that the plants have a chance to get their roots into their new surroundings and start to establish before the weather gets too hot or the soil too dry.

❀ If the weather is already getting warm, plant on as cool a day as possible. If that is not possible, plant in the early evening so that the plants are not subjected to the hottest part of the day right away.

The size and condition of the hole are the keys to success.

Prepare holes well

❀ Make sure that each plant has a planting hole a bit larger than the plant's root-ball.

❀ If the weather is dry, fill each hole with water just before you put the plant into the hole. A bit of localized watering works wonders for its establishment and reduces water wastage.

Last-minute moves

Keep all plants in their pots until you are ready to put them in. If you remove them from the pots in advance of planting, their roots are more likely to get dry, especially if you unexpectedly take longer than you had anticipated.

Hold your position

Leaving the plants in position while you start to plant makes planting quicker and easier. It also makes it easier for you to ensure that each one goes in exactly the right position in relation to its neighbor.

Don't dig too deep

Don't be tempted to plant at anything other than the depth the plant was at in its pot. Planting too deep may cause rotting and death; planting too shallow makes a plant more susceptible to drought.

Be a tease

Once you have taken the plant out of its pot, you will be able to check the roots. If the roots are very congested in the pot, gently tease out a few of the outer roots before the plant goes in the hole. This will help to ensure that the roots spread through their new surroundings more rapidly.

Matted roots may stay that way after planting.

Keep cool

If the weather is already quite warm and the plants have a lot of leaf growth, they could suffer quite badly, particularly in the first few days after planting. Erect some temporary shelter to give them a bit of light relief.

Get rid of the competition

Once all the plants are in position, top off all the soil surface with a bulky mulch, such as cocoa shell or bark. This will reduce weed growth dramatically, saving you time and reducing any competition between your plants and the weeds, and will help to keep the soil relatively moist. Top off the mulch as soon as it starts to thin out, first pulling out any weeds that have appeared.

A good layer of mulch is invaluable for keeping competition out and moisture in.

Have fun with fillers in a young border: they may spark new ideas.

Keep the labels

It is worth keeping a record of exactly what you planted, but I can't stand seeing plant labels in flower beds. If you're like me (but also too busy to staple them all into a special folder!), then simply put all the labels into a jar or an envelope labeled with the area of the garden they are from so you have a record.

Fill the gaps

A newly planted bed of herbaceous plants will have a lot of gaps in it for the first few years. If you don't like all that gappiness, use seasonal bedding and bulbs, and perhaps some hardy annuals, to create color that won't affect the border in the longer term but will look great while the bed develops.

Use landscape fabric

Planting through holes in a landscape fabric can serve all sorts of purposes. On a slope, it can help keep the soil in place. (See page 15.) In other places, fabrics can suppress weeds, reducing maintenance. They also prevent decorative materials, such as bark or pea gravel, from working their way into the soil.

Caring for established beds

Once a flower bed starts to grow and develop, it will soon begin to look great. But this movement means that you will need to keep an eye on the plants and supply the TLC they deserve!

Plants will quickly conceal any frames that they grow through.

Stop the flop

Many herbaceous plants, and indeed many annuals that you may be using as temporary display plants, are a little too tall for their own good and have a tendency to flop. This not only spoils the way they look but may damage adjacent plants (including the lawn) and makes them more prone to slug attack. A bit of hidden support is worth its weight in gold.

Get it in early

It always pays to insert plant supports as early as possible. If you put in supports once there is quite a bit of foliage on the plant, the job takes longer as you try to avoid damaging the plant, which is always inevitable, and the support tends to be less well hidden. As soon as the plant appears aboveground and you can gauge fairly accurately just how wide it will spread, you should start staking.

Stop supports from rooting

With heavier plants or where you actually want the support to be an integral part of the look you create, supports such as freshly cut willow or hazel stems fit the bill perfectly. These only pose one problem; if they left are in the soil for more than a month or two, they may root and quickly develop quite extensive root systems. Wrap layers of packing tape tightly around the entire length of the wood that will be in contact with the ground before you insert the stem into the soil; this should prevent it from taking root.

Natural materials make virtually invisible stakes.

Subtle staking

Most plants look better if the support that they need is hidden away. Twiggy sticks, cut to a length to suit the individual plant but generally about 18 inches (45cm) tall with the lowermost 4–6 inches (10–15cm) driven into the soil, work well.

Make your own supports

If you plan in advance, there should be no need to buy special stakes for plants; just save prunings when cutting back shrubs, trees, and hedges.

Proprietary supports

There is a whole host of supports available from garden centers and mail-order catalogs, and it is well worth shopping around for good deals. Choose supports in sizes and colors to suit the plants you are growing, and if they are metal make sure that they are either galvanized or plastic-coated.

Use any soft material for ties: the softer the stem, the softer the tie should be.

What to use for plant ties

You can use a variety of materials to tie plant stems to supports: soft garden twine, raffia, proprietary plastic ties, foam-covered wire, open wire circles, or even a short section taken from the leg of a pair of stockings or tights.

Tall stems

Some plants, such as hollyhocks (*Alcea*) and delphiniums, may not need general support, but their tall and sometimes slightly fragile flower spikes may need it, especially if the plant is in a particularly windy spot. A single bamboo cane usually does the trick, but take care not to damage the crown of the plant as you insert the support into the soil. Tie the plant in using a figure eight to allow room for expansion and reduce the risk of the stem being damaged.

A figure-eight knot allows movement.

Keep plants under wraps

Flower buds, flowers, and soft foliage are especially vulnerable to frost damage. Protect them by draping with horticultural fleece, old net curtains, or even newspapers; the edges must be properly anchored with metal pegs, hoops, or large stones and bricks to be effective. Fleece bags with drawstrings are now available, making protecting larger tender plants or their flowers much easier, quicker, and more effective.

Be prepared for cold

Changes in temperature, when tender plants are subjected to frost, can do a lot of damage, especially if the arrival of frosts is sudden. Make sure that you have all you need for protection ready and waiting, and keep listening to the weather forecasts.

Keep on top of weeds

Hoeing is a great way to kill off annual weeds, but can do a lot of damage in a crowded flower bed. Invest in a tiny hoe, such as an onion hoe, and you will be able to hoe quite safely in tight spaces.

You will need all the tricks there are to keep hostas hole-free.

Slugs, snails, and other problems

❀ The soft, young foliage produced early in the year is a magnet for certain pests, in particular slugs and snails. Some plants, such as dicentras, seem to be damaged only rarely, but check all plants regularly so that you can collect and dispose of the pests.

❀ Mulching with cocoa shells seems to reduce slug and snail damage; barriers such as crushed shells, pine needles, or proprietary copper rings also help to keep the slugs and snails away from your plants.

❀ Later in the year, large, floppy foliage from herbaceous perennials makes a perfect place for slugs and snails to hide, so check beneath large leaves around the bases of the plants, and collect any lurking pests.

❀ In any area of your garden, you can be sure that there will be a fair selection of pests and pathogens that could attack your beloved plants. See pages 218–223 for more tips on some of these problems.

Allow plants to toughen up

Although it may be tempting to keep fleece or other protection on plants, doing this means that the plants will not be able to harden off naturally. It may also become rather damp beneath some forms of frost protection, making pests and infections all the more likely to become a problem. During mild weather, or at least during the warmer part of the day, remove or partially remove frost protection—but don't forget to get it back in place on time!

Water well

❀ Flower beds and borders will need some water, especially during the first few months after planting while the plants get established. For watering, see pages 176–178; most importantly, water thoroughly and less often (avoid frequent sprinklings), and water in the evening or early morning.

❀ Many herbaceous plants are prone to fungal infections that thrive on wet foliage. Try to get water direct to the roots, not on the leaves—this is less wasteful, too.

❀ Both rainwater and "gray" water from baths or sinks are fine for using on flower beds and borders. So collect all you can and make use of it!

Using a can is a slower but efficient way to water.

Deadhead to keep displays tidy and make them last.

Faded flowers

❀ As flowers start to fade, make sure you regularly deadhead the plants. Removing these faded blooms helps to avoid the plant wasting energy-producing seeds.

❀ Regular deadheading is the key to success, but if a lot of flowers have faded simultaneously and there are not many more to come, you can often save time by giving the plant a "haircut" with sharp scissors or, in the case of tougher plants, a pair of shears.

Feed with care

❀ If the soil has plenty of organic matter, it should be healthy and full of nutrients, but occasionally it may be necessary to use fertilizers. These are generally best applied in spring or early summer—put them on too late in the season and they may encourage soft, new growth, which will be hit by frosts.

❀ If spraying a foliar feed onto the leaves or applying nutrients such as a magnesium solution to the leaves, do it on a cloudy day or when the leaves and petals will have dried completely before the sun gets hot, to avoid scorch. Water drops focus the sun's rays, like tiny lenses.

Make a soil mound

It is normally bad to mound soil around plant stems and crowns, but in very cold weather it can help to protect the plant from frost and reduce any heaving of the roots. With heavy soil or in wet conditions, mound up compost or composted bark. As soon as it warms up, scrape the material away from the stems.

Mound up soil ahead of heavy frosts.

Autumn tidying

❀ At the end of the season you can tidy up beds and borders a bit—removing faded leaves helps to clean up residues of pest and pathogen problems from earlier in the year. Use sharp scissors or pruners to ensure that you don't damage the crown of the plant as you remove infected foliage.

❀ It can be worth leaving some old leaves on herbaceous plants because they often help to protect the crown from winter cold.

❀ Leave in place the seedheads of sedums and others that look good or provide useful food for the birds. They can be removed in the spring.

Brown, dried leaves should be promptly removed.

Creative containers

Containers are well worth the effort they take to create and maintain, and they allow you to grow things that would perhaps not naturally suit your garden soil, such as the ever-popular camellias, rhododendrons, and azaleas. They would not be a wise choice if you garden on an alkaline or chalky soil, but if you are prepared to get some ericaceous compost, these once-impossible plants become proud features. Containers can rapidly transform a garden; you just have to remember to water them!

Using containers to the fullest
For many years people thought of container gardening as inextricably linked with summer bedding, but more and more of us are now exploring its full potential. Not only summer bedding, but indeed any seasonal bedding will look great, and will look stunning if combined with seasonal bulbs. Longer-term containers are well worth considering too, perhaps for shrubs or small trees underplanted with bedding and bulbs, making a miniature garden in itself. Then,

of course, there are the vegetables and herbs—most of these are perfect candidates for life in a good-sized pot or planter and will allow you to grow root vegetables or slug-prone crops whatever your soil and its population of problem creatures. You can create numerous mini-gardens, of a wide range of plants, regardless of your natural garden soil. If you choose attractive containers, then these too can help to bring color and interest to your garden, even when the plants themselves are not at their best.

This chapter shows you how to
❀ Choose containers—different plants have different needs.
❀ Choose baskets and liners—which are best for which purpose?
❀ Plant containers—get the best compost and the right plants for you.
❀ Cultivate crops in containers—which fruit, vegetables, and herbs thrive and how to care for them?

Choosing your containers

The size and type of containers you use can make the difference between your plants surviving and thriving. Pots should be big enough for good root growth and contain adequate planting medium to act as a reservoir for water and soil nutrients.

Frost-proof pots are fired at a higher temperature.

Frost-proof containers

Unless you're willing to move containers to a frost-free place over the colder months, look out for those described as frost-proof. The beautifully decorated, wonderfully colored glazed pots that are usually sold at knock-down prices are rarely even frost resistant. Frost-proof terra-cotta emits a higher-pitched "ting" if flicked hard with a finger nail.

Think big

For ease of maintenance, choose larger pots and tubs. They hold a greater volume of soil, protecting plant roots from the effects of extreme heat and cold.

Several holes help to ensure good drainage.

Avoiding a bog garden

Unless you want to produce a miniature pond or bog garden, it is essential that your container has plenty of drainage holes. Terra-cotta or stoneware pots often have one single, central hole, while containers made from artificial materials may have more. But whatever you choose, they must be there, so don't get taken in by some of the gorgeous-looking but drainage-hole-free pots that are on sale!

A straight-sided or outward-flaring pot makes repotting possible.

Pots for long-term plants

Containers for plants such as small trees or shrubs, which may need to be moved into larger containers or open ground in a few years, need to be chosen very carefully. Use pots with upright sides or sides that flare outwards—never pot-bellied pots, because it is nearly impossible to remove a well-established plant from one of these, unless you're prepared to smash the container!

Making pots look attractively aged

If brand-new terra-cotta, stone, or concrete pots just look too new and perfect, the trick of painting them with a solution of manure or yogurt really does work. Manure does not tend to smell as you might imagine and is less likely to be licked off by passing cats! The pot should be dry when you start, to help the manure or yogurt to adhere better.

Pots will age faster if they are left in a damp place.

Protect roots from extreme temperatures

Thicker-walled containers, perhaps made from wood or double-skinned plastic, are the best for keeping roots insulated against temperature extremes. To give extra protection, you can line the inside of the container with a sheet of bubble-wrap polythene, but ensure that the drainage holes are not covered.

A layer of bubble-wrap inside the pot makes great insulation.

Special care for acid-loving plants

Concrete containers are fine for most plants, but avoid them if you are planting an acid-loving plant, such as a camellia, pieris, or azalea (*Rhododendron*). The concrete may gradually weather and leach an alkaline solution into the soil, resulting in yellow-leafed, miserable plants. If you're desperate to use a concrete container for an acid-loving plant, line the inner surface with polythene, keeping the drainage holes clear.

Acid lovers are happy in ceramic or synthetic pots.

Top ten plants for year-round interest

1. *Arbutus unedo* (Strawberry tree)
2. *Buxus* (Box)
3. *Ericas and Callunas* (Heaths and heathers)
4. *Euonymus fortunei* (Spindle tree)
5. *Ilex* (Hollies), especially variegated forms
6. *Laurus nobilis* (Bay laurel)
7. Pieris species and cultivars
8. *Pinus mugo* (Dwarf mountain pine) and other dwarf conifers
9. *Trachycarpus fortunei* (Chusan palm)
10. Yuccas (Hardy yuccas)

Customized wooden planters

Most garden paints are also suitable for using on wooden containers to add color or hide stains and blemishes, but always check the label. Make sure the paint has dried completely before you start to plant.

Choosing baskets and liners

Hanging baskets can transform the front of your house or a bare fence in your back garden, and they are the perfect gardening answer when space is tight. There are many different basket and liner options, so make sure you choose what works best for you.

Check the chains

When buying a hanging basket, choose one that has removable hanging chains. This makes it much easier when it comes to planting: you can simply do the planting without having to work around the chains, and plants are less likely to get damaged.

Look for wide planting holes

Planting around the sides and even the base of a hanging basket makes it look really impressive. To make this easier, choose a basket with widely spaced wires—they do vary a lot.

The wide spaces between the bars on this basket will allow plenty of planting around the sides.

How long will it last?

The longest-lasting baskets are those with plastic-coated mesh; choose carefully, and they will blend in well. Baskets made from natural materials do have a certain rustic charm, but they rarely last more than a year or two.

Metal and plastic baskets should give several years of service.

Holes in liners

If you want to do a lot of side and base-planting, you will need holes in the liner. If you use moss as a liner, it can be built up in layers, leaving holes as you plant. Otherwise go for one, such as foam or compacted wool, into which it is easy to cut holes. Coconut fiber (coir) can be cut, but it is much tougher, and cutting accurately is difficult.

The easiest liner to plant through is loose moss.

Time-saving liners

For speed of planting, choose a wool, foam, or preformed cardboard liner. Cardboard liners often come with ready-made gaps for planting; they are certainly time-saving, but they restrict what you can do. Cardboard also has a tendency not to fit as snugly into the basket as you'd hope.

Measure your basket before buying a liner—it is easy to get it wrong by eye.

Recycled liners

As an alternative to coir or other artificial liners, you could also use a circle cut from an old sweater or cardigan. Ideally use real wool, which will rot down naturally in the compost heap afterward. Whether you go for bold and brash or a more subtle, natural color is up to you.

Once covered with moss, a plastic liner is hidden.

Homegrown moss

If you like moss but are unhappy about it having been taken from the wild, you can use the stuff you rake out of your lawn, as long as it has not been treated with a moss-killing chemical. This works well but is rarely as moisture-retentive as the moss sold especially for basket lining. Use a thick layer or an inner liner to keep moisture and soil in the basket.

Hiding an ugly liner

Double liners in baskets can be useful—a very sturdy but unattractive liner can have an outer, thinner layer of real moss added. And in the winter, two layers make for warmer, better protected plants and better displays.

The ultimate recycled liner

If you have a pond, drape several layers of blanket weed pulled from it over an upturned hanging basket. Allow each layer of the weed to dry before you add another layer, and keep adding until it is at least ¼ inch (6mm) thick. When dry, it can be used as a good, natural-looking basket liner.

Homegrown moss can look every bit as good as sphagnum moss.

Planting your containers

Now that you have chosen your containers, it is time to plant them, which is the exciting part. Spend time thinking about the kind of plants you want, their requirements, and color schemes—and don't forget to water them when finished.

A large pot may be all but impossible to move once planted.

Watch your back

If you are using a big, heavy container, get it in exactly the place you want it before you add the compost and plants—this will save a lot of potential backaches. Once the container is full of plants and moist soil, it will weigh much more.

Keep out pests

To reduce the number of pests, such as slugs, entering through the drainage holes, cover the holes with fine, strong mesh before you add the drainage stones to the bottom of the container. Doing this will also help to keep out some of the other less-troublesome garden creatures, such as woodlice.

Keep drainage holes open

❀ Many different materials can be used for drainage—broken terra-cotta pots are not the only option. Try broken household china or large irregularly shaped stones or rocks. Just make sure you position them so that they do not block the holes.

Water your empty pots

Unglazed terra-cotta absorbs a lot of water when new, often causing new plants to suffer from drought almost immediately. Water the empty pot thoroughly several times before you add the soil. Once wet, it won't cause any problems.

❀ If you need to keep the weight of the container to a minimum, use crunched up polystyrene plant trays or packaging material to create a low-weight drainage layer. Make sure you dispose of it properly when you eventually empty the pot. Do not leave it around the garden—polystyrene is not biodegradable and may prove hazardous to the local wildlife.

Frost-damaged, broken pots make excellent drainage.

Don't fill to the brim

Leave about a 1-inch (3cm) space at the top of the pot, otherwise it will overflow when you water it.

Gappy half barrels

Wooden containers, such as half barrels, may have the odd gap in them when new. Don't be tempted to line these with polythene in an attempt to keep the soil in, as this has a drying effect. Instead, wet the wood thoroughly before you plant; it should swell as it absorbs the water, closing the gaps.

Barrels become gappy when standing empty and dry, but when wet should rapidly swell up to seal tightly.

Choosing your potting mix

❀ Don't be tempted to use garden soil in containers. Although you may get away with it, it rarely keeps its structure well in a container, and the plants often end up suffering from root rot. It really is best to buy fresh, new mix every year. Reusing potting soil makes it much more likely that the plants will suffer diseases or vine weevil attack in the second year.

❀ For short-term containers, such as those filled with summer annuals, a standard, multipurpose, loam-free mix usually fits the bill. I always add the larger chunks left after sieving for seed sowing—bedding plants don't need such perfect conditions, and I think these chunks make for even better drainage.

❀ For longer-term containers, it is usually best to choose a loam-based mix with plenty of fertilizer. If you find this tends to get a bit airless, add up to 50 percent multipurpose loam-free soil, plus some grit. The added weight of the loam also helps to prevent pots containing taller plants from toppling over.

Save on potting mix in tall pots

If you've fallen for a long, tall container for your summer bedding, it's easy to save on the amount of mix you'll use. Place an upside-down flowerpot over the drainage hole, so only the upper part of the container needs filling; shallow-rooting and short-term plants don't need deep soil and won't suffer. If the pot is to stand in a windy spot, reduce the risk of toppling by filling the bottom half with stones or gravel.

Feed in advance

Make life easy by mixing in feed before planting.

To save time later on, you can add controlled-release fertilizer granules to the mix at planting time; these usually supply food for about six months. For summer bedding I still add regular applications of a high-potash liquid feed because this will ensure an even better display of flowers.

51

Improve moisture levels

Moisture-retaining granules can prevent plants from suffering from water-stress—great if you are out at work all day. Make sure you follow the instructions with regard to quantities, and don't be tempted to add more than suggested—otherwise, as the granules absorb water and expand, you may end up with a volcano effect. I prefer to hydrate the crystals thoroughly and then add them to the potting mix. This makes it easier to get them evenly distributed; dry crystals tend to fall to the bottom more easily.

The granules grow 30 times larger once wet.

Choose plants carefully

Creating your own container display is great, and you can do exactly what you like in terms of color combinations. Don't forget to check what each plant will look like when it is fully grown and in flower. Consider height, spread, and brightness. If necessary, amend your lineup before you plant rather than after.

Think about colour combinations

When planting for a single-season display—for example, when you plant seasonal summer bedding—it generally looks best to stick to just two or three types of plant and to restrict the color range—unless, of course, you want to create an "Aaagh, where are my sunglasses" effect! If the plants will be in flower at different times, it is a different matter.

Because containers are much smaller than borders, keep combinations simple.

Pale colors and white make a serene combination.

Odd numbers cover up any variations

If you want to ensure that uneven plant growth is well hidden, use odd, rather than even, numbers for your larger more high-profile plants. This way it should not look as if an attempt at symmetry has gone wrong!

Cooling colors

It can look great to have really bold colors, but if you are not careful you can end up with just too many. For a cooling effect in your plantings, use plants with either silver foliage or white flowers. These are calming on their own, but they can also add some contrast and a bit of light relief to a bright color scheme. There's a wide range of likely contenders.

Plants on higher steps need to look good from below as well as above.

Looking good from all angles

When you are planting a container, make sure that it looks good from all the angles at which it is likely to be seen, not just from your view when you're doing the planting. A pot on the doorstep, for instance, needs to look good as you approach the door, from above, and from the doorway.

Starting the cascade effect

If you want to make trailing plants around the edges of the container start to perform a little sooner, angle the plants out slightly when you plant them. This way, they are leaning in the right direction from the start.

Remember where your plants will be sited

It is all very well falling for the plants you see in your garden center or those that are growing fantastically well in someone else's garden, but make sure that they will also perform well in the spot you have to fill. The amount of sunshine or shade the site receives is hugely important to a plant's success.

Will you water it enough?

If you know you may not be able to water the container quite as often as you should, it is no use going for the real moisture lovers like monkey flower (*Mimulus*), lobelias, and azaleas (*Rhododendron*). Instead choose plants known to be more drought tolerant, such as pelargoniums or herbaceous geraniums.

Don't skimp, pack them in!

Provided you make sure that there is some fresh compost between all the root-balls of adjacent plants and between the root-balls and the container, you can really use as many short-term bedding plants as you can pack in. The normal rules for long-term planting do not apply here.

The pelargoniums that form the backbone of this display will tolerate fairly dry conditions.

Many small bulbs are happy planted in layers.

Planting for long-lasting displays

❀ Make any container look good for longer by underplanting with seasonal bulbs. Choose smallish varieties, such as miniature daffodils (Narcissus), iris, or perhaps crocus, to extend the season of interest. Make sure you plant them deeply enough, and avoid putting very dense-rooted plants, such as heathers, directly on top of bulbs—they may not be able to make their way through the mat of roots. The roots of seasonal bedding plants should not be a problem.

❀ In longer-term containers, where bulbs could last for more than one season, you can also underplant with seasonal bedding to provide even more color and impact, but take care when planting these, or else you may damage the roots beneath.

Get plants off to a good start

Pinch out leggy shoots and fading flowers before planting in the container; it's easier than doing it once planted, when you're all too likely to dislodge the plant. Doing this will also allow the plants to concentrate on producing good, sturdy, bushy growth, and will help them to get established.

Make sure all the plants look their best at the start.

Keep moisture in and pests out

When the planting is complete, try dressing the soil surface with a layer of sharp grit. This serves two purposes: it helps to keep moisture in and decreases the risk of vine weevils laying their eggs.

Night-scented stocks are compact enough for most containers.

Complete with some perfume

Bedding plants may look good, but not many are scented. Sprinkle seed of night-scented stock (*Matthiola bicornis*) into gaps in the soil to provide fragrance during warm summer evenings.

Plant in advance

Try to plant containers of bedding a few weeks early. Provided they are kept in a sheltered and, if necessary, frost-free spot, the plants will establish better than if the container is put out in its final position immediately. Be prepared to wait.

Success with hanging baskets

Take care not to plant trailing or very bushy plants right next to the points where the chains will be attached. If you do when you hang the basket, you are likely to damage the plants as the chains swing into place.

Cultivating crops in containers

Tasty tomatoes, succulent cucumbers, aromatic sage, and juicy apples are just four of the many edible crops you can grow in containers, providing you match the pot to the plant. Here's how to make the leap from pot to plate!

Any vessel with drainage holes that holds soil will be good for growing edibles.

What can you use as a container?

You can use pretty much anything that's a suitable size with adequate drainage holes to contain your edibles. There are even plenty of good-quality fabric "planter bags," complete with drainage holes and handles for ease of use. The advantage of these bags is that you can fold them up over winter when they are not in use.

Big pots make a big difference

❀ By definition, cropping plants need to be productive. If your expectations are to be met, it's essential that they have a decent-sized container. Small containers are hard to keep moist, so avoid pots smaller than 12 inches x 12 inches (30cm x 30cm). Big is invariably best.

❀ Drought-tolerant plants, such as many of the Mediterranean herbs, cope happily in a smaller container, or several can be planted together.

Finding big pots

Recycle those huge flower pots that are used for sizable shrubs and trees—either after you have planted them yourself or if local landscapers and tree surgeons have any to spare. For those who do a lot of planting, big pots can become space-wasters, and they may be very happy to part with them.

Growing bags are great

❀ Growing bags can be bought in just about every garden center or DIY outlet. They offer the lowest-cost option and work especially well with crops such as tomatoes and peppers.

❀ The soil in a growing bag is often extremely compacted. Luckily the plastic of the bag tends to be tough, so make sure you thoroughly work the bag over to fluff up the contents before you start planting. This will also ensure that the soil is evenly distributed within the bag.

Before cutting or planting make sure you fluff up the planting mix.

How to use growing bags

❀ Most standard-sized growing bags will fit three tomato plants, but I find it much easier to restrict myself to two: it keeps the plants healthy, and I always get a heavier crop.

❀ Before cutting planting holes in the bag, make sure it is in exactly the spot you want it. Unless supported by a board, open growing bags are impossible to move without losing soil.

❀ Make an H-shaped cut for each plant; rather than removing the two flaps of plastic this creates, fold each back on itself. This leaves a slightly protruding "lip" on the outer edge of the cut, which will help deflect a lot of water, decrease runoff, and make it much easier to get all the water into the soil.

❀ If you plan to support taller crops in bags, you need to put support structures in place before cutting holes and planting. Inserting them once the plants are in the growing bags makes excessive root disturbance more likely.

❀ If you tend to overwater plants in containers, then it may be worth making a couple of holes in the base of the growing bags to allow surplus water to drain off. Otherwise, with this type of container, you are essentially planting in an impervious plastic bag.

Pot feet really can make a difference.

Drainage means life or death

Drainage is important for any plant, so make sure that drainage holes in the base of a container do not become obstructed or clogged. This is easily prevented by using a layer of crocks in the bottom of the pot or by raising the pot off the ground onto "pot feet," bricks, or even an old pallet to keep the holes clear of any debris.

Chillies can be an attractive crop for the patio.

Suit the potting mix to the crop

❀ The choice of potting mix you use will depend on whether you plan to grow crops permanently or temporarily. Apples and other permanent crops will benefit from a loam- or soil-based blend, while crops such as annual vegetables grow perfectly well in a good-quality multipurpose mix.

❀ For lime-hating plants, such as blueberries, an ericaceous mix is vital. If they are grown in standard soil, they may develop lime-induced chlorosis, which is an iron and manganese deficiency that results in leaf yellowing between the leaf veins.

Top ten crops for containers

1 Carrots
2 Chard 'Bright Lights'
3 Chili peppers
4 Dwarf French beans
5 Dwarf runner beans, such as 'Hestia'
6 Eggplant
7 Any herbs
8 Sweet or bell peppers
9 Potatoes
10 Tomatoes such as 'Tumbler' or 'Totem'

Given enough water and feed, almost any crop can be grown in a pot.

Which crops are suitable?

Just about any vegetable or fruit, including tree fruits, can be grown in a container. The only conditions are that the container must be large enough and filled with a suitable growing medium, and that you must be prepared to put in that bit of extra work required to produce successful crops in containers.

Add some manure

If you have access to well-rotted manure, add it to your potting mix. It will help to improve moisture retention and provide a feed for the crops as they develop. I add about 30 percent manure or garden compost to containers when growing vegetables.

Potted potatoes

❀ You can grow potatoes in a container and produce a very acceptable crop. I use a container with a minimum size of 18 inches (45cm) each way, and if you choose an attractive container, it can even look good on a patio or terrace.

❀ There is no need to plant more than one or two potatoes in each pot of this size; more than this will not actually give much more of a crop because the plants will compete too much with each other.

❀ It's often said that main-crop varieties work best in containers, but I have grown early and salad varieties in good-sized containers with great success—so grow what you actually like to eat!

❀ If you plant the tuber approximately 6–8 inches (15–20cm) below the rim of the container, you can gradually build up the soil level in the same way that you would "earth up" a crop of potatoes growing in open ground. This will help to keep the plant cropping well and greatly reduces the risk of light reaching the developing tubers, which would cause them to turn green and poisonous!

Make watering easier

Generally speaking, as far as the pots are concerned, big is always better. Large pots full of a lot of soil will be much easier to keep adequately watered, making your life easier and greatly increasing the chances of a healthy, heavy-cropping plant.

Tree fruits need the largest containers of all.

Thriving beans

❀ Runner beans will do well in a container, but as they are a really thirsty crop, keeping them well watered to produce a good crop can be difficult. Use as large a container as you can—the greater volume of soil means that it will dry out less readily—and line the inside walls with bubble wrap.

❀ Water in the evening to give the beans a chance to take up more water.

❀ Beans growing up a tepee of bamboo canes creates an attractive bit of vertical gardening.

❀ The dwarf runner bean 'Hestia' is perfect for smaller pots; it does not even require a support and has attractive red and white flowers.

❀ French beans are not only stringless but much more tolerant of dry soil than runner beans.

❀ Make successive sowings of dwarf French beans for an extended cropping period. The seeds can be sown direct; pests are less likely to eat the emerging seedlings.

❀ Get an extra early crop of dwarf French beans by sowing early and keeping the pot in the greenhouse. Once the danger of frost is passed, bring it outside.

Small containers are difficult to maintain.

Tips for tomatoes

❀ Tomatoes are the classic container vegetable, so simply choose any variety sold as being suitable for growing outdoors and get going.

❀ The "patio" varieties, which are generally particularly compact, are easier to keep happy in the confines of a smaller container.

❀ If you want attractive tomato plants for a hanging basket, then try the cascading varieties such as 'Tumbler' or 'Tumbling Tom'; the latter is available in red or yellow fruiting varieties. These also look good trailing over the edges of a container.

❀ Tomatoes are particularly intolerant of fluctuating temperatures, especially when the weather gets a bit cold. If planted out too early, the foliage often turns a miserable shade of purple! Always harden off the plants thoroughly and, unless you provide temporary protection, don't risk putting the containers out until early summer or even later.

Miniature or trailing tomatoes flourish in baskets.

❀ Choose a "bush" variety if you want to have a more compact tomato plant that does not need to have its sideshoots removed and only requires a bit of staking. "Cordon" or "indeterminate" types need more support.

Potted peppers

❀ Both sweet or bell peppers and chili peppers can be grown in containers. If you want a decent crop, choose a well-protected and sheltered spot with plenty of sun.

❀ If you're growing hot chili peppers and children also use the garden, position the pots well out of reach!

Try growing attractive peppers as a focal point next to a sunny bench.

Eggplant

❀ I find that eggplant grows well in pots, but the plants need a lot of natural light and plenty of warmth, so choose a site with care and make it as sheltered and sunny as possible.

❀ The pretty purple flowers (and sometimes purple stems too) make eggplant an attractive patio plant, but remember most varieties have sharp thorns, so think carefully before you put the pots in position.

Carrots and parsnips

❀ Both these crops are best sown directly into the compost; the seedlings can then be thinned to the spacing indicated on the packet.

❀ If you want to avoid carrots becoming infested with the maggot-like larvae of the carrot fly, growing them in a container makes the task easy. Choose a container more than 18 inches (45cm), tall and the crop will be too high for there to be much chance of the carrot fly laying her eggs on it.

❀ Parsnip seed should germinate fairly reliably under suitable conditions in well-drained soil, but it is still worth "station-sowing the seed." This means sowing two or three seeds in each spot where you would like one parsnip to grow—you can always thin out any extras.

❀ Parsnip seeds are particularly slow to germinate, so why not sow a few lettuce seeds where you sow each batch of parsnip seeds? This makes it clear exactly where the parsnips were sown, and makes good use of the pot until the parsnips start to grow. Once the seedlings begin to appear, simply use a sharp knife to cut the lettuce off just below the soil's surface.

Beets

This is a crop I thoroughly recommend for pot growing, especially if, like me, you have a high population of slugs and snails in your garden. These pests are less of a problem in pots.

❀ It is best not to try to transplant beets; they rarely produce as well. Sow the seed directly into the container; then thin out the seedlings as you would if they were in open ground.

Try red-leaf beets like 'Bull's Blood'.

Melon, zucchini, and squash

❀ All these related, heavy-cropping plants can be grown in containers, but they all do far better when supplied with lots of moisture and food, so I strongly advise using the largest container you can get.

❀ These crops are both hungry and thirsty, so they definitely benefit from some well-rotted manure incorporated in the potting soil.

❀ Zucchini are the easiest to grow in a container; the plants are relatively compact, and the fruits are small enough not to need supporting. The others will need more attention and work.

❀ If you grow squash in a container, remember that the plants generally produce plenty of wide-ranging, trailing stems. Try placing the container close to a hedge, trellis, or fence, which the plant can use as a support through which to scramble.

Zucchini plants can spread out quite a bit, so give them some space.

Salad leaves and lettuces

❀ Lettuces and other cut-and-come-again salad leaf crops do very well in containers and are so easy to harvest if you put the pot close to the house.

❀ Choose some varieties with colored or interestingly shaped leaves, and the crop will have double value, being both decorative and tasty. Grow single varieties; mix up the seed from a few of your favorites; or use one of the packets of mixed variety leaves.

❀ Reduce the risk of the lettuces running to seed by keeping pots at least partly shaded to help prevent the soil from drying out.

Using containers can help keep slugs off.

Colorful chard

❀ To make a productive patio pot full of chard look particularly gorgeous, choose a very colorful variety, such as 'Bright Lights'.

❀ For some jazzy color effects or serious color coordination, you could grow the crop in a contrasting or matching colored container.

'Bright Lights' has stems in a range of eye-catching colors.

Plants per pot

This is approximately how many plants fit a 12-inch (30cm) pot:

1 plant: Eggplant, zucchini, melon, squash, pepper, tomato

1–2 plants: Potato

3 plants: Strawberry

4–5 plants: Runner bean and climbing or dwarf French bean

8–10 plants: Beet, chard

12 plants: Parsnip

35 plants: Carrot

Lettuce: depends on variety

Look for attractive crops

It is worth looking around for especially ornamental varieties of your favorite plants. For instance, you could have yellow, striped, or purple tomatoes. And why grow the standard gray-green sage when you could have it with purple, or purple, cream, and green variegated leaves?

Herbs

❀ Herbs make great pot plants and most look really attractive, too. Combine their good looks with a stunning terra-cotta pot, and presto, you have something seriously ornamental, aromatic, and tasty.

❀ Herbs need excellent drainage, so incorporate plenty of horticultural grit into the mix before planting; I add about 25 percent by volume.

Terra-cotta suits herbs, both in terms of their looks and needs.

❀ Make a pot of herbs look all the more attractive by dressing the surface of the soil with a thick layer of attractive horticultural grit. This will also help to ensure good growth by reducing the risk of stagnant conditions around the plant crowns.

❀ If your garden soil is heavy and inclined to be moist, your herb growing may need to be restricted to pots. Make it even easier to get the most from what you grow by positioning the pots in a lovely sunny spot that is easily accessible.

❀ Growing mint in a pot is the one absolutely foolproof way to ensure that it does not start to take over your garden, as it does when grown in open ground.

❀ Make a container of assorted herbs look especially attractive by including a few trailing or sprawling varieties of thyme planted close to the edge, where they can cascade downward.

❀ If you want to keep a record of exactly which varieties of herb you have in the pot, remove the plastic labels when planting and slip each into the soil close to its plant. This way you need not see the label, but you can retrieve the information easily.

Mint should be kept in a container to control it. You can plunge a pot into the ground if you want it in a bed.

Strawberries

❀ Strawberries are the favorite fruit for growing in containers, largely because they really seem to thrive, whether they are in a special strawberry planter, a window box, or just a good-sized pot.

❀ The advantage of growing strawberries in a pot is that because the plants are raised off the ground, the fruits are far less likely to be nibbled by hungry slugs and snails. This is the perfect way to grow them if you want undamaged fruits and don't like using slug controls.

❀ I find strawberry planters, with their flange-shaped holes, really difficult to plant in and maintain, though other peoples' efforts certainly look good. You can make your own tiered planter from three shallow terra-cotta pots of decreasing sizes. Fill each with soil, then stack them on top of each other, with the largest at the bottom. You can plant around the edges of the lower pots, and in the center of the top one. A perfect strawberry mountain!

Give strawberries plenty of water and feed, and they'll guarantee a juicy crop.

Keep crops watered

Some flowering plants might cope with drought, but crops in pots need a good, regular supply of water. Drip irrigation systems can make all the difference, and most can be fed from outside spigots.

Tree fruit

❀ It is possible to grow tree fruit in containers, but you are not likely to get a heavy crop and, for me, the maintenance is a job I would prefer to avoid. If space is limited but you do have some open ground, it is easier and more productive to grow fruit trees in fan, espalier, step-over, or cordon forms.

❀ If you really want to use a pot, perhaps to move more tender trees under cover for winter or to make a fig fruit better, the container must be large, ideally a full-sized half barrel, not one of the dinky sort about 18 inches (45cm) across.

❀ The potting mix needs to be loam-based, but add extra grit to keep the compost structure open and adequately drained.

You may want to keep trees near house walls and foundations in pots, but you will get smaller crops.

Trees & shrubs

Trees and shrubs form the "backbone" of a garden, providing structure and giving form 12 months of the year. Trees and many shrubs too can be quite pricey, so it is all the more essential that you get the right ones.

Over the years, trees will change their shape and size, and the effect they have on the garden will subtly change, too. Being the largest plants in the garden, trees also tend to have the greatest influence on what other plants will grow and how they will flourish. Choosing the most suitable ones, and making sure that they grow and develop to create just the effect you had dreamed of, can be one of the most important gardening tasks.

Choosing your trees

Choosing trees should be a pleasure, as they are plants that may be there for generations and will help to make your garden that perfect haven that it has the potential to be. This is probably the most significant purchase you will make

because the trees will have such a huge impact on your garden over the years. A tree has the potential to grow to many times the size it was when you bought it. So when you decide you need some trees, make sure you do your research and try to avoid those impulse buys.

Every now and then established trees may need the help of an arborist or tree surgeon. This is an expense that you should try not to resent, because when properly looked after, those trees will give you untold pleasure in return.

This chapter shows you how to

❀ Choose a new tree or shrub—getting the right species for the site.

❀ Maintain trees and shrubs: how to plant them, care for them, and prune them.

❀ Choose what to plant under the tree canopy.

❀ Deal with tender species.

❀ Buy, plant, and care for shrub roses.

Choosing a new tree or shrub

Trees and large shrubs often act as focal points within the garden's design, so you need to spend time researching before you buy. Make sure the species you have in mind will thrive in the conditions you can offer and that they won't grow too big.

Seeing trees in full leaf does make choosing easier.

Convenience plants

Container-grown trees and shrubs are popular because they are convenient. They can be bought and planted at any time of year, but there can be hidden drawbacks. Avoid buying them either during or just after extremely cold weather, when their roots may have been frozen in their pots, or during or after a long period of hot weather, when plants may have become stressed by drought.

Autumn is best

There is no doubt that autumn is the best time to plant trees and shrubs. This allows the plants time to acclimatize before facing the stresses of the following summer. More importantly, it also gives the roots time to move out into the soil while it is still relatively warm and moist.

Bare-root or balled?

Bare-root plants, lifted from open ground, are sold from late autumn to late winter or very early spring. The roots of root-balled plants are put into moist soil and wrapped. They are often a very good value, but the roots must be kept moist. Both may be planted while dormant and leafless to limit root damage and help them to establish.

Nurseries may prune roots to help plants establish.

See its true colors

If you would like to plant a tree or shrub with colorful autumn foliage, then autumn is the best time to buy. Autumn color is influenced by several factors, including weather and soil conditions, but if you see the plant in its full autumn glory before you buy, then at least you'll know it has the potential to do great things.

Because maples can vary quite a bit, pick your plant when in leaf.

Paying for delivery

Although getting sizable shrubs or trees delivered may add quite a bit to the cost of buying them, the cost of delivery may well be worthwhile. If you have not got the right type of vehicle, you can end up damaging the stems or having the top growth blown to bits in the wind!

Cutting down to size

It is important to choose a suitable size of tree for the space you are planting. If you fall in love with a tree that is likely to get too big, you could consider treating it as a short-term resident, perhaps planning to fell it after ten years or so. Alternatively, consider having it pruned and shaped regularly so that it retains its shape. Some trees respond better than others to this treatment, so check before you buy.

Top ten trees for small gardens

1. *Acer griseum* (Paper-bark maple)
2. *Acer negundo* 'Flamingo' (Ash-leaved maple)
3. *Acer palmatum* (Japanese maple)
4. *Acer pseudoplatanus* 'Brilliantissimum' (Sycamore)
5. *Cercis siliquastrum* (Judas tree)
6. *Koelruteria paniculata* (Golden-rain tree)
7. *Magnolia stellata* (Star magnolia)
8. Many *Prunus* species (Cherry)
9. *Pyrus salicifolia* 'Pendula' (Pear)
10. *Robinia pseudoacacia* 'Frisia' (Black locust)

Acers are perfect for small spaces.

Be a choosy shopper

❀ To pick the healthiest plants, inspect stems for signs of die-back, pests, or infection; check that the leaves are in good condition; and look for plump, vigorous buds. Put back anything that does not look in perfect health.

❀ Avoid plants with moss, weeds, or lichens on the soil—it suggests they have been poorly cared for.

❀ Excessive pruning may have been done to remove die-back; the problem may not be there anymore, but the plant is weakened.

❀ Slip off the pot: soil that falls apart indicates recent repotting or maybe root die-back; congested roots suggest a plant has been in its pot too long.

Bigger isn't better

The size of the tree or shrub you buy will affect its price. A big tree will make more impact when it's planted, but may also cost you ten times the price of a smaller one—and need more looking after than its smaller versions. Staking is rarely advised for average-sized new purchases, but it may be essential for a big tree when the size of root-ball cannot support the top growth. Watering needs are also greater, and the tree will establish more slowly, so think hard before buying big.

The growth below the surface is just as vital as what's above.

Planting time

Plant your trees and shrubs as soon as possible after you have bought them so that there is less chance of their being damaged or suffering from drought. This is equally important when planting in containers, as you are unlikely to water as regularly as the nursery.

Look after container-grown plants

If you can't plant new pot-grown trees or shrubs straight away, water them well and stand them in a sheltered spot where they won't be knocked or blown over. If necessary, carefully tie taller plants to a support, or even lay them down so they're less likely to get damaged.

"Heel in" bare-root trees or shrubs

Bare-root plants need to be "heeled in" or temporarily planted to prevent their roots drying out. If you are sure that you can plant within 24 hours, cover the roots in damp rags overnight. Dig the planting hole before lifting them so that they can go straight in.

Heel in on a slant to avoid root disturbance.

Making a moat

If the site is dry or likely to become dry, scrape out the soil around the planting hole to create a slight depression and encircling bank that will funnel the water toward the roots. If this slight depression is maintained, it should continue to direct water inward for years to come.

The roots should grow out into a zone of planting mix.

Dig a big hole

Make sure that the hole you dig is bigger than the rootball of the plant. If possible, aim to make the planting hole at least 50 percent bigger than the existing pot. This will give you plenty of space to spare in all directions and allow you to add plenty of planting mix.

Planting on heavy soils

Dig as large a hole as possible, and mix grit and planting mix with the natural soil to reduce the contrast between it and the contents of the hole. This dramatically reduces "sump" problems. Sumps are the result of planting a container-grown plant in a smallish hole in heavy soil with normal planting mix. The root-ball can act like a sponge, drawing in excess moisture when the soil gets wet, and drowning the plant.

Mound planting

In very heavy soils or those that are prone to waterlogging, it is best to plant trees and shrubs on a slight mound to reduce damage. Be careful not to leave any of the roots exposed, as that will have disastrous results. Hedges planted in a wet site will have a greater chance of thriving if planted higher than normal; plant them along a slight ridge, rather than trying to make a series of individual mounds.

Planting mixtures

A good mixture for planting consists of soil from the hole that is mixed with some well-rotted manure or garden compost, plus some general fertilizer. This should help to improve the soil texture and provide nutrients to get the tree or shrub started. Make sure that any fertilizers are mixed in thoroughly and don't come into direct contact with the plant, and that you water the tree or shrub well.

Extra care on dry soils

Fill the planting hole with water on a dry site, and allow the water to drain away before you plant. This should help the surrounding soil to become thoroughly moistened without wasting water.

Planting checklist

❀ If the roots are tangled, teasing them out will really help the plant to establish quickly. Soaking the root-ball in water for a couple of hours, or at most overnight, makes it easier to untangle the roots without damaging them.

❀ It is essential that you do not set plants too deeply, or you will run the risk of stem bases rotting and the roots not getting all the oxygen they need.

Using a cane across the hole is easier than judging depth by eye.

❀ Plants from a reputable garden center or nursery should be potted at the correct depth, but there's no harm in checking—just the roots should be belowground, not part of the stem or any of the trunk above the roots.

❀ To ensure you plant at the right depth, place a cane across the hole and use this as a guide for the positioning of the root-ball.

❀ As you add the planting mix, periodically check the planting depth; it is a lot easier to adjust it at this stage.

❀ Firm the mix around the roots as you fill to prevent settling and ensure that the roots make close contact with the soil.

❀ As soon as the plant is in, water thoroughly, topping up the soil carefully if the level drops.

Care after planting

Once a tree or shrub is in the ground, you can't just walk off and completely forget it. Huge numbers of potentially lovely (and often rather pricey) plants are lost every year because they're not given enough aftercare.

When to stake

❀ You need only stake large trees, which are vulnerable to wind-rock before their roots become established and can support their own top growth.

❀ If you do need to stake, drive in a short stake at an angle. This encourages better root development and a stronger trunk than longer or upright stakes.

❀ Take great care not to damage the roots when you are driving the stake into position. It is best to hammer the stake into the ground before the plant goes in the hole.

Water deep down

If you are worried about drought after planting, why not bury a piece of pipe at an angle (say, a length of downspout) next to the roots of the new plant? Keep the pipe in position as you back-fill the hole, and leave the top end protruding just above the soil surface. You can pour water straight down the pipe, avoiding wastage and ensuring that the water goes straight to the roots quickly and effectively.

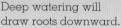
Deep watering will draw roots downward.

Rabbit damage

If there is any chance of rabbit damage, take precautions immediately, using at least one spiral tree guard or erecting a rabbit-proof cylinder around the base of the plant. For multistemmed trees or shrubs, you may need to use a wire mesh to protect the base of the plant, or perhaps try several spiral guards.

Spiral guards may not be attractive, but they work.

Tie time

When choosing a tree tie, look for one that is easy to adjust and which avoids constriction as the trunk expands. It must also have a "buffer" or spacer block on it; this should be placed between the tree's trunk and the stake to prevent chafing when the tree sways.

Check ties regularly, and loosen as the trunk thickens.

Mulching last

❀ When planting is complete, apply a mulch 3½ inches (8cm) deep to cover the entire root area, and ideally a little farther. This will help to both decrease competition from weeds and reduce moisture loss from the soil by evaporation.

❀ Make sure that the mulch is not in contact with the tree's trunk or the shrub's stems because this may cause rotting and stress, possibly even death.

❀ Don't be tempted to use an impermeable material, such as sheet plastic, beneath the mulch. This might stop weeds from growing, but it will also dramatically reduce the amount of oxygen and moisture that can get through to the plant's roots.

Woven plastic covered with bark is very effective.

Under the mulch

There are plenty of weed-suppressing fabrics on the market now. These will allow moisture and air to get where they need to go, and can be used on the soil surface and then concealed beneath a layer of more attractive mulching material.

Weather damage

Occasionally, even a perfectly hardy tree or shrub may suffer damage from cold or wind shortly after planting. If there is any risk of this happening, drape horticultural fleece over it, or use a fleece drawstring bag large enough to keep the whole top growth snug. Regular watering is a must during windy weather as well as in dry spells.

What can go wrong?

❀ Woody plants can suffer from replant disorder, in which a perfectly healthy new plant deteriorates rapidly when planted in the same spot from which a closely related plant has been removed. This is especially common with roses, apples, and pears, and can occur even when the plant looks in perfect health. The precise cause is uncertain—it may be nutritional or due to the buildup of soil bacteria or fungi—so never give it a chance to happen.

❀ Roots of woody plants can be surprisingly springy and may tend to curl back into their compacted or restricted shape. Make sure you re-spread them carefully before backfilling the planting hole.

Banana fertilizer

If you eat lots of bananas you can make good use of the skins, which have a particularly high potassium content. When roughly chopped and added to the planting hole, they will improve the organic content and provide extra potassium as they break down, which will encourage both wood ripening and an excellent flowering display.

Pruning trees and shrubs

Always check the pruning needs of your trees and shrubs, either on the label or in a reference book, before you attack them with any sort of pruning tool. If in doubt, wait—too often, plants are spoiled by unnecessary or excessive pruning.

Neat cuts without long stubs are the key to good pruning.

Cut at an angle

Make pruning cuts at an angle so that rain can roll off the surface rather than remain on it. Cut close to the bud, but not so close that the bud itself could be damaged.

Pruning directions

Always cut back to a good-looking, healthy bud facing in the direction you want any new growth to go. This is almost always going to be an outward-facing bud.

Keep tools sharp

Sharp pruning tools are vital; it is easy to create a horrendous, crushed mess with badly designed or blunt pruners. The damaged stems not only look awful but are also more prone to infection by fungi that cause die-back.

Pruning for health

❀ Remove weak and spindly wood, pruning back to an outward-facing bud. This should help to promote the development of healthy new growth.

❀ Dead wood can and should be removed promptly, regardless of the time of year, but it is easier to spot what is dead or dying when the plant is in leaf.

❀ If you are pruning out dead or dying parts of a stem, make sure you cut well past any signs of the problem, into completely healthy growth, and then clean the pruning tool before using it again.

Always remove sickly or dead growth quickly.

Pruning for flowers

When pruning to encourage new flowering stems or to rejuvenate a neglected shrub, you can remove up to one in five of the old stems, pruning back to within about 2–3 inches (5–7.5cm) of ground level.

Checks and balances

When pruning, take your time and stand back from time to time to check that you are achieving a well-balanced look and removing stems evenly over the entire plant.

Ten common shrubs pruned in spring

1. *Buddleja davidii* (Butterfly bush)
2. *Caryopteris*
3. *Ceratostigma* (Plumbago)
4. *Cotinus* (Smokebush)
5. *Forsythia*
6. Hardy *fuchsia*
7. *Hydrangea*
8. Shrubby *lavateras* (Mallow)
9. *Perovskia*
10. *Spirea*

Fuchsias flower on new growth.

Remove suckers

Some trees are notorious for producing suckers or unwanted growth from the base or at some distance from the trunk—watch out for this especially on Sumac (*Rhus*), cherry (*Prunus*), robinias, lilacs (*Syringa*), and poplars (*Populus*). Suckers need to be dealt with promptly: cut or pull them off right up close to the root from which they came, but be warned you may need to do this regularly. The very action of removing them often stimulates more to grow!

Removing branches

If you cut a whole limb from a tree at one time, the bark underneath may be torn, unless you "undercut" it first. Use a sharp saw to make a cut into the bottom of the limb about 12 inches (30cm) from the trunk, cutting about quarter of the way through. Next, saw down through the branch about ¾ inches (2cm) further away from the trunk until you can lift the branch away. Now make another undercut 1–2 inches (3–5cm) from the trunk, then saw down from the top of the limb, joining the two cuts. Make sure you do not damage the swollen "collar" at the branch base where the wound heals. Finally, neaten off the newly created cut.

A short stub is easy to remove cleanly.

A cut away from the collar will heal well.

Ten common shrubs pruned in summer/after flowering

1. *Buddleja alternifolia*
2. *Chaenomeles* (Flowering quince)
3. *Cotoneaster*
4. *Deutzia*
5. *Kolkwitzia* (Beauty Bush)
6. *Magnolia x soulangeana* (Magnolia)
7. *Philadelphus* (Mock Orange)
8. *Photinia*
9. *Prunus* (Ornamental cherry)
10. *Ribes* (Flowering currant)

Under and through the canopy

Make the best use of every scrap of space by underplanting shrubs and trees, and growing climbers as well. Obviously this increases competition for moisture and nutrients, but as long as you supply plenty of both, everything should grow really well.

A few bulbs tucked around a sapling can spread to form a whole colony under the mature tree.

What plants can you use?

It is best to use relatively small and shallow-rooted plants for underplanting because they will make fewer demands on the soil and everything it contains. Bedding plants, herbaceous perennials, and bulbs generally work fine.

Plant together

Minimize damage to the tree or shrub roots by getting your permanent underplanting, such as bulbs, in place when planting the tree or shrub. This makes the planting easier, and means there is no possibility of any root damage.

Drifts of bulbs

Bulbs planted in drifts look wonderful beneath trees and can really transform any part of your garden. Try to plant the bulbs in a random, scattered effect so that they look natural. Straight lines or spacing that is too perfect really looks peculiar and certainly spoils the effect.

Purple crocuses look natural under trees.

Keeping to scale

If you want to plant beneath a shrub, you can still use bulbs to great effect. To keep everything in scale, stick to smaller types such as crocus, snowdrops (*Galanthus*), cyclamen or grape hyacinths (*Muscari*), or use miniature narcissi such as 'Tête a Tête'.

Making space

If there is no space beneath a shrub, why not do a bit of crown-lifting? Just remove the lowermost branches. Provided you don't overdo it, the shrub should still look great, but there will be space for a lovely drift of bedding, bulbs, or small herbaceous perennials.

Best climbers for scaling shrubs

1. *Clematis*
2. *Cobaea scandens* (Cathedral bell)
3. *Eccromocarpus scaber* (Chilean glory flower)
4. *Ipomoea* (Morning glory)
5. *Lathyrus* (Sweet pea)
6. *Thunbergia alata* (Black-eyed Susan)
7. *Tropaeolum speciosum* (Flame creeper)

Protecting the roots

To ensure that both the tree and the climber do well, each needs an adequate root run. Therefore the climber needs to be planted at some distance from the trunk of the tree, not right up close to it. Make sure that there is plenty of bulky organic matter in the planting hole, too, and pay extra attention over the first few years while the plants get established.

Supporting act

❀ To get the climber going in the right direction, run wire or rope from its base to the lowest branches; remove it once the climber is established.

❀ Thread the wire or rope through a length of old hose where it goes over a branch, to prevent chafing.

Ascending color

❀ If you want more color and interest in a limited space, give a tree or shrub extra value by growing a climber through it. A climber will increase the seasons of interest and, provided you use one that is not too heavy and is in proportion with the shrub or tree, both should grow well together. Such mixing is best done with fully established shrubs or trees, and any shrubs that are used as supports need to be quite large.

❀ Annual climbers can look great, particularly on relatively small shrubs, and will not pose significant competition.

❀ If you go for a clematis, unless it is an extremely large shrub or preferably a tree, avoid the very vigorous *Clematis montana*; its rampant growth may prove just too much!

A clematis in a tree gives it a whole new look.

Will they survive?

Choose plants that can either put up with the degree of shade cast by the tree or shrub or guarantee an adequate amount of time when the shade is not excessive. Underplantings and climbers are likely to need a bit of extra moisture and food, so keep the area well watered and mulched.

Best climbers to grow into trees

1. Chilean glory flower
2. Clematis
3. Flame creeper
4. Honeysuckles (*Lonicera*)
5. Roses including 'Rambling Rector', 'Albéric Barbier', 'Bobby James', 'Paul's Musk', and for large trees only, *Rosa filipes* 'Kiftsgate'

Honeysuckles in trees near seating give fragrance.

Tricks for tender species

If you've fallen for a tree or shrub that is a bit tender, do your utmost to provide it with what it needs, or be prepared to take the risk that it will be damaged or even killed when the weather turns particularly cold.

A warm wall helps
Cytisus battandieri.

Siting with care

Choose the planting site with extra care: consider how much protection is offered by nearby hedges, large shrubs, trees, boundaries, or heated buildings. Planting on a sheltered, sunny wall may make the difference between survival or die-back.

Tougher with time

Many marginally hardy plants are much hardier once established. Provide extra cold protection in the first few years, but often this won't be necessary after a few seasons.

Make a base camp

Create a seasonal shelter using galvanized chicken wire made into a tent over the shrub and filled with dry leaves, fern fronds, or straw. This works well on wall-shrubs because the cage or tent can be fixed to the wall or fence. Avoid using hay or other material that is inclined to hold moisture; this will encourage stem deterioration.

Wrap up warm

Cover potentially tender shrubs or small trees with a few layers of horticultural fleece, making sure that they are well anchored. Fleece drawstring bags are very useful for shrubs because they can simply be popped over them to provide a few degrees of frost protection.

Fleece bags are the most convenient protection.

Let them breathe

Never be tempted to wrap tender plants in plastic or other non-breathable material because condensation will build up, shortly followed by rotting and deterioration. Plastic can be used, but only in the very short term.

Wrap tree fern trunks with breathable fabric.

Tender tree ferns

Stems or bases of tender shrubs, such as tree ferns (*Dicksonia antarctica*), can be wrapped in burlap or old sacking held in place with twine.

Shrub roses

Roses are deservedly popular garden plants, but don't forget that most of them are well armed with thorns. Think about their proximity to paths or other places where they could regularly pose a danger to young children, or even you.

Shopping around for variety

The biggest range of roses is available from specialist growers and nurseries, so make sure you look through few a few catalogs or websites—the range is staggering.

Bare-root roses aren't expensive and establish well.

Buying bare-root

Most people agree that it is best to buy bare-root roses, ready to be delivered and planted in the late autumn and winter. Most of the specialist nurseries supply them this way.

With such a huge variety of roses, you will certainly find a favorite.

Planting depths

Roses generally have a clear graft-point where the rootstock has been grafted onto the chosen cultivar. When planting a rose, this swollen area should be at or only just below soil level; if it is buried too deeply you are much more likely to get unwanted sucker growth from it later on.

Know your roses

Roses differ in more than just their flower shape and color. For example, musk roses are best where you need scent to carry on the air. If you live in a damp climate, rugosa types are the most resistant to fungal diseases and are also surprisingly hardy. There are roses suitable for drier and wetter gardens, too, so it is worth doing a bit of research. Good nurseries can advise if you tell them your conditions.

Special treatment for roses

Roses really do benefit from a specially formulated rose fertilizer, which has just the right balance of nutrients. These include potassium and magnesium, which encourage flowering while preventing the foliage from yellowing as a result of magnesium deficiency.

Climbers & wall plants

Whatever your personal style may be, it is great to be able to garden not just on the horizontal but also to include a little vertical gardening. Any garden has its fair share of vertical surfaces, and most of them will have the potential to become new planting spaces, so why not make use of them all? If you have always hankered after a larger garden than you have, or perhaps your gardening is restricted to a yard enclosed by fencing or walls or maybe even a balcony, then making use of each and every one of those potential planting sites that are on the vertical is even more important.

In this chapter take a closer look at how to ensure you succeed in making the best possible use of each surface, whatever its size, structure, shape, or aspect. Some of these surfaces are best suited to being covered with climbing plants, while others can be made beautiful using wall shrubs. It is well worth doing a little research into what is available before you go shopping.

Bringing height to your garden

Climbers and wall shrubs are not difficult to grow. Provided you plant properly in the right position and keep them in good shape, they can totally transform dull expanses of wall and fence. Many walls, especially those that are south or west facing, will offer you warmer and more sheltered growing conditions not available in other parts of your garden. They should be cherished and used to their very best advantage.

This chapter shows you how to

❀ Support climbers with different kinds of structures.

❀ Choose climbers and wall shrubs—assess your needs and conditions to make the best choice.

❀ Plant climbers—tips and tricks for the best results.

❀ Prune and train climbers at the best time of year.

How to support climbers

Some climbers are able to cling to surfaces and need no additional support, but most need a means to help them cover the surface. Generally speaking, the larger and woodier the stems of the established plant, the stronger the support will need to be.

Self-supporters

Self-clinging climbers include Chinese trumpet creeper (*Campsis grandiflora*); the ivies (*Hedera helix* and *H. colchica*); climbing hydrangea (*Hydrangea anomala* subsp. *petiolaris*); Virginia creeper (*Parthenocissus henryana, P. quinquefolia*); Boston ivy (*P. tricuspidata* 'Veitchii'); and *Pileostegia viburnoides*. All of these plants may need some minor support until they start to cling.

Use a climbing hydrangea to cover a shaded wall.

Order of priority

If the climber you are planting is quite small, it may not be able to make much use of the support system initially, but always get the trellis or wires in place before you plant. It is simpler to work without the plant, and there is less chance of damaging it.

Anyone for trellis?

Trellis panels are a useful way to partially obscure a view or unsightly area while also providing a good surface up which to grow climbers. Choose light- and medium-weight climbers, which should be fine on a trellis. Avoid the most vigorous ones such as Virginia creeper (*Parthenocissus quinquefolia*) or some types of clematis, and the heaviest, such as wisteria.

Thunbergia alata 'African Sunset' is suitable for a trellis.

Leave a gap

A trellis panel on a wall should be fixed so that as much air as possible can circulate behind it. The easiest way to do this is to fix wooden battens about 2 inches (5cm) thick to the wall, and then attach the trellis to these battens.

Think about access

Walls or fences will need maintenance at some stage. Make this easier by hanging the trellis so that it can be lowered if necessary. Fasten horizontal battens to the wall, and attach the trellis to the lower batten with hinges and the top batten with hooks and eyes.

Curves and panels fit together to make interesting outlines.

Any shape, any size

Trellises come in many different shapes and designs. If you thought it was always in squares and oblongs, take a look at what's available: there are sizes and shapes for just about every vertical surface imaginable.

Detachable panels

If you need to be able to remove the trellis from the wall completely, then you can still use the basic system of attaching it to battens. Use heavyweight hooks and eyes on both the top and bottom battens to attach the trellis panel. It is certainly easier to repaint or treat a trellis off the wall, and it reduces the risk of damage to plants below.

Creating a supporting framework

❀ Heavier plants need something sturdier than a trellis. If you have your eye on such a plant or if you simply don't like the look of trellis panels, then a system of wires is the answer. If you use suitable materials and do the job well, this will support anything from the lightest to the heaviest climber.

❀ You can use any type of wire, but for the strongest and longest-lasting support system, galvanized straining wire—available from garden centers—is best.

❀ Straining wires can be stretched between vine eyes, either horizontally or at any angle up to vertical to create a fan-shape. This provides the plants with room to grow and minimizes the build up of stagnant air behind the plant (which would encourage disease development). The wires need to be about 2 inches (5cm) from the surface of the wall.

❀ For the support to work, it is essential that the wires are kept taut; if necessary, use a pair of pliers to tighten the wires, making sure that they are extremely taut when installed. Adjustable straining bolts will help to tension heavy wires. It is worth buying good-quality and rust-resistant hardware for this sort of job: go for galvanized or brass screws, and galvanized wire and vine eyes.

The extra-long shafts of vine eyes hold the wires away from the surface of the wall.

Choosing climbers and wall shrubs

The general rules for choosing a healthy and worthwhile plant apply when it comes to selecting a climber or wall shrub. (See page 67.) If you start with the best quality plant and look after it well, you should soon be rewarded with plenty of new growth.

Do your homework

With climbing plants, it is important that you research before you buy. Make sure you get a climber whose growth suits your surface area: too vigorous or heavy a climber can be potentially disastrous.

Annual changes

Concentrate on annuals if you want to have a regularly changing display. Try morning glory (*Ipomoea*), sweet pea (*Lathyrus odoratus*), or Chilean glory flower (*Eccremocarpus scaber*).

Morning glories produce bright, trumpet-like blooms throughout the summer.

Climbers for shady places

1. *Akebia quinata* (Chocolate Vine)
2. *Celastrus scandens* (American bittersweet)
3. *Clematis alpina* (Alpine clematis)
4. *Clematis macropetala* (Clematis)
5. *Humulus lupulus*
6. *Hydrangea anomala* subsp. *petiolaris* (Climbing hydrangea)
7. *Lonicera japonica* and varieties (Japanese honeysuckle)
8. *Lonicera periclymenum*
9. *Parthenocissus tricuspidata* (Boston Ivy)
10. *Schisandra chinensis*

Honeysuckles have the bonus of superb scent.

Climbers for a sunny spot

1. *Actinidia kolomikta* (Kiwi)
2. *Passiflora caerulea* (Blue Passion Flower)
3. *Solanum crispum* 'Glasnevin' (Chilean potato tree)
4. *Trachelospermum asiaticum* (Jasmine)
5. *Vitis* 'Brant' (Grape Vine)
6. *Wisteria*

Wisteria needs sunshine to perform to its full potential.

Make the most of shelter

Walls, especially those that are in a sheltered spot, often allow you to grow shrubs that might otherwise suffer in your garden. When deciding what to grow on these surfaces, remember that this is where you can choose something that will really benefit from the luxuriously protected conditions available.

Climbers favoured by birds are ideal on a fence or screen, but not near doors.

Climbers for perfume

1. *Clematis armandii*
2. *Clematis montana* 'Elizabeth'
3. *Lonicera japonica* (Japanese honeysuckle)
4. *Lonicera periclymenum* (Common honeysuckle)
5. Roses
6. *Trachelospermum asiaticum*
7. *Wisteria*

Evergreen *Clematis armandii* flowers in early spring, with a sweet perfume.

Walls for wildlife

❀ Climbers and wall shrubs can provide great resources for wildlife, adding height and volume of plant cover.

❀ Scented flowering plants will attract insects: even humble ivy (*Hedera*) is a wonderful source of nectar in the winter months.

❀ Mature climbers may be used as roosting sites.

❀ Sturdy, leafy shrubs or climbers, such as Virginia creeper (*Parthenocissus quinquefolia*), provide a great roosting spot for local birds.

❀ Avoid placing climbers favored by birds close to a doorway, as your doorstep will be constantly covered with their droppings. Plant a lighter or less leafy climber.

Planting climbers

The same basic planting techniques apply to climbers as to trees and shrubs. (See pages 68–69.) Remember that climbers often need to be gently untangled from their canes; planted at an angle; and tied into new support systems in order to achieve a good start.

Siting climbers near a wall

When planting against a wall, you need to take extra care because the site is likely to be less hospitable than one in a flower bed. Dry soil is the main problem: the foundations of the house tend to have a drying effect, pulling in moisture from the surrounding soil throughout the year. The wall itself may act rather like a storage heater, absorbing heat and then releasing it later—great for those plants that need it, but perhaps a little too much for those that don't. The area close to a house wall also suffers from serious rain-shadow effects: the presence of the wall means rain cannot hit the soil from one direction, and the overhang of gutters and roof eaves creates further problems.

Planting distance from a wall

The planting hole should not be any less than 18 inches (45cm) from the house wall. At this distance, all the drying effects of the wall and foundations will be less of a problem.

A few canes and plenty of care should guide your climber to its support quickly.

How to avoid mildew

Plants growing in dry situations tend to be more susceptible to powdery mildew infection. To avoid this problem, do not choose mildew-prone plants, such as the honeysuckles (*Lonicera*) and many of the roses, for a potentially dry spot unless you are sure you will be able to keep them adequately supplied with moisture.

Mildew is often a sign that plants are dry at the roots.

Easy early training

Initially you may need to use a cane and some twine or wires to train the plant toward the wall and the support system. You can remove this once the plant is established, but it should ensure that it starts to move in the right direction from the start.

How far to plant near a fence

When climbers and wall shrubs are planted against a fence, you should still try to plant them about 18 inches (45cm) away. This will give the plants a chance to put on a bit of growth in the direction of the wall and will make training easier.

Getting the climber at the right angle

Once the plant is in the hole, angle it at about 45 degrees, leaning it toward the wall to encourage it to start off in the right direction. Take extra care to ensure that the stems are not in contact with the soil surface.

Remove support before planting

Climbers are often wrapped up with mesh or attached to a framework when you buy them. It's easier to remove this before you get the plant into the ground; often some fairly time-consuming and intricate work will be needed.

Adding nutrients to planting holes

When planting close to a wall, it is especially important to incorporate plenty of bulky organic matter into the surrounding soil and into the planting hole, whatever the soil type. Matter such as garden compost, well-rotted manure, or proprietary planting compost works well.

The young growth of climbers is soft, but older stems can be brittle, so tie shoots carefully, ideally when young.

Dig deep for the healthiest clematis

Clematis benefit from deeper planting than other climbers. Plant them about 2 inches (5cm) deeper than they are in their pots. The stems are well adapted to growing up through some soil, and deeper planting means that they are less prone to damage by heat or soil dryness. It also seems to help reduce the risk of clematis wilt.

Spread out and tie in

Make sure that you spread out the existing growth as well as you can because this should help to ensure that good coverage is made from the start. The young shoots will need to be attached to the support using foam-covered wire, soft twine, or proprietary ties. Any tying needs to be done carefully because the young shoots are likely to be very tender and easily damaged.

Long-term feeding

For the first couple of seasons, a climber planted in a well-prepared planting hole may not need any extra feeding beyond a small amount—about 2 ounces (50g)—of a balanced fertilizer sprinkled around the root area and then watered in. Once it is better established, any suitable slow-release feed should do perfectly. Apply this in the spring for the best results.

Early watering

Climbers are likely to need above-average attention when it comes to watering, especially when they are still becoming established. A weekly heavy drench is often needed: make sure it gets to the roots by carefully clearing away the mulch. After watering, carefully re-apply the mulch.

Cut back to healthy growth

Any stems that are dead or badly damaged are best cut out either before the plant goes into the ground or immediately after planting. If you have about five good, sturdy, and apparently healthy stems, you should get an excellent spread of growth.

Delicacies for slugs

Young clematis in particular are very prone to damage by slugs and snails, which eat away at the stems, effectively ringing them often in the space of just a few days. Large sections of the plant may be killed. Either apply slug-killing biocontrol, or put in place copper rings or other suitable barriers to prevent this from happening. The damage is generally only very severe in the first year.

Deadhead for a longer display

Regular deadheading of flowering climbers and wall shrubs prevents the plants from wasting energy making seed and seedheads, allowing them to form new growth or flowers.

A snail is thwarted by a copper barrier.

Some remove just the rose flower, others cut to a full five-leaflet leaf; see what works for you.

Covering an arch or pergola

When training a new plant to grow over an arch, arbor, or pergola, it is best to tie the stems to the upright or else they will be inclined to flop outward. Tie the main stems evenly to achieve a uniform spread of growth. Check and retie repeatedly as the plant makes new growth.

Pruning and training

The exact pruning and training needs of climbers and shrubs vary, so make sure you know what's needed. In the first few years, aim for a good framework of balanced growth and the potential to cover the wall or shed, even if the plant is still too small to achieve it quite yet.

Immediately cut out old stems of climbing roses showing any dieback.

Remove sickly growth

Always remove any dead, diseased, damaged, or dying growth, and do so promptly, even if it is not the suggested time for pruning your particular plant. If left in place diseased areas are likely to encourage dieback infections, such as coral spot or gray mold, which may then cause more stem dieback.

Pruning basics

When pruning, always use sharp tools and cut back to a vigorous-looking, plump bud. Choose a bud that is facing the direction that you need the stem to go—this way you will get quicker and more effective coverage, ideally without too many gaps.

Always make a slanting cut just above a bud.

Shorten lanky growth

If the new growth is rather sparse or excessively long, carefully cut back or shorten it; this will stimulate branching. Always cut back to a suitable sturdy bud or sideshoot.

Check flowering habits

Before you grab the pruning tools and attack an innocent shrub, remember that unnecessary and incorrect pruning can easily destroy all the flowering potential of some plants that year. Check what each plant needs in a reliable book, making sure you know whether it flowers on the current season's new growth or last season's old wood.

Tie in new shoots

Throughout the growing season, regularly inspect the climber and direct any new shoots that have developed. It is far easier to do this regularly when the stems are pliable than trying to force (and possibly damage) a woodier stem to grow where you want it to.

Plants will recover

If you do have to prune at the "wrong" time of year or you simply make a mistake, there is rarely any need for panic. Getting it wrong generally only means the loss of one year's flowers.

Two-step pruning

If you need to prune a plant such as a firethorn (*Pyracantha*), where you want to be able to enjoy both the berries and the flowers, try doing half the job after flowering. This gives you a chance to enjoy at least some berries, and after that you can complete the pruning.

Wait for winter

If you want to see what shape the pruning you are carrying out is creating, it is often easier to prune during the winter months when the branch structure is more readily visible.

Pruning when stems are bare gives a good idea of the plant's shape.

Flowering hormones stay in the tip of an upright stem; a horizontal stem spreads them evenly.

Lay low for more flowers

Training the stems of climbers, shrubs, or trees into a more horizontal position helps to encourage more flowering and fruiting. This makes it a useful technique for plants whose main appeal is their display of bloom or berry.

Tie with care

When tying in stems of a climber, wall shrub, or other trained specimen, you can minimize the risk of branch or stem injury if you use foam-coated wires, or very flexible and stretchy ties. For larger stems, cover standard wire or cable with a length of old garden hose to help spread the effect of the taut tie.

Bigger jobs need bigger tools

Even the best-quality, super-sharp pruners may not be sufficient for larger pruning jobs. Be prepared to invest in a good-quality pair of loppers or even a pruning saw, and leave the major pruning jobs at the greatest heights to the professionals.

Lawns & grass care

Most gardens have a lawn of some sort. Yours may be a beautifully manicured, perfect sward of lush green, or it may be a functional—and by extension, less than perfect—surface used by all the family. Whatever it is like and however big it is, the lawn often has such a central role that there is no ignoring it.

In many gardens, a lawn is key to the whole design, so decide what percentage of the garden you want as lawn and its location early on in the planning process.

Sometimes the existing lawn is so weedy that there seems no option but to start again. If this sounds familiar, all the tips you might need to create a new lawn from scratch are here.

Maintaining your new lawn

Once your new lawn is in place, you will need to maintain it and keep it in general good health, or else it will soon start to look patchy and thin and will become more prone to attack by pests, pathogens, mosses, and weeds. Lawn

maintenance need not take up all of your gardening time—in this chapter there are plenty of time-saving tips.

If your gardening time really is short but you desperately want a good-looking lawn, you may even decide to get someone else to do the time-consuming job of regular mowing during the growing season. That way, you can have more garden time and the choice to do the lawn maintenance, such as edging, feeding, and weeding, yourself.

This chapter shows you how to

- ❀ Make a new lawn from scratch, from seed or sod.
- ❀ Combat pests and diseases.
- ❀ Mow, water, and feed your lawn.
- ❀ Look after your lawn.
- ❀ Identify and solve lawn problems.
- ❀ Create a wildflower meadow.
- ❀ Naturalize bulbs into your lawn.

Making a new lawn from scratch

Making a new lawn is the perfect opportunity to start with a weed-free blank canvas and create a fine level sward. You can choose from hard-wearing to fine lawn seed mixes, depending on how much wear and attention your lawn will receive.

A simple expanse of uniform green sets off plants—and provides an ideal place to sit or play.

What shape of lawn?

You may be tempted to create a really intricately shaped lawn, but remember that the simpler the shape, the easier it will be to mow—all those twists and curves that look so interesting on paper can make for a real nightmare.

Prepare the ground

Preparation is the key: it may seem like an endless process—and it does take a lot of time—but however much time and money you spend on the sod or the seed, it will all be wasted if you skimp on the preparation.

Choose the right spot

❀ Try to avoid putting your lawn in a shaded area. Lawn grasses are much less likely to succumb to pests or competition from weeds and diseases if they are growing in a reasonably open, sunny, adequately drained (but not too dry) spot.

❀ If you do need to create a lawn in a shaded spot, it is essential to use a lawn seed mixture specifically for shady areas. This will contain varieties of grass much better able to cope with the conditions.

Sod or grass seed?

❀ Lawns from sod or from seed need a very similar amount of preparation work, and this is the time-consuming part. Both will initially need extra care, especially watering.

❀ A sod lawn is much more expensive than one raised from seed.

❀ A new lawn from sod is generally ready for use much faster than one from seed.

Seed is ideal if you can wait a bit longer.

Reduce compaction

Compaction of the soil causes poor aeration and poor drainage in new lawns, which in turn causes poor grass growth and increases problems with moss and weeds; so try to break up any compacted areas before you start. Small areas can often be dealt with using a garden fork or a cultivator.

Fork over the ground thoroughly first.

Using power tools

If your soil is heavy, take care with powered cultivators; they can cause a "pan" or layer of compacted soil lower down in the soil, especially if used when the soil is wet. If necessary, delay using power tools until the soil has dried out.

Do some serious weeding

❀ Make sure you remove all pernicious weeds—those with fleshy root systems that are extremely difficult to control. Take time doing this because you need to get every tiny bit of root out: if you break the root of a weed, such as a dandelion, into pieces as you remove it, each piece left in the soil has the potential to become a new plant, so it is easy to make the problem worse!

❀ If you use a weed killer, make sure that it is formulated to control the weeds that are there; not all products control the same range of weeds.

Remove stones

Fork out all large stones and other debris. It may seem that each time you rake the area, more stones appear, but you will get there eventually. If you end up with lots of stones, don't discard them; save them to use as drainage material in the bottom of containers.

What type of grass?

Be honest about how much wear and tear—and how much maintenance—your lawn is likely to get. Fine grasses make the most elegant lawns but require more maintenance. With enough water and food, a bit of autumn care, and regular cutting, a tougher "utility lawn" can look really good.

Is your soil good enough?

If you're in any doubts as to the soil's fertility, use a balanced fertilizer before you sow or lay a lawn. This should make up for any shortfalls and get the grass growing and establishing well. Raking the fertilizer in helps to distribute it evenly and reduces the risk of it coming in direct contact with the roots of the grass.

Tread to make sure the soil is evenly firm.

Treading the surface

Try to get the area as level as possible. Once you've achieved this, firm the soil by using a flat-footed walking movement over the entire surface. Any humps or hollows can then be filled in before you start to sow the seed or lay the sod.

93

A new lawn from seed

Early autumn is the best time to sow a new lawn. The soil is warm and seasonal weather will help the seed to germinate quickly. Late spring is also a good time, but the soil is colder and there will be a flush of new weeds competing with your seed.

How much seed?

❀ Measure the area accurately before you buy your grass seed, and don't forget to subtract the area taken up by any features such as paths or island beds.

❀ The seed box usually states the weight of seed needed per 1 sq. yd. (1m²) of soil. As a rough guide, a good handful of seed is approximately the right amount for this area.

❀ If you want to be more precise, mark out a trial area of 1 sq. yd. (1m²) and weigh out the seed. Distribute the seed very evenly. Use this square to remind you what the correct sowing rate looks like when the seed is on the ground.

❀ If you can't do it by eye, mark out the area with 3-foot-long (1m) stakes, and weigh out the seed.

Where to start

Always start sowing the seed at the far end of the area to be sown—this way you won't end up walking on the areas that you have just sown. Wear flat boots or garden shoes so you won't create any serious bumps and hollows as you progress.

Avoid thick and thin

Don't try to economize by sowing the seed too thinly. Sparse grass is more readily colonized by weeds, algae, and moss, and may make more work for you later on. But don't be tempted to sow the seed too densely; overcrowding will cause weaker growth.

Seeds should be well spaced, but not sparse.

Don't breathe in

Even the freshest of grass seed from a great supplier tends to be very dusty, and it is worth wearing a simple face mask when measuring it out and sowing it, especially if you are inclined to be sensitive to dust.

Sow a straight line

Make sure that straight edges are really neat and totally straight—lay a sheet of plastic or a lightweight board with a straightedge over the area that you don't want to sow; then sow the seed right onto the board or plastic. Lift it off carefully, and you should be left with a perfect line. Any grass seed on the plastic sheet or board can then easily be tipped off and reused.

Raking settles the seeds into the soil.

Rake after sowing

You'll get far better germination rates if you lightly rake the soil after sowing the seed. This helps to cover the seed, protecting it from birds and helping to keep it moist.

Keep a record

I'm not a great filer of gardening information, but it is really worth keeping a note (or the old box) of the grass seed you used. If you ever want to extend the lawn or, more likely, simply patch it or overseed it, you'll get a much better result if you match the grass seed mixture exactly.

Don't hand out a free lunch

Reduce bird damage to small areas of grass by netting until the grasses are growing. Use scarers, such as buzz-lines or old CDs, suspended from canes on large areas.

Watering after sowing

Plenty of moisture is essential for the grass seed to germinate and the grass seedlings to establish well. Make sure the area is kept just moist at all times—if you're away and the weather is warm, get someone to do it for you! Use a watering can for small areas or a medium-fine nozzle on a hose so that you don't disturb the lightweight grass seed with aggressive watering.

Gentle watering leaves the seeds in position.

Be patient!

❀ Don't mow a new lawn created from seed for several weeks after it is sown; mowing too soon can cause serious damage. For the first cuts, leave the grass longer than you would normally.

❀ Avoid weed killers or heavy use of the lawn for the first year. The young grass takes time to knit together.

A mowing strip allows you to mow the edges easily.

At the edge

When a lawn is surrounded by flower beds, established plants often hang over the edge of the lawn or even flop onto the surface. This causes shading, which increases the chances of moss and weeds invading and of the grasses failing because they do not have enough light. Edge the lawn or at least the sides adjacent to flower beds with a neat "mowing strip" consisting of a line of paving, and this problem is instantly avoided.

95

A new lawn from sod

Sod is best laid before the weather gets either too wet or too dry—early autumn or early spring is ideal, and it is easiest to get it to establish properly and rapidly at this time. But sod can be laid at other times, as long as it is well watered and not frost has not set in.

Rolls should be moist, green, and healthy.

Check the sod quality

Always examine a few rolls of sod before the whole delivery is unloaded; you need to be sure that they are of the quality you expected. Reject sod showing signs of deterioration, such as excessive yellowing, rotting grasses, or fungal growth, and any with weed infestations. It pays to check.

Ordering sod

❀ Measure the area you need accurately; then add a yard or two of extra sod to allow for the odd mis-measurement or awkward ends of roll lengths.

❀ Try to order the sod so that it arrives on the day you are sure you can lay it—sod deteriorates fairly rapidly.

Laying the sod

❀ Lay the first piece of sod against a straight-edge if your new lawn has one. This will make it easier to get subsequent sections in place.

❀ Lay the second piece of sod while kneeling on the first one; this causes less damage than if you kneel on the bare soil.

❀ Kneeling on the newly laid lawn is going to cause dents unless you kneel on a wide plank or board. Doing this helps to distribute your weight more evenly and so prevents dents.

❀ If you can, get someone to pass the sod to you. Otherwise, getting up and down repeatedly increases damage to the new lawn and makes it all much more time consuming.

❀ The edges of the sod will need to knit together, so place each piece with its edges flush with those of the neighboring ones.

Delays in sodding

❀ If you have to delay laying a lawn, then don't risk leaving it rolled up for more than a day or two; the grasses will soon yellow, and fungal threads are likely to appear.

❀ If you need to delay for more than a couple of days, lay out a sheet of plastic and unroll the sod on to it, grass side up. Water well before using and as promptly as possible.

Use a plank for straight edges and to kneel on.

Butt up edges tightly for a solid surface.

Staggering joints while not wasting sod can be a bit of an art.

Stagger the joints

You are less likely to get unacceptable gaps in the surface of your new lawn if you stagger the joints in adjacent rows, laying them like bricks in a wall.

Marking a curve

❀ For a circular curve, use a peg and line with a funnel full of dry sand on the end. Drive the peg in to the soil; pull the string taut; fill the funnel with the sand; and pull the funnel end around to draw a sand-curve.

❀ For other curves, you can use a hose laid out on the grass to form the perimeter. Anchor it well in the ground with wire bent into U-shaped pins that will fix in place while you cut. Carefully check the shape before you start cutting.

No cuts at the edge

Avoid using a small piece of sod right at the end of a row. This area is prone to damage, and a tiny bit of sod laid at the edge will be all the more susceptible. Instead, use a full-length piece of sod at the end, and fit the smaller piece further in along the row.

Make contact

Make sure that the roots of the grass are in firm contact with the moist soil beneath. Tread the surface of the lawn carefully once it is all laid. With small lawns, you may be able to use a flat-headed rake to tamp down the surface and so avoid walking on it.

Fill the cracks

Ideally, there will be no gaps between your pieces of sod. But if possible, having some finely crumbled or even sieved soil to sprinkle or sweep into the joint areas never hurts. It will fill any cracks, and the grass will soon spread into it.

Using a guide for a straightedge

For straight edges, use a gardening line—two pegs with string between them—held taut along the edge-to-be. Then stand on a plank, to minimize damage to the lawn, and make sure you are looking straight down at the string to cut an accurate line.

Shaping the edges

❀ It is always best to shape the sod to form the outline you want once it is in place, not before you lay it.

❀ You need to have a very sharp cutting tool, ideally a half-moon edger, to make a firm, neat, vertical cut, or else the edge will look messy.

❀ If you do not have and cannot borrow a half-moon edger, then you can use a sharp spade, but the line will not be quite as smooth.

❀ When using a half-moon edger, position yourself so that you are standing immediately above the line you are cutting. This makes it easier to cut accurately and ensures that the cut you make along the edge is truly vertical.

For the neatest edges, try to use a half-moon edger.

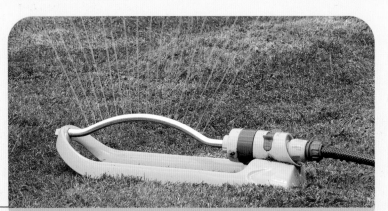

If it does not rain, water the lawn well every two to three days, gradually tapering off over a month.

When to water

Never water a new sod-laid lawn until you have finished the edges; cutting wet sod is much harder and more likely to make a messy edge. At the same time, standing on the adjacent sod increases the chances of you damaging it.

Keep watering

Keeping the newly laid lawn well watered is especially important while it is establishing itself and the roots are growing down into the soil. If they are allowed to dry out at all, the grass may never successfully root. If there's no rain, it's up to you.

A thorough soak

Once all the sod is in place and cut to shape, give the lawn a really thorough soaking. The water needs to penetrate right through the grass and the root layers into the soil beneath. Although a new lawn won't appreciate waterlogging, it is better to overdo this first watering than risk the soil beneath not being adequately wetted.

Aftercare

❀ A new lawn created from sod should not be cut for at least two weeks after it is laid. Make the first cut higher—that is, longer—than normal.

❀ Keep off the lawn for at least two weeks, and treat it gently for the first couple of months. After this, it should be well established and tougher.

Lawn pests and diseases

Keeping the lawn well maintained can greatly reduce the amount of damage from pests and diseases, so make that your first task. If you find you have a problem on your hands, deal with it promptly before it gets out of control.

Toadstools appear rapidly and need to be removed promptly.

Fungi on the march

If fungi appear on the lawn in a line, they are often growing from buried tree roots; the long-term solution is to remove the tree root.

Pick off fungi regularly

Fungi often spread effectively using spores produced from the lower surface of their caps. If you can, brush off toadstools growing in lawns as soon as they appear, and certainly before the caps open fully.

Fairy rings

Fairy rings are pretty much impossible to kill, but they do get wider every year. When the edges of the ring eventually reach adjacent borders or paths, the fungus usually dies out.

Fairy rings have a charming name, but they can be a nightmare.

Practice good hygiene

If you do have fairy rings in your lawn, the spores can be spread on feet and on mowers, so make sure you mow the infected area of the lawn last, and clean the mower thoroughly afterwards.

Keep off the grass

If you can manage to avoid walking on the lawn when it is snow covered, frosted, or extremely wet, you will find that it remains more vigorous and is less prone to damage by fungal infections, such as snow mold.

Wildlife vandals

If your lawn is being ripped up or dug up by birds or small mammals, the chances are that they are looking for grubs. This tells you that you have a problem, and the only solution is to control the grubs. Biological nematode control drenches work well.

Mowing, watering, and feeding a lawn

Sowing grass seed and laying sod is only the beginning of the story. When the grass takes off, you then have to maintain it during the growing season—mowing, watering, edging, and feeding as required.

An unmown lawn looks conspicuous.

Little and often

However boring you may find mowing a lawn, it really is a job you need to tackle fairly regularly when the grass is growing. If left too long, the lawn will look awful for a while when you do finally cut the grass, and it will take a long time to recover. Don't try to save time by cutting the lawn too short (also known as scalping it) because this will put the grass under a lot of stress, making it more easily invaded by weeds.

Don't cut too short during dry weather

If the weather is very dry, it pays to leave the blades on the mower slightly higher than normal. Keep mowing regularly so that you only ever remove tiny, short clippings; these can safely be left to fall on the grass, where they will act like a miniature mulch and help to preserve moisture.

Finishing touches

If you want to make your lawn look really tidy, neaten up the edges with a half-moon edger or, if they are still in shape but a bit overgrown, use edging shears.

Edging is a quick way to tidy up a lawn.

Don't mow when wet

When the weather is very wet and the lawn is sodden there is an excellent excuse for not doing the mowing: you are likely to do more harm than good. The surface will become compacted, and drainage and aeration will be impeded.

Walking the plank

When edging the lawn use a straight-edged plank as a guide—lay the plank on the lawn with its long edge exactly where you want the lawn edge to be. Stand on the plank, and cut directly along its edge. Trimmings from a repaired or edged lawn make a great addition to your compost heap, so don't waste them.

Watering

Lawns are more resilient than you might think. In most cases, even if they become brown and miserable looking following a drought, they will re-green later in the year, especially if you ensure they get a bit of extra maintenance.

An evening drink

If you need to water your lawn, try to do this in the evening. As the day cools down, less water is lost to evaporation, and the grasses have a chance to take up the water more efficiently.

Lawns get the longest drink overnight, without evaporation caused by the sun.

Lawn stripes can be created with rotary and cylinder mowers, and can hide irregularities.

Keeping tabs on watering

If you are unsure about how much water a sprinkler is applying, once it is set up, leave a straight-sided jar or bowl on the grass within the range of the sprinkler. This will show you just how much water is being applied—it will be more than you think, so make sure you don't leave the sprinkler on for too long.

Feeding the lawn

Grass will survive perfectly well without being fed, but if you want a lawn that looks great and is better able to fight off problems, such as weeds, moss, pests, and pathogens, you should feed with a specially formulated lawn fertilizer.

Feeding season by season

There are different formulations of lawn feed for the various times of year, so make sure that you use the appropriate one. For instance, if you applied a spring feed in the autumn, you would be stimulating soft, lush grass growth at just the time of year when you need to be toughening up the grass in preparation for winter.

Some feeds come with devices to scatter them.

Using a dry fertilizer

When using a dry form of fertilizer, it is especially important to water it in well shortly after application. This minimizes the risk of scorching and increases the ability of the grass to make use of the feed. Avoid fertilizing a lawn suffering from drought stress; it is better to wait until it has recovered before applying the fertilizer.

Quantity control

Grass can be seriously damaged by excessive doses of fertilizer, so you must apply it at the correct rate. If you are using an applicator to spread granular feed, always make sure that it is correctly calibrated for the product that you are using.

Caring for your lawn

As your lawn matures, it may need special attention in places or you may want to make design changes. Whatever you do though, always remember that you can change your mind later.

Reshaping an existing lawn

Mark out the edges of the shape you have in mind, and stand back and look at it from all windows of the house, upstairs and downstairs, to make sure you have got the shape right—and don't start cutting until you are sure.

Make sure you are happy with the curve before you cut.

Cutting edge tools

A half-moon edger or a sharp border spade is the best tool to trim edges or cut a new shape. Try to keep the cut totally vertical and sharply defined.

Mix and match grass

In extreme cases of wear and tear, it may be necessary to re-sod parts of the lawn. Make sure that the new sod matches the type of the original lawn, and that you keep the patches extremely well watered and regularly tamped down until their roots have established.

Keep it simple

If changing your lawn's shape, think about why the old shape didn't work. Often, the problems are complex outlines or awkward corners that make mowing difficult.

Lawn repairs

Heavy foot traffic to get to frequently used parts of the garden or the house itself often means far more wear and tear along those routes. Laying stepping stones in the lawn to allow direct access to these areas should keep the lawn in better condition, and means that you can even walk on it during wet, frosty, or snowy weather without feeling guilty.

Set slabs low enough to be mown over.

Sowing on the side

For extra-quick replacement seeding that is less reliant on the weather, chit or sprout the lawn seed first. Just mix the grass seed with some moist compost in a plastic bag and allow it to germinate before mixing with the soil on the bare area.

Seed fills gappy, sparse patches.

Overseed sparse grass

Areas that have become thin and sparse may respond well to overseeding. Just loosen the soil surface of the bare or sparse area; sprinkle on a matching grass seed; rake the soil over again; and water well. Overseed patches at the same time of year that you would sow a new lawn—but you can risk sowing much later into spring or even early summer if you can keep the new seed well watered.

Filling minor hollows

If minor hollows have developed, you may be able to even up the lawn surface by gradually filling the dents with a topsoil mixture in the autumn or spring.

Use garden soil to fill in any hollows beneath the sod.

Leveling hollows and bumps

Where hollows have developed in a lawn, cut an "H" shape in the sod, centerd over the hollow. Peel back the flaps of sod, and add soil until the hollow is filled. Replace the sod; tamp it down well; and water it thoroughly. If raised areas or humps have developed in the lawn, follow the same procedure in autumn or early spring. Remove excess soil from below the flaps of sod; then replace it; tamp it down; and water it.

Reversing bad edges

Where lawn edges become worn or broken, cut out a square of sod, including the damaged area. Lift it carefully, with the roots, and rotate it so that the damaged area now faces inward and a new, perfect edge is on the outside. You can easily overseed the bare patch, and the cut edge will be much more resilient.

When to give up

If your lawn is persistently thin and miserable in shady, damp, or dry areas despite all your care, try planting ground cover instead.

Patch and mend

If your lawn gets damaged in a highly visible area, you can cut out the damaged patch and swap it with a matching piece of grass lifted from somewhere less obvious in the lawn. Tamp both pieces in well, and water; then sow fresh seed on the damaged patch—it will recover quickly.

Lawn problems

No matter how hard you try, it is nearly impossible to keep a beautiful, uniform lawn for long—weeds can't seem to resist marring the landscape, and bad drainage may cause mossy patches. Learn how to stay in control with these helpful troubleshooting tips.

Dandelions' foliage rosettes escape mower blades.

Weeding

Deep-rooted perennial weeds can do a lot of damage to a lawn, not only spoiling its appearance but competing with the turfgrass for light, moisture, and nutrients. Even if you are not after a prefect sward of green, it is worth removing these weeds, especially those that are low-growing or rosette-forming, such as dandelions, as they will not be affected by mowing.

An invaluable weeding tool

An old, sturdy kitchen knife is a great tool for removing shallow-rooted lawn weeds. Make sure you ease the knife right down around the roots, so that you can remove the whole root system, because some weeds are capable of regenerating a new plant from each chunk of root left in the soil.

A knife is useful for removing weeds.

For every weed, a killer

If you opt for the weed-killer approach, check the label of the product very carefully before you buy. There are numerous weed killers, available alone or in combination, and different products will not control precisely the same range of weeds. Make sure you know which weeds you have, and that the product will control all or most of them.

Cutting coarse grasses

❀ If coarse grass has developed in the lawn, it is especially difficult to control, and weed killers are obviously not an option. Instead, try fluffing it up before mowing; this ensures that more weed grass is cut by the blades and, if repeated each time you mow, it will have a seriously weakening effect and the problem will diminish.

❀ Use a sharp knife to slash closely spaced parallel lines across the patch of coarse grass. Repeat this every few weeks over the growing season, and the problem will start to die out.

Weed killers kill more than weeds

Every year a lot of damage is done to garden plants by careless weed-killer use, especially when weed killers applied on windy, gusty, or very hot days drift onto neighboring plants. Only spray during calm weather, and read the instructions carefully.

A spring-tined rake is the
perfect tool for scarifying.

Dethatching

❀ When you dethatch the lawn, you are
aiming to remove dead grass and other
debris from the base of the lawn. The best
tool for this is usually a spring-tined rake
with long, flexible tines, but if you have
a dauntingly large job to do, it may
be worth hiring a mechanical dethatcher.

❀ After you have detatched your lawn, it
invariably looks worse than it did before
you started. Don't panic—this is how it
should be, and the lawn will soon green up
again, especially if it is kept well watered
for the next few days.

❀ Provided the moss in
your lawn has not been
treated with a chemical
moss killer, you can
add it to your compost
heap or use it as an
attractive mulch for
container plants.

Use lawn moss to
create a mulch.

Improve aeration and drainage

❀ Fallen leaves
from nearby trees
can seriously damage a
lawn, so it is important
to rake them up
regularly in the autumn.
A spring-tined rake is
the best type for the
job, but if the area is
large you could use a
leaf vacuum or blower.

Fallen leaves make a lawn
prone to fungal diseases.

❀ If you really want to save time and effort, do two
jobs in one. Provided you mow your lawn regularly,
the mower will pick up and cut up fallen leaves
that have not become firmly matted on the surface.
This saves you having to rake up the leaves, and
the ready-chopped leaves will rot down even more
quickly in your compost bin because they have been
chopped and are mixed with the moist, nitrogen-rich
grass clippings.

❀ Poor drainage and aeration leads to poor
grass growth and other problems. If time is short,
concentrate your efforts on the areas that have
become most compacted, such as areas near the
barbecue and any children's play equipment.

❀ For the best long-term improvements in drainage,
use a hollow-tine aerator. This removes plugs or
cores of soil from the sod, and the holes created can
then be filled with sand to create drainage channels.
Otherwise, use a fork.

❀ If you have
used a hollow-
tine aerator,
sweep up all the
soil cores and
add them to the
compost heap.

Ease your fork back
and forth to aerate.

Creating a meadow

A clipped and manicured patch of green is attractive and functional, but it can look a little formal and take hard work to maintain. If you want to go for the low-maintenance option that attracts local wildlife, create a wildflower meadow.

A haze of wild flowers in tall grass brings a natural tranquility to any garden.

The meadow effect

A wildflower meadow—or something to create that feel, however small—will help attract wildlife to your garden and provide a welcome relief, especially in a town garden.

Starting with plug plants

You can buy various formulations of wildflower lawn mixes, but the easiest way is to buy small plug plants. These tend to be far easier to establish and to keep than those raised within a developing lawn.

Natural methods

If you want to encourage natural wild flowers, it is essential that you ignore all the usual instructions for lawn care, especially feeding. The grass needs to be treated more like natural sod and, if fed, it will simply swamp out wildflowers.

Keep choices local

When choosing flowers, consider the local environment and the soil type you have to offer. Annual poppies (*Papaver*), cornflowers (*Centaurea cyanus*) and pincushion flower (*Scabiosa*) like a well-drained, sunny spot; ragged robin (*Lychnis flos-cuculi*) and meadowsweet (*Filipendula ulmaria*) prefer damp sites.

Cornfield flowers suit drier sites.

Spring meadow color

For spring color and interest in a meadow-style planting, try growing wild daffodils (*Narcissus pseudonarcissus*) and species crocus, such as *Crocus tommasinianus* and *C.vernus*.

Keeping a meadow looking good

Regularly remove pernicious weeds before they start to take over. Either cut them out carefully with a transplanting trowel or kitchen knife, or spot-treat with a weed killer.

Mowing your meadow

Mow your meadow twice a year, in early spring and autumn. This will prevent the wildflowers from being dominated by weeds.

Naturalizing bulbs

You can make a lawn much more interesting by planting it with bulbs, which look great growing through grass. As you need to allow the bulb foliage to remain on the plants, plant the bulbs in an area that you are happy to leave the grass to grow long.

Do not plant bulbs under evergreen trees; they will not get enough light.

Where to position your bulbs

Before you go over the top, consider the site. Avoid areas where deteriorating foliage will be too unsightly or mowing around bulbs will be too time-consuming. Remember that soil under a tree is likely to be dry and in shade for much of the year.

Large or small?

Consider the site and the scale of the nearby plants when deciding what to plant. For a small-scale, delicate look, crocus, snowdrops (*Galanthus*), or miniature daffodils (*Narcissus*), such as 'Tête-à-tête', are ideal. For a really bold planting on a larger scale, daffodils work well and are also a very good value. If you hanker after a naturalistic meadow effect, snake's head fritillary (*Fritillaria meleagris*) is perfect.

Planning drifts

❀ Mow the lawn before you start to plant the bulbs. This makes it much easier to create the planting holes and to see what you are doing.

❀ Bulbs in grass look best if given the appearance of being a totally natural occurrence. Aim for random planting without even the slightest hint of regimentation.

❀ If you are planting more than one drift of bulbs of the same type for naturalizing, make sure that the drifts are not of exactly the same size and number of bulbs and that each drift has a slightly different outline.

Snowdrops multiply of their own accord.

Stay on the level

Try to use either a single type of bulb or at least varieties of a very similar or identical height so you'll be able to enjoy them all. Avoid golden and yellow forms of crocus; these are always the first target for the birds, especially sparrows, who often shred them before they are even fully open.

Useful equipment

For planting larger bulbs in grass, you need either a very long transplanting trowel or a bulb planter. If you have more than a few to do, a long-handled planter, which you drive into the soil with your foot, saves a lot of strain on your back and knees—and a lot of time.

Scattering small bulbs

❀ Scatter bulbs and plant them where they fall, only moving any that fall far beyond the planned area or that are much too close to their neighbors.

Plant bulbs using the H-shape cut.

❀ Small bulbs, such as crocus, are time-consuming to plant in individual holes. Instead use a sharp spade or half-moon edger to cut an 'H' shape in the appropriate place. Peel back the two flaps of sod, gently fluff up the soil beneath, and scatter the bulbs. Plant in the usual way, and then replace the flaps of sod. Water well, so that the roots of the sod don't suffer too much and quickly reestablish.

Protect early leaves

As the bulbs start to grow in the spring, the first leaves are easily hidden by the grass, making them an easy target for passing feet, or even car tires if they are next to your driveway. A temporary fence of bamboo canes and twine helps to keep them from being damaged. It can be removed simply and quickly once the leaves are large enough to be impossible to miss.

Bed bulbs in firmly

When you are using a bulb planter or trowel, you are unlikely to be able to see the bottom of the hole clearly. Make sure that the bulb base (the root end) is pressed down fully so that it's in contact with soil at the bottom of the planting hole.

Use a bulb planter to remove a plug of soil that you put back on top of the bulb.

Divide to maintain flowering

Bulbs such as daffodils (*Narcissus*) planted in fairly dense drifts soon need more space if they are to continue to flower well. Every five years or so, lift the bulbs (or at least half of them, randomly scattered through the planting) and replant in a new site. Why not plant at the edge of the drift to make it bigger?

Feed and water

Bulbs in grass need extra watering, particularly near trees or during dry spells. Without moisture, they can't take up the nutrients they need to flower well the next year. They also need feeding; they are competing with each other and the grass. Apply foliar feed during the growing season while the leaves are green, or water in a granular fertilizer.

When to lift bulbs

Ideally, lifting bulbs for replanting should be done in the autumn, but at that time of year there will be no aboveground sign of where exactly each bulb is growing. Either mark the positions with sticks before the foliage dies down, or lift the bulbs "in the green," when they still have green leaves.

The kitchen garden

One of the most satisfying things you can do in your garden is to grow at least some of the food you eat. It is a fundamentally appealing activity, and there is no doubt that when you grow some of what you eat, it not only feels good, but tastes excellent, too.

Whatever the size of your garden, try to find space for at least a few vegetables, herbs, or fruit. If you garden purely in containers, then see pages 56–63 for some tips on growing a gorgeous selection of edibles in containers.

If you are worried that crops will be less appealing to look at than flowers and shrubs, then I say, think again. Many vegetables look stunning, whether they are grown among other vegetables or integrated into a flower bed.

Growing your own crops

If you have never entered into this exciting area of gardening, make this the year you start, because the rewards are huge. Once you've begun you'll find it truly addictive.

You can easily grow just about any of the mosts popular vegetables, and you'll be surprised at how straightforward it is to grow some of the more exotic ones. Make sure you start with the easier crops such as beans, tomatoes, and potatoes, plus perhaps a few fresh herbs. Once you've realized how easy these are, and gained some experience, you'll be even more likely to succeed with others. It is important to grow things that you really enjoy eating, and less rather than more of each crop, so you can avoid seasonal gluts.

This chapter shows you how to

❀ Grow and care for herbs. .

❀ Grow and maintain tree and soft fruits.

❀ Plan a vegetable garden.

❀ Grow vegetables from seed.

❀ Sow and grow under glass.

❀ Grow vegetables from sets, tubers, and young plants.

❀ Get the best from all your crops.

Making space for herbs

The easiest way to liven up an otherwise run-of-the-mill meal is to add some freshly picked herbs. Even a humble sandwich can be transformed into a truly delightful feast if you add some fresh, home-grown basil.

A mixed container of herbs near the kitchen door can be ideal, but remember to repot as the plants outgrow the space.

Basic soil requirements

Most herbs need very free-draining ground and will not last long if planted in a heavy, damp soil. If your soil doesn't fit their requirements, grow the herbs in either a container or a raised bed, or make sure you dig in lots of grit, sand, and compost before planting so that drainage improves. (See pages 62 and 119.)

Not all herbs are hardy

Some herbs are not hardy, and if planted out too early in the year or left in too late in the year, they will die. Check the seed packet or plant label carefully.

Dressing the soil

Dressing the soil surface with grit after planting slightly shallowly ensures a free-draining surface layer at the collar of the plants. This makes them much more likely to thrive, even when it's very wet. Always buy horticultural grit, and never use leftover builder's grit, shingle, or gravel because it can contain damaging materials.

Mint is invasive

The roots of mint are notorious for being aggressively invasive. Either grow mint in its own container above-ground, or plant it in a bed but keep it in its original container plunged into the soil. When planted in a pot, the roots are much less likely to escape. The variegated mints are generally far less vigorous, and much less inclined to cause problems.

Different mints vary in flavor, so have a nibble to be sure the one you buy is to your taste.

Keep cats off your basil

Basil has an aroma that you either love or hate, and cats seem to love it. Perhaps because it is (to me at least) somewhat reminiscent of cat's urine, male cats in particular often spray or urinate on basil plants, so make sure that your basil is kept out of their way.

Statuesque and graceful, fennel is a herb that is worth growing in an ornamental bed or border.

Starve herbs for stronger flavor

Most herbs have a more intense flavor if they are not grown too "soft," so hold back on general or higher nitrogen feeds. Either don't feed at all, or use a high-potash fertilizer.

Herbs reach many heights

Make sure you check the ultimate or potential heights and spreads of the herbs you use—some, such as fennel, may look delicate in the garden center, but check the label, and you'll discover that it can grow to 6 feet (1.8m).

Keep cutting herbs back

Even if you're not eating the herbs quickly, it pays to cut them back regularly. This will keep the ones with woody stems compact with plenty of new growth, and prevent them from becoming leggy.

Sweet bay (*Laurus nobilis*) is a much more handsome plant if regularly harvested.

Ten great herbs to grow at home

1. Basil: mainstay of Italian cooking.
2. Bay: add to soups and stews.
3. Chives: garnish for salads.
4. Coriander: use in curries.
5. Mint: make into a sauce for lamb.
6. Parsley: garnish and fish sauces.
7. Rosemary: add sprigs to roast lamb.
8. Sage: use in savory stuffings.
9. Tarragon: perks up egg dishes.
10. Thyme: delicious with fish.

Tree fruit

There is no flavor quite like fruit grown in your garden and eaten straight from the tree or bush. Almost no garden is too small: pick your crops carefully, and consider growing in shapes other than the traditional tree, and you can grow fruit wherever there is sun.

White reflects light onto ripening fruit.

Best sites for tender fruits

Some of the more exotic fruits, such as nectarines, peaches, or vines, can be grown well out of doors in most areas, but for the heaviest crop, a greenhouse or conservatory will help. A wall that receives all-day or afternoon sunshine is a good compromise because it acts as a heat store, accumulating warmth during the day and gradually releasing it when temperatures fall. A wall like this also provides some protection from bad weather.

Get the site right

❀ Fruits invariably do better in a spot with plenty of sun; they won't crop that well if planted in a shady position.

❀ One of the more shade-tolerant fruits is the 'Morello' cherry. This does very well even on a north-facing wall.

❀ A moisture-retentive soil that isn't likely to get waterlogged is perfect for most fruit. In very dry weather, it will often need watering; otherwise, the crop will be smaller and often a bit distorted or cracked.

Prune for productivity

Pruning fruit bushes and trees can make a phenomenal difference to the size of the crop. Make sure you do your homework for the fruit you're growing so that you know exactly how and when it should be pruned.

What to buy

When choosing fruit crops, consider whether they need a second plant as a pollinator. Some fruit is self-fertile, so only one tree is necessary for fruit set, but most need another pollinator. To be suitable, this must be in flower at the same time. Suppliers and nurseries should be able to tell you what they stock that would fit the bill.

Pruning the cherry family

Many fruit trees, particularly cherries, plums, peaches, nectarines, and almonds, are prone to silver leaf, a potentially fatal fungal infection. The spores gain access via open wounds. Infections are hugely reduced if trees are only pruned during the summer months, and if pruning cuts are kept as small as possible.

Using a wound paint may reduce the risk of silver leaf.

Hold the fruit, and give the stalk a firm but gentle twist to test if it is ripe.

Pollination improves productivity

Although so-called self-fertile trees can crop on their own, I always find that they crop much more heavily when there is a pollinator close by. Make sure the extra pollinating tree is not removed if you can, otherwise you may find that your crops decrease.

Keep it in the family

If space is limited but you want several different varieties of apple, or to be sure that you have a suitable pollinator, then you could consider a "family tree" of different cultivars that have been grafted together to form one tree. Provided that they are all of a similar vigor, such as 'James Grieve', 'Sunset', and 'Egremont Russet', these can be fun. But if cultivars of different vigor have been used, pruning and fruiting can be a problem.

Spur and tip bearing apples

Most apples are "spur-bearers," producing crops on spurs along the shoot. Others are "tip-bearers," carrying much of their crop close to the shoot tip. Common tip-bearing apples include 'Discovery', 'Tydeman's Early Worcester', 'Worcester Pearmain', and 'Bramley's Seedling'. Avoid tip-bearers if you want to train your tree as an espalier, cordon or fan: they are much harder to train into these shapes, and will have a lot of unproductive wood. A tip-bearer is better grown as a bush, half-standard, or standard.

Training the branches of spur-bearing trees away from the vertical increases yields.

Fitting fruit in

❀ Fruit trees are not grown on their own roots but are grafted onto a "rootstock" to limit their size. Broadly speaking, M26 means large apple trees, MM106 medium-sized, and M9 dwarf trees. With pears, Quince A and C are similar to an apple's M26 and M9, respectively.

❀ If space is limited, avoid apples described as biennial bearing: they often only bear a useful crop every other year. Ideally, choose one that is described as "dual purpose": this means it can be used as a dessert apple or as a cooker.

❀ Fan-trained plums or cherries, and cordon or espalier apples or pears, can all be grown on a fence, trellis, or wires, and so take up very little room.

❀ Why not train a pair of cordon apples over a simple arch? If chosen well, they will pollinate each other, look great covered in blossom in spring, and fruit in summer, taking up little garden space.

Soft fruit

Soft fruit, such as strawberries, raspberries, and blueberries, add another dimension to your garden and certainly make a delicious addition to mealtimes. Most soft fruit is relatively compact, making it ideal for growing in the smaller garden.

Extending the strawberry crop

If you want to have lots of strawberries over a long period, choose the varieties carefully to include early-, mid- and late-season types. Remember that the yield from a single plant on any one day is never going to be that great, so ideally you should grow several of each variety.

Raspberries need support

Raspberries are a crop I would recommend to anyone, but they do take up quite a bit of room. If you want to cut back on the preparation for growing these gorgeous berries, grow autumn-fruiting varieties; they do not need to have a support system like the summer-fruiters do.

Try tougher raspberries

If you garden on soil that is too alkaline and too heavy for raspberries, autumn-fruiting types may be the answer. For me, summer varieties never perform well after their first year, whereas autumn-fruiting ones seem much better able to cope in adverse conditions, and just keep on fruiting.

Soft fruit and birds

Raspberries, especially summer-fruiting types, are well loved by garden birds. I love feeding them, but there is a limit—I also love my raspberries. A fruit cage, netting, or scarecrows mean more of the crop goes to the humans.

A netting alternative

Standard fruit netting drives me crazy, because it tangles and tears so easily; it is also easy for birds to become entangled in it. I prefer pond netting; it is less expensive, much easier to set up, doesn't tangle, and still has a small enough mesh to work brilliantly.

Pond netting is good for protecting fruit.

Build a fruit cage

To make a small cage, use narrow, flexible hose; sturdy stakes; and pond netting. Cut the hose into lengths long enough to make a hoop over the plants, under which you can move to collect fruit. Push a stake into each end, leaving about 8 inches (20cm) protruding. Drive one cane into the ground; bend the pipe into an arch; and drive the other stake into the ground. When all the hoops are up, attach the netting.

Make sure you leave a way into your cage.

Leave access for pollinators

Whatever method you are using to protect fruit, remember that to get a crop the flowers have to be pollinated, so don't put fine netting over the plants until most of the flowers have been pollinated.

Blueberries like it boggy

Blueberries are popular for their lovely taste and texture and their brilliant antioxidant benefits. They perform well, but for the best crop, grow several plants, and remember that these are lime-hating, boggy-ground dwellers. Unless you have or can create a suitable spot, they won't succeed. The best garden blueberries I have ever seen were in a compost bin full of

A bush can yield 11 lbs. (5kg) of blueberries.

acidic compost and soil. The compost volume was so great that it stayed moist.

Feed your fruit

With crops, you get out what you put in.

Most fruit produces a far lower or less appetizing crop if it is not well fed. Feeding needn't be complicated: give a general fertilizer in the early spring combined with a nutritious mulch, such as well-rotted manure or garden compost, and follow with sulphate of potash in early summer to encourage flowering and wood ripening.

Remember to water

In very dry years, water will also be needed if you want a good crop that is relatively free from problems such as bitter pit (apples) or cracking (apples, pears, nectarines, plums, and cherries). Avoid frequent but light watering; a thorough and deep watering at longer intervals is of much more use.

Some fruit announces its ripeness through color, smell, and softness.

Don't overfeed

Although feeding increases productivity, excessive feed, especially if it includes quite a bit of nitrogen, is likely to cause soft growth that is damaged by pests, pathogens, and weather. It is generally better to err on the side of caution.

When is it ripe?

With raspberries or strawberries, the change in fruit color tells you when the crop is ripe; in gooseberries, look for a slight yellowing and give the fruits a gentle squeeze—if they don't give, wait.

Planning a vegetable garden

Choosing a spot for growing vegetables is really important, but it's also vital that you then spend time preparing the soil. Last but certainly not least, plan what you want to grow. Get it right now to save problems later.

Textured leaves and dramatic colours make many vegetables attractive.

Get the site right

To grow vegetables easily and get a good crop, you need a sunny spot, and ideally a well-drained but fairly moisture-retentive soil. Everything will struggle if there is too much shade. But if the classic space for edibles, confined to the back of the garden, is not sunny enough, don't forget that crops can look great among flowers and other ornamentals—or even in a prominent place of their own.

Adding lime

Most vegetables do best on a neutral to slightly alkaline soil, so adding lime may be necessary.

Watch out for wind

Windy spots are best avoided because they can cause a dramatic decrease in cropping. Even a slight to moderately windy spot may reduce yields by an average of 30 percent.

Shield your crops

If there is no choice but to grow your vegetables in a windy location, erect a windbreak fence or plant a shrubby windbreak before you start. Whatever you use, make sure it is at least partially permeable: a solid wall may cause problems as wind swirls over it. The effort really is worthwhile: every 3-foot (1m) height of windbreak provides about 16 feet (5m) of protection behind it.

A dense hedge slows the wind, reducing moisture loss from plants and raising air temperatures in the sheltered area.

Rotate your crops

However small your crop area, it is well worth using a rotation system. Ideally, move crops around three or four beds or areas in sequence, but always avoid growing the same or a closely related crop in the same ground two years running. This helps to reduce pathogen and pest problems and maintain fertility.

Crop rotation for weed control

Rotation can also help with weeding. If a plot is rather weedy, grow a crop of potatoes in it. These have a good weed-smothering effect, which saves you time, and makes them a good crop to precede a difficult-to-weed crop, such as garlic.

Companion planting confuses pests' sense of smell and their visual targeting of your crops.

Make a deep bed

You can create a "deep-bed" system, starting with very thorough soil improvement using a lot of organic matter. Avoid disturbing this soil over the coming years, only doing so when planting, and only add organic matter to the surface of the soil. This way you can save yourself a lot of work: firstly, there is a lot less digging and secondly, because the soil is not disturbed by digging, dormant weed seeds that are already in the soil do not germinate (as they do if the soil is dug over), so only weed seeds that are blown in need to be dealt with.

Natural pest control

There are advantages to growing onions and carrots together—something a classic rotation system wouldn't allow. If you want to reduce the risk of carrots getting carrot fly and onions getting onion fly, grow these two crops on the same plot, perhaps even in alternating rows: the smell of the carrots masks the smell of the onions and *vice versa*, making both crops less likely to be tracked down by these pests.

If you do not need to step into them, raised beds can be planted more densely than open ground.

Use raised beds

If the soil is very stony, heavy, or light and sandy and you cannot improve it by the usual methods of digging in organic matter and/or grit, consider creating raised beds. Sink 6-inch x 1-inch (15cm x 3cm) boards about 2 inches (5cm) into the soil as edging; then fill with a more suitable soil.

Rotate crops for soil fertility

Rotation can help with soil fertility. Crops such as pea and bean (legumes) have the ability to "fix" nitrogen from the air into a form that is available to plants. This makes them a great crop to grow on a piece of soil, which is then to be used for a nitrogen-hungry crop, such as cabbage, cauliflower, Brussels sprout, broccoli, potato, spinach, or chard. Because these crops use so much nitrogen, it makes sense to grow a crop that does not need a lot of nitrogen, such as carrot or parsnip, on the same ground after them.

Keep a notebook

I'm not a great list-keeper or note-taker, but I would thoroughly recommend keeping a notebook if you grow vegetables. Recording the basics, such as varieties grown, sowing and planting dates, and perhaps even cropping dates and yields, makes decisions and planning easier the following year. It also ensures that you have a definitive record of the variety names, so you know what to choose (or perhaps what to avoid!) the following year.

Be adventurous

Try to be a bit adventurous if you're an experienced vegetable grower—by all means regularly grow those varieties that you know will do well and that have the flavor you love, but try some of the new varieties too. Each year there is a whole host of new varieties put on the market, so don't miss out. F1 hybrid seed may seem expensive compared with standard seed, but for uniformity and vigor, it may be money well spent.

Winter shopping

Raising your own vegetables from seed is very good value and immensely satisfying. Over the late autumn and early winter when things are generally a little quieter in the garden, take time to study seed catalogs and start to make lists of what you need.

As long as you group several plants in a clump, sweet corn will crop well.

Grow beyond the vegetable plot

Some surprising vegetable crops can be used in ornamental areas of the garden. Sweet corn, with its rustling leaves and feathery flowers, can make an architectural impact in a border.

Read catalogs carefully

To make your life easier and to reduce the risk of pest and pathogen problems, take note of comments made in catalogs about each variety's resistance to common problems. Those sold as "suitable for beginners" or "for organic growers and gardeners" are generally good choices.

Space-saving plot design

If you are creating a vegetable plot from scratch, you'll want to maximize the amount you can cram into the space you have available—but don't forget to allow enough space on paths for a wheelbarrow to be pushed with ease and without damaging nearby crops. All areas of the beds should be easily accessible from the path: if they are too wide for this, lay a line of bricks or stepping-stones to create an access route for maintenance and harvesting.

Vegetables from seed

If you don't have a greenhouse, cold frame, or propagator, there are still plenty of vegetables you can grow by sowing the seed directly into the soil or by investing in a few "starter plants."

Get the soil ready

Make sure that the soil has been cleared of weeds, and if necessary, incorporate some bulky organic matter. Digging in well-rotted manure or garden compost can make a huge difference to poor soil.

Don't work wet soil

Avoid working on soil that is very wet: it will be compacted readily, and this damages the soil's structure, increasing the chances of it becoming poorly aerated and waterlogged. In any case, many seeds will rot if the soil is too wet. It is better to wait for a week or so, even if this means sowing later than the suggested sowing times.

A plank will fit between rows of young plants.

Walking the plank

If the soil is nearly ready but you still think it might get compacted if you stand on it, lay a plank or board down, and stand on this. The plank spreads your weight over a much larger area and reduces the risk of compaction.

Attending to distances

No matter how pressed for time you are, always take a moment to check the suggested sowing depths and seed spacings. If buried too deeply or too shallowly, some seeds may germinate very poorly or even not at all. But don't get too worried about being precise—a hairsbreadth here or there won't be significant.

How thin is thin?

Seed packets often suggest sowing "thinly"—a vague term, but one you should note well. The thinner you sow the seed (within reason) the less thinning out you will have to do later. However, don't sow so thinly that there is a risk of the final spacing being too wide!

Sow three parsnip seeds together and thin to one.

Station-sowing

For some crops that are notoriously temperamental, such as parsnip, it is worth station-sowing. This is sowing about three seeds together, but with the suggested final spacing distance between each trio. It allows for one seed to fail, one to be a bit wimpy (and be removed) and the other to thrive, and it avoids any more thinning!

Sow a marker crop

If you are sowing slow-germinating and somewhat erratic seeds, why not sow a fast-germinating crop, such as lettuce, along the row too? It'll be up and harvested before the slow crop needs all that space. In addition, it serves as a great marker, making it easier to see exactly where the crops and the emerging weeds are.

Coping with dry conditions

In very hot, dry conditions it can be difficult to keep the top layer of soil adequately moist. If it does not remain moist for long enough, the seeds may not germinate, or they may germinate but the seeds or young seedlings may then die. There are several things you can do to avoid the problem.

✿ Make areas of newly sown seed and young seedlings high priority when it comes to watering.

✿ Make the furrow into which you sow the seeds about ½ inch (1cm) deeper than normal; then put a layer of very wet soil in the bottom of it to a depth of about ½ inch (1cm) and sow the seed on this. Top the drill off with dry soil.

✿ After sowing, water well and then cover the soil surface with newspaper, a couple of layers of fleece, or similar material. This should help to reduce moisture loss from the surface. Make sure that you remove the covering before the seeds germinate, or they will perish.

Some seeds don't like it hot

If the weather is very hot and dry when you sow the seed, prepare for heat-sensitive seeds, such as lettuce, to be slow and erratic in their germination. Ideally try to avoid these conditions because overall results tend to be very disappointing.

Water will drain very rapidly through a layer of sand under your seeds.

Use sand when it's wet

If the soil is really too wet for sowing seed but you have no option but to plant, make the furrow a tiny bit deeper than usual, and line it with horticultural sand before you sow the seed. This should prevent the seed from actually sitting in water and rotting.

Cover rows with fleece

To get direct-sown seeds off to a somewhat speedier and more reliable start, cover the row with fleece held in place with metal pegs or weighed down with large stones or bricks at the edges.

Thinning tips

❀ Seeds sown direct will need some thinning out unless you are unbelievably good at sowing thinly and have been lucky with your germination rates. But don't thin crops in very hot or wet weather; either extreme is more likely to result in inadvertent damage to the seedlings you want to keep. Hot, dry weather is the most dangerous.

❀ When choosing what to thin, always take out the weakest-looking seedlings or any showing signs of stunting, discoloration, or other problems.

❀ The thinnings of crops that transplant well (most things except the root crops) can always be used in other areas, if for some reason you suddenly find you need more of the crop or it has failed unexpectedly elsewhere.

❀ After thinning a row of seedlings, water the row right away, even if the soil seems adequately moist. The water you apply now will help to resettle the disturbed soil around the finer roots, allowing the remaining seedlings to continue to grow.

❀ Always thin carrots in the evening because, however careful you are, you will bruise the foliage, and this releases an aroma that attracts carrot fly, a serious pest of carrots. At night there are fewer flies around, and less aroma is released into the cooler air.

A lollypop stick, seed label, teaspoon handle, or even a pencil helps to ease out roots.

Handling small seeds

Sowing all but the largest seeds direct from your hand can be tricky because if they are clammy or damp, the seeds will stick to your hands. When they do leave your hand, they will do so in clumps. Mixing the seed with plenty of dry horticultural sand will help. Alternatively, take a clean, dry piece of paper, and fold a sharp crease down its center. The seeds can be evenly distributed from this if you hold the paper in one hand and tap it sharply with the other as you move it along the row—although it takes a little practice.

Protecting seeds against birds

If wild birds have a habit of eating seeds before they germinate, temporarily cover the bed with fleece, newspaper, or netting held taut between pegs. The netting must be kept taut to prevent birds from getting tangled in it.

Protecting seeds against cats

Cats are not interested in your seeds, but they do find finely raked, crumbly soil irresistible and see it as a huge litterbox. Lay lots of twigs over the newly sown ground to deter them from destroying your efforts.

Save your seed

If you have seed left over, it can often be saved easily and effectively from one year to the next, so don't waste it. Seed is most likely to remain in good condition if kept in cool, dry conditions, perhaps even in a sealed box in the refrigerator. If you keep spare packets of opened seed, wherever you store it, make sure that it's safe from rodents.

Black plastic is best for warming soil. If you use a heavy-duty sheet, you can pack it away and use it again for years.

Using old seed

If you find a packet of seed that has been open for some time or one that has passed its suggested use-by date, there is no harm in sowing it anyway. Being opened or being old is likely to have reduced the percentage of viable seeds in the packet, so either sow more than you usually would or be prepared to buy more if not enough germinate.

Save silica for seeds in storage

The packaging for electronic equipment, musical instruments, cameras, and other high-value items often contains small sachets of silica gel. Don't toss these: save them for use in the container in which you store your seeds because the gel helps to absorb moisture from the atmosphere around the seed packets and reduces the risk of dampness building up and damaging the seeds.

Extend your cropping season at both ends

❀ Successional sowing means sowing a relatively small proportion of the seed at, say, two-week intervals. It helps to reduce the extent of the seasonal gluts that are so common when you grow your own and extends the period over which you can harvest each crop.

❀ Search the catalogs and take note of suggested harvest dates for any one crop: there are often distinct early, midseason or main-cropping, and late-cropping varieties available. Choosing one from each category can increase the harvest period.

❀ Covering the soil with plastic sheet or fleece before you sow allows it to warm up slightly and may keep off excessive rain. This allows earlier sowing and improves the chances of some crops, such as carrot and parsnip, which often fail due to damp, cold soil. Seeds germinate much better in the warmth.

❀ At the end of the season, cover developing crops with fleece to keep them viable and cropping for longer.

❀ Always start harvesting as soon as the vegetable is ready, or else the plant tends to slow down. With some crops, such as pea and bean or zucchini and melon, this really makes a huge difference to the cropping season's length and the total yield.

Sowing under glass

Some seeds need to be sown in a greenhouse or cold frame for a bit of extra heat; others that could be sown direct may give better results if protected from erratic temperatures or slugs and other pests. Whatever the reasons, try to supply suitable temperatures.

Using a heated propagator

❀ You get more reliable results for crops such as tomato, pepper, and eggplant if you can supply some bottom heat. Investing in a heated propagator may seem daunting, but it'll be less expensive than you might think and owning one opens up a whole new range of growing opportunities. If necessary, put it on your birthday or Christmas list!

Extra heat is invaluable for seeds of tender crops.

❀ If you have two or more types of vegetable seed that need slightly different temperatures to germinate, set the thermostat at the higher temperature or only very slightly lower, and stand the pots of those seeds requiring lower temperatures on inverted pots inside the propagator. Being raised off the capillary matting on the tray at the base means they are heated to a lesser degree.

❀ Seedlings soon suffer if kept in a heated propagator for too long. Once the majority of seedlings have appeared, gradually acclimate them to a cooler life, and then place them in a suitable position to grow.

Small trays for small crops

If you only want small numbers of a crop, either use quarter-size seed trays (harder to get a hold of but well worth looking for) or sow in pots. Growing more than one type of seed in a single tray spells disaster.

Sow rows in gutters

Sow in lengths of plastic gutter; but be careful not to over-water. To plant, squeeze the gutter to loosen the strip of compost and roots, and slide the row of young plants out into a channel dug in the soil. It saves time, and the plants suffer little if any damage.

Use multicell seed trays

I'm a real fan of multicell trays for seed sowing. They allow you to sow just one or two seeds in each cell (rather like a mini pot). This reduces the time spent thinning and minimizes the disturbance to the seedling or small plant.

Module trays are ideal for tomato plants.

Potting crowded seedlings

I usually carefully thin out the grass-like seedlings of leeks into individual holes in new pots for growing before planting. But one year I ran out of time and simply pulled the potful of tiny plants apart, replanting the whole lot in to a larger pot of fresh soil. Freed (to a degree), they grew brilliantly, making plants just as good as those that had taken hours of work. This is only suitable for pretty chunky, tough seedlings such as leeks.

Water before thinning

Make sure the soil in trays or pots is moist before you attempt to prick out seedlings. Dry soil means more root damage.

Sow thinly

If you sow seed in a tray, try to sow thinly. This will dramatically reduce overcrowding and the time you later spend thinning out congested seedlings. It'll also mean an easier and less damaging move for the seedlings, and consequently better crops for you.

Sowing thickly may save space, but it will cost in time and yields.

Exposure to outdoor temperatures lets plants toughen up or "harden off" naturally.

Acclimate seedlings

❀ Move seedlings raised under protection outside during the day and back in at night for a week, to acclimatize them before planting.

❀ Use bell cloches, a transparent plant cover, or fleece draped over a frame as protection if you are worried, but don't leave them on for too long.

Planting

❀ You can plant most vegetables a bit deeper than you might expect: the extra depth gives them more support in the soil. Some, such as tomatoes, will form additional roots at the base of the stem.

❀ Avoid extreme conditions for planting. Too much heat, cold, or wind, or a soil that is too wet or dry, will cause a check in growth that sets plants back. Wait a day or two until conditions improve.

❀ If the weather suddenly turns too hot, protect transplants with shade netting or even a sheet or two of newspaper for a few days. This gives their roots time to establish, and they suffer less in the heat.

Vegetables from sets, tubers, and young plants

Some plants are generally grown using tubers (potato) or sets (garlic, onion, and shallots), while others are bought as young plants. This is a very easy way to raise an impressive crop, and the range of varieties available is huge, so take advantage of it.

Ridges give good drainage

If your soil is rather heavy and inclined to become very wet in winter, grow crops that don't appreciate these conditions, such as garlic, on raised ridges for better drainage. I draw up a ridge of soil, about 6 inches (15cm) tall and 8–10 inches (20–25cm) wide at the base, and plant the individual cloves in the normal way, but into the top of the ridge. This works well—far better, I find, than the oft-quoted method of raising individual cloves in pots and then planting once the soil conditions have improved.

A ridge of soil will be drier and warmer.

Use proper seed potatoes

It really isn't worth trying to economize and use potatoes that have started to sprout in your kitchen instead of buying certified disease-free tubers. Kitchen potatoes are much more likely to be infected, and also they are often covered with shoots that are much too long and break off when you try to plant them.

Protect sets with netting

When you plant onion or shallot sets, the necks of the bulbs will protrude slightly above the soil surface. This is a serious temptation to birds, which pull them out of the soil, so they don't get a chance to root, and you end up with gappy rows and fewer onions than you expected. For the first four to six weeks after planting, keep the sets covered with netting—it'll keep the birds away and help your crop to get established.

Netting is the best way to keep birds off.

Choosing garlic

Garlic bought for cooking is best not used for planting. It might work fine, but there is also a significant risk that it may be diseased or that the variety itself is not actually a good performer in your climate. Buying special planting stock avoids both these problems.

For best crops use planting stock.

Planting leek seedlings

When you are raising leeks, wait until they are at least 8 inches (20cm) long before you plant them in the open ground.

Allow for leek growth

After you have made a deep, narrow hole and placed a leek transplant into it, it is definitely best not to fill in the gap between the leek and the sides of the channel. Instead just wiggle it around a bit to ensure that the roots are right at the base of the hole. Water it well. This initial watering and any subsequent waterings will be enough to settle the soil around the root while allowing maximum sideways expansion of the stem.

Watering leeks and chives

Leeks and chives often succumb to devastating attacks of fungal rust. This is always worse when the foliage is damp, so always water these crops directly at the base.

Water leeks only at the base.

Toughen up plants to avoid rust

Fungal rust thrives on soft foliage, so avoid excessive feeds of nitrogen-rich fertilizers or manure. Instead apply sulphate of potash to the soil. Potash helps toughen up the growth and minimizes the risk of a fungus attack without affecting the flavor in any way.

Buying young vegetable plants

Buying young vegetable plants is not a sin. If you've run out of time, missed sowing dates, or simply don't have the specialty equipment required for good germination, such as a heated propagator or a frost-free or heated greenhouse, then young plants are a good idea. Don't be put off by people who say you should always do everything "properly"—shortcuts can be equally successful.

Raising plants in the house

If you are keeping plants on a house windowsill, they are at risk of becoming "drawn" or leggy because of the lack of natural light. Keep them as close as possible to the window, and stand them on a sheet of aluminium foil (shiny side up); this will help to reflect light back onto the plants.

Keeping tender veg warm

If you do buy plants of tender vegetables, such as eggplant, pepper, or tomato, make sure you have somewhere suitable for them, with plenty of natural daylight and adequate warmth, until it is time for planting. If you can't provide the accommodation they need, delay buying them.

These tender crops really need a nighttime minimum of 60°F (16°C) to thrive.

Top of the crops

Each and every crop you decide to grow will be worth the effort, but to get the best possible results—whether you're a first-time vegetable grower or a well-seasoned hand—give each what it needs.

Sweet corn can be raised in pots; it prefers a warm start.

Grow sweet corn in blocks

Whether you sow sweet corn direct, or plant the seedlings, always do so in blocks, not rows. This wind-pollinated crop gets much more thoroughly pollinated if grown in blocks, giving much higher yields.

Stick to one sweet corn

Avoid growing more than one variety of sweet corn, unless you have a very large garden, because cross-pollination between varieties often causes loss of quality. This is especially true if you are growing a "super-sweet" variety.

Avoiding tough tomatoes

You can reduce the likelihood of tough skins developing on tomatoes growing in your greenhouse by doing your best to avoid excessively high temperatures. Shading on the glazing both reduces the temperature and prevents too much direct sunlight from hitting the developing fruit.

Greenhouse soil care

If you grow tomatoes in the soil in a greenhouse border, you are likely to start to get problems after a few years, particularly with soil-borne infections. Although it is very hard work, you will have to change the soil completely. Do this either as soon as problems start to occur, or preferably, every three or four years, before crops start to fail.

Thinning tomato leaves

You can thin out the foliage on tomatoes, but don't go overboard. By all means, remove some leaves if they are so numerous that they are shading the fruits heavily, but make sure there are still plenty left—they're needed to feed the plants.

Looking after cordon tomatoes

Cordon-type tomatoes, also called vine or indeterminate, such as 'Tigerella', 'Gardener's Delight', 'Mirabelle', and 'Shirley', need their sideshoots removed regularly so that the energy available can go to the developing fruit trusses. When the plants are as tall as you want them to be, usually toward the end of the summer, pinch out the top of the plant, leaving a couple of leaves above the uppermost flower truss.

Limiting the size of a tomato plant means fewer trusses, but the fruit may be larger.

The bush-type tomato varieties are ideal for growing in containers.

Bush tomatoes

Bush-type or determinate tomatoes, such as 'Tumbler' and 'Totem', do not need pinching back and sideshooting—doing this would mean a lighter crop.

Pinching back shoots

Sideshoots are best removed when they are 1 inch (3cm) or shorter. If they are any bigger than this, you can easily damage the plant when removing them. Never cut off sideshoots; instead, hold the shoot between finger and thumb and quickly and firmly bend it down until it snaps off cleanly.

Snapping a sideshoot makes a clean break at a natural weak point that will heal quickly.

Supporting large tomatoes

Large-fruiting tomatoes, such as the beefsteak types, can produce very heavy fruit capable of breaking the stem to which they are attached. If you are worried that this might happen, place inverted flower pots beneath the lower trusses to support them, and either thin out upper trusses slightly or rig up a net to support them.

Use stakes for support

When tying tomatoes to stakes, or canes, for support, always use a figure-eight system. Loop the string around the stem; then cross the two ends over; then pass them around the cane, and tie them on the far side of it. The string must be loose around the stem to allow for plenty of room for expansion. Do not tie the knot next to the tomato: you are much less likely to injure the stem if you tie the knot against the stake.

Crossing the strings reduces the risk of the stem being chafed against the cane.

Avoid blossom-end rot

Avoid the black, leathery sunken patches known as blossom-end rot developing on the tomatoes by growing them in larger containers or ideally in the open ground. Erratic and inadequate watering causes this disorder, so plants in containers are more susceptible, especially if the containers are relatively small. Keeping the soil barely moist is the key to avoiding the problem.

Avoid skin splitting

Erratic watering makes tomato skins split, so keep moisture levels even and never allow the soil to get too dry before you apply the water. Consider a simple drip irrigation system if watering tomatoes in containers is difficult.

The right level of feed maximizes yields without losing flavor.

Feeding tomatoes

Regular applications of a liquid tomato fertilizer containing plenty of potash really help to maximize the crop. However, they often result in magnesium deficiency, showing on the leaves as yellowing or purple areas between the veins on the older or lower leaves. This rarely effects the cropping, but if it is severe, treat by watering the foliage with a solution of Epsom salts.

Magnesium deficiency is common later in the season.

Green tomatoes

If you have green tomatoes on the plant late in the season, when temperatures have dropped, you may be able to ripen them if you carefully lay the plant down onto a mat of dry straw and then cover with a cloche.

Everyone has encountered this end-of-season problem.

Ripening the plant

You can ripen healthy green tomatoes once picked—just put a few in a dry paper bag containing a slightly overripe banana. The ethylene gas produced by the banana is a natural ripening agent.

Watch the temperature

Erratic temperatures can cause distorted fruit, so try to ensure even, warm temperatures all summer.

Blighted tomatoes

Outdoor tomatoes often succumb to the ravages of potato-blight infection. If you want to avoid spraying against this infection, check catalogs regularly for varieties showing high levels of resistance.

Dealing with blight

If blight does hit your tomatoes, promptly cut off the top growth, and dig out the stem bases to reduce the risk of the spores getting into the soil. Discard or burn the infected material; do not compost it under any circumstances.

Ten great tomatoes

1. 'Gardener's Delight' (cherry, cordon)
2. 'Legend' (salad, bush)
3. 'Marmande' (beefsteak, cordon)
4. 'Oxheart' (beefsteak, cordon)
5. 'Piccolo' (cherry, cordon)
6. 'Sweet Million' (cherry, cordon)
7. 'Tigerella' (striped salad, cordon)
8. 'Tornado' F1 (salad, bush)
9. 'Totem' F1 (salad, bush)
10. 'Tumbler' (cherry, bush)

Feed your pepper plants

Make sure that peppers are fed regularly with a liquid feed containing plenty of potash to keep them flowering and fruiting.

Try eggplant

Don't be deterred from growing eggplant—it's as easy to grow as indoor tomatoes. The plants need greenhouse protection and perform best with plenty of natural light. If you have the luxury of space, they are ideally grown in a separate greenhouse from tomatoes, which develop tough skins in too much light.

Zucchini, melon, squash, and pumpkin

All these crops need plenty of moisture if they are to produce a really heavy crop, so make sure they are planted in moisture-retentive soil and that the surface is kept mulched.

Pick crops when young and shiny; older ones turn bitter.

Don't overwater

Eggplant is much easier to overwater than tomato or even pepper. Make sure the soil is just dry to about 2 inches (5cm) depth before you water.

Harvesting aubergines

Always keep a pair of secateurs or a sharp knife to hand when it's time to harvest aubergines. They are extremely spiny around the calyx or stalk end, and the stems are very tough.

Zucchini flowers

❀ If conditions are too dry, plants form more male flowers. This means fewer fruit, but it does make for good eating picked fresh and fried in batter; leave some to fertilize female flowers.

❀ Male flowers are easily identified by their slim, straight-sided stem; there is a slight swelling just below the base of female flowers.

❀ One of the most common causes of damage to fruit is rot from a wet flower spreading into the developing fruit. You cannot stop rain, but you should only water at the base of the plant. When flowers start to deteriorate, quickly pinch them off.

Only a few males are needed for fruit.

Remove leaves dusty with mildew, but don't worry about these silver marks.

Don't panic over leaf markings

Many zucchini and melon varieties form distinct silver markings on their leaves. This is perfectly natural and nothing to worry about, but it is often mistakenly thought to indicate mildew or, worse still, virus infections.

Dealing with blighted potatoes

If potato blight strikes, immediately cut back all the haulms (top growth) of infected or suspect plants and toss out or burn them; never compost diseased material. If this is done rapidly and if conditions are relatively dry, you can prevent the tubers from becoming infected. Lift the crop as soon as possible, and make sure it is thoroughly dry before storing.

Brown patches spreading on leaves are the depressing symptom of blight.

Potato and lime

Avoid growing potato on ground that has just been limed for a year or two. Limey soil is more likely to produce potato tubers infected with scab—not a major problem, but best if avoided!

Resistant varieties

There are a few varieties of potato now available, such as 'Sarpo Mira' and 'Sarpo Axona', that show good resistance to potato blight. They are well worth tracking down if your potato crops are always badly damaged by blight.

Avoid wireworm tunnels

Soil that has only been cultivated for a year or two is very likely to have a high population of wireworms. These small, ginger-colored pests tunnel into the tubers and can wreck the crop. Try to avoid growing potatoes until the third or fourth year: if you just cannot bear to wait, concentrate on early potatoes, which can often be lifted before the wireworms have had time to do much damage.

Mildly blighted potatoes may look sound but will soon deteriorate.

Early potatoes make efficient use of space.

Choose early potatoes

If you are short of space but still want to grow potatoes, then early varieties are best. They take up less room, and because they are in the ground for a short time, the site can be used for another crop once they are harvested.

Earth-up potatoes

Potato blight fungus is the most serious problem affecting potatoes, and earthing-up well will help to reduce the likelihood of it infecting the tubers when the spores are washed down through the soil.

Plenty of earth above developing tubers helps stop them turning from green and possibly toxic.

Try sweet potato

❀ If you want to branch out a bit, try growing sweet potato. You raise the plants from "slips" (rather like cuttings), but they need warmer conditions than standard potatoes.

❀ To increase the chances of a heavy crop, move the slips to individual pots before planting in very early summer.

❀ Planting through thick, black plastic (such as cut-open soil bags laid black-side up) and covering with horticultural fleece really helps to increase soil and air temperature and makes for a better crop.

Slug control

Large, deep tunnels in potatoes are caused by keeled slugs, probably the second most serious potato problem. Try using a biological control nematode, growing the varieties described as relatively slug-resistant, or growing mostly early varieties that can be lifted before the worst of the slug damage can occur.

Check stored potatoes

Checking stored potatoes regularly is always a good idea: infections often spread rapidly with so many tubers in close proximity. It is essential to check regularly if your crop had blight because this infection makes the tubers very prone to secondary bacterial rotting.

Sort your potatoes

When sorting potatoes for storage, it pays to have at least three grades—seemingly perfect, minor damage (such as surface slug or wireworm attack), and eat now (more seriously damaged). I have kept slightly damaged tubers for months with no problem, provided the tubers were perfectly dry when stored.

Harvest potatoes on a dry day, and dry them before storing in breathable sacks or

Choosing lettuce

If your lettuce crops are often ravaged by slugs and snails, try to choose at least some varieties that have red or purple leaves. I find that they are rarely as badly damaged by these pests as the green varieties.

Ten great lettuces

1. 'Bijou' (red loose-leaf)
2. 'Chartwell' (romaine)
3. 'Corsair' (cos)
4. 'Freckles' (red-freckled romaine)
5. 'Little Gem' (mini-cos)
6. 'Lollo Rossa' (red loose-leaf)
7. 'Mascara' (red oak-leaf)
8. 'Revolution' (red loose-leaf)
9. 'Salad Bowl' (oak-leaf)
10. 'Sioux' (iceberg)

Grow a range of lettuces for colorful salads.

Sow cool

Lettuce seed is unusually sensitive to heat and does not perform well if the conditions are very hot, so plan your sowings accordingly.

Protecting Asian vegetables

Flea beetle—a tiny pest responsible for causing numerous equally tiny holes in the foliage—is a serious problem on many of the leafy Asian vegetables. Before it gets a chance to attack, cover the crop with fleece. This serves a dual purpose, because many of these vegetables enjoy the somewhat more protected and slightly more humid conditions beneath the covering. If you can, cover the row right after sowing.

Horticultural fleece or mesh are perfect alternatives to pesticides.

Cut and come again

Many leafy vegetables can be cropped more than once. Loose-leaf lettuces, which don't develop a tight, dense heart, are ideal, as are chard, spinach, and even kale. Three to six weeks after sowing, when the young plants have reached about 4–6 inches (10–15cm) in height, simply cut them off 1 inch (3cm) above ground level with a sharp knife. The stump will regrow, giving enough for a second crop of baby leaves within another few weeks, and a third after that.

Avoid bolting

Lettuces will bolt, rocketing up into tall plants and turning bitter, if they become too hot or dry. Keep moisture levels constant, and be prepared to harvest before bolting strikes in a hot spell.

Avoiding pea moth

Pea moth, which leaves tiny maggots to develop within the pods, can be avoided by growing the crop beneath a layer of fleece or very fine mesh. Making sowings early and late in the day also helps avoid the problem.

Mulch peas and beans

Mulching beans will make a huge difference to the crop, especially during dry weather. Always mulch when the soil is really moist.

Climbing French beans have greater yields than dwarf types.

Try French bean

If runner bean regularly disappoints because the young beans abort, this is almost always due to dryness in the soil. If lots of organic matter and mulching don't do the trick, grow climbing French bean; this is far more tolerant of slight dryness.

Pick peas

It is essential to keep on picking peas and sugarsnaps as fast as the pods develop. If the seeds within are left on the plants to ripen, the flowering will diminish and the yield will suffer accordingly.

Frequent picking means tender peas and high yields.

Prepare a bean trench

Beans are a very thirsty crop, so do all you can to prepare the soil well before sowing or planting, incorporating plenty of bulky organic matter. It is often said that you must prepare the bean trench the autumn or winter before, but I regularly do it minutes before planting and find it works just as well.

Ten great beans and peas

1. 'Aquadulce Claudia' (broad)
2. 'Blue Lake' (climbing French)
3. 'Borlotti' (climbing French)
4. 'Cobra' (climbing French)
5. 'Kelvedon Wonder' (pea)
6. 'Meteor' (pea)
7. 'Oregon Sugar Pod' (mangetout)
8. 'Pickwick' (dwarf runner)
9. 'Purple Teepee' (dwarf French)
10. 'Red Rum' (runner)

Fleece tunnels are quick to put up and provide warmth as well.

Avoiding carrot fly

Carrot fly is a serious pest. The maggot-like young pests tunnel into the root, making it more prone to rotting and a lot less appealing to eat. Avoid by covering the crop with fleece or very fine mesh as soon as the seed is sown, or as the seedlings start to emerge. To make weeding and harvesting easier, put an open-topped barrier of fleece or fine mesh around the row. If this is at least 18 inches (45cm) tall, the low-flying carrot fly will not be able to fly over it to lay her eggs.

Sowing times for carrot

If the soil is too wet and/or cold, carrot seed readily rots. Ignore the directions on the packet; make a decision about sowing times on the basis of the soil conditions.

Grow shorter carrots

Try the stump-rooted carrot varieties if your soil is shallow, rather stony, or in any other way not great for growing carrots. They naturally produce shorter, stubbier roots, which may not look as elegant, but they taste just as good and will perform better in less than perfect soils.

Stump-rooted carrots are best in stony soils and even containers.

Try a range of carrots

❀ It is worth trying carrot varieties, such as 'Flyaway', 'Sytan', or 'Resistafly', sold as showing a degree of resistance to attack.

❀ Round-rooted varieties of carrot include 'Parmex' and 'Paris Market'. These work relatively well in stony soil.

❀ Different carrots suit early and late crops. Try 'Amsterdam Forcing' or 'Nantes' types for summer salads, and 'Autumn King' or 'Chantenay' for later in the season.

❀ For different colors, try 'Purple Haze', 'Purple Dragon', or 'Yellowstone'.

Water features & ponds

Having a pond or water feature in your garden adds a certain touch of magic. There is nothing quite like the sound of gently moving water to add to the feeling of tranquility that being in a garden brings.

Bringing water into your garden need not be hugely time-consuming or expensive. You can scale up (or down) what you create to fit in with the size of your garden and your budget.

If your garden is on a slope, you will have to take this into account in the design you choose.

If you just want a single pool or pond, make sure you are prepared to create an adequately sized level area first. To make a pond with pools leading to or from it look relatively natural, think carefully about where you position each part.

Planning each element

If you want moving water, you will need to have a power source close by. If you are just starting to plan a new garden, take this into account, perhaps trying to keep your water

feature close to any other part of the garden that will need an exterior power source. This may influence where you make your water feature.

Water, particularly in the form of ponds, can pose a serious and potentially life-threatening risk to children. If you do introduce water to a garden that young children use or might visit, bear this in mind and perhaps choose a self-contained feature that has no significantly deep water.

This chapter shows you how to

❀ Choose a water feature.

❀ Plan a pond.

❀ Choose a liner for your new pond.

❀ Edge a pond with plants and boulders.

❀ Plant your new pond, and the best plants to use.

❀ Look after your water feature.

❀ Care for your pond year-round.

Choosing a water feature

There is such a huge choice of ready-constructed and kit water features available these days that you will have no difficulty finding something to suit your garden. Look through catalogs, and then visit a supplier for advice.

The importance of proportion

Powered water features, such as fountains, can only spray or move water to a maximum height or spread. Always check what it is, whether this force is appropriate to your pool or pond, and whether the feature is in proportion to the pool and the rest of the garden.

Self-contained features

For small gardens or for use within a small area of a garden, look for the many self-contained water features available. These will allow you to have moving water despite these limitations.

Safe features

If you have small children or are likely to have any visiting your garden, then always consider the safety aspect. You may dream of a large pond, but perhaps this could replace a safer short-term feature in a few years, when the children are older.

Pebble fountains are safe and simple.

Go with the flow

If, like me, you garden on a steep slope, a pond can be an extremely difficult feature to create. Better to make use of the natural slope and instead make a stream or even a waterfall that can come down the slope, end up in a small pool, and then be pumped back up to the top again.

Submersible pumps are simple to install.

Types of pumps

There are two main types of pumps you may come across in a garden center. A submersible pump is installed so that it works from under the water, while surface pumps need to be sited out of the water and so need to have some sort of housing created for them. Surface pumps generally create a noticeable noise.

Water can be directed down a slope through a natural-looking stream.

You can fit a surprising amount into a simple, small pool of still water.

Make a mini-pond in a container

❀ If you don't have enough space for a pond, you can make a mini-pond in a large ceramic container. It should be at least 18 inches (45cm) deep; any shallower, and the water will get too warm and may turn green.

❀ A half barrel makes a good miniature pond, but make sure that it is totally water tight—ideally, line it with butyl. Fold down the liner at the, so that it does not quite reach the rim; then use short, galvanized tacks to hold it in place.

❀ Choose a container that is frost-proof. If you get extremely cold weather, be prepared to insulate the sides of the container, too.

❀ A pot or container with drainage holes in it will be more difficult to use, but you can often achieve a watertight effect if you plug the holes with corks from bottles of wine.

❀ Ceramic containers that are not glazed on their inner surface will need to be made waterproof by treating the unglazed surface with neoprene paint.

❀ In a small container pool there will be no space for planting shelves, but you can create these by submerging bricks.

❀ Make sure you choose suitably sized plants for a very small water feature. Check the ultimate heights and, even more importantly, the spreads of the plants carefully before buying.

Adjustable pumps

If you are buying a pump to power a cascading water feature, spouting gargoyle, or miniature fountain, make sure that you check the pump's flow rate and that it can be adjusted if necessary, allowing you to create just the right look.

Pump power

To check if the pump you have in mind will be powerful enough, work out the volume of your pond: this is its depth x length x width. For a pump to work well, its flow rate per hour must be greater than the total volume of the pond.

Plan your power

Powered water features and fountains will need to be connected to an electricity supply. Consider the distance from the house and the time, trouble, and expense needed to extend the existing supply. Installation of proper shielded cables is a specialized business, and cables need to be labeled and buried at the correct depth by a qualified electrician.

Always use clean, mortar-free bricks.

Planning a pond

A pond is a long-term addition to any garden, so make sure you spend plenty of time working out what will work best, look most appealing, and be of maximum benefit and least risk to your garden.

A good site means less maintenance.

Where to site your pond

❀ Avoid a position beneath or even very close to deciduous trees: this will obviously increase the problem of leaves falling into the pond when the autumn arrives.

❀ Too much sunlight will increase the rate at which algae build up. A partially shaded spot is ideal: it should have enough sunshine for healthy plant growth without encouraging algae growth.

How to keep shapes smooth

If you are aiming for anything other than a straight-edged pool, make sure that the shape is flowing and smooth. The easiest way to achieve this is to make the edges relatively simple and to use a flexible garden hose to mark out where the outline should be. This will allow curves and smooth lines without sharp angles.

Design intricacy increases costs

Flexible liners can be used to make an elaborately shaped pond, but a simple design will use up considerably less butyl and underlayment. This allows you to save money or have a bigger pond for the same budget.

Simple shapes, like a circular pool, create the greatest impact.

Shelf planting

Make sure that you create or install your pond so that most of the shelf-planting will be at the back, making it easier to enjoy the water and shallower planting in the foreground.

Put the widest part of the shelf at the back of the pond.

Hidden depths

Design your pond with water of varying depths. This allows you to use a wider range of plants and attract more varied wildlife. (See pages 150–151.) Remember that the shallower water will heat up more rapidly in the summer and so be more likely to become breeding grounds for algae.

Shaping your steps or shelves

Steps or shelves at the sides of large ponds are invaluable for plants that require shallower depths of water. Make sure that the horizontal surface of each planting shelf is wide enough to hold a planting basket and that it is either totally level or sloped very slightly, with the lip edge very slightly higher; this makes it even less likely that the pond basket will fall off.

Plants like this gracefully nodding *Dierama* love the moist conditions of a bog garden.

Plan your shelves

Before creating planting shelves, try to decide, roughly, which plants you intend to use and make sure you create enough shelves at suitable depths to have what you want. It is much easier to get it right at this stage than to alter shelf heights later on.

Create a boggy area

❀ A pond looks more natural with a bog garden beside or around it. This creates perfect conditions for plants from hostas up to a giant gunnera.

❀ If you are creating boggy areas at the edges of, or adjacent to, your pond, these will need some sort of liner, perhaps off-cuts of the main piece of butyl. (See page 146.)

❀ To keep the area boggy but not too wet, use a garden fork to puncture the liner. With no holes, the water and soil would soon become unsuitable for plants, and be likely to get rather smelly as oxygen levels drop.

❀ Keep these mini-drainage holes open and prevent them from becoming blocked with silty soil by placing a 2–4-inch (5–10cm) layer of stones in the base of the area that you have punctured.

Level off

It is essential that you create a pond on a totally horizontal site: whatever you do, the water will always find the level, and a lopsided pond looks awful. Make things easier for yourself and choose a relatively level spot.

Check the levels

At regular intervals as you dig out the pond, check that the top is level. If you are installing a rigid preformed liner, it is vital that it, too, is level. An ordinary spirit level will do—lay a plank across the pond, and place the level on it.

Never rely on judging the horizontal by eye.

Filling your pond

Ideally, ponds should be filled with rainwater, but it may be difficult to acquire adequate quantities. If you resort to tap water, allow it to stand for at least a week before you start to plant. This will allow at least some of the additives to disperse.

Choosing a liner for a pond

Many garden centers supply some pond equipment, but if you want the best selection of liners of any type, and often at the most reasonable prices, it is generally best to go to specialized suppliers, many of which offer a mail-order program.

Rigid liners

Rigid, preformed liners provide the easiest way to create a pond and generally come complete with shelves to allow for planting at varying depths. Their main disadvantage is that there is a limited range of shapes.

Draining rigid liners

Some preformed liners have a drainage hole built in to them to allow you to empty and clean the pond relatively easily. For this to work, it is essential to make a small sump, or pit, beneath the plug hole when you install the pond—a rubble filled pit is perfect.

Protect the liner from stones

Remember that for flexible liners, such as PVC, butyl, or plastic, you will need to put down some sort of underlayment. Otherwise there is a great risk of the liner being punctured by underlying stones, tree roots, or other sharp objects. You can buy special underlay, or use old carpet padding; for smaller areas, a thick layer of straw will work well.

A layer of sand and underlayment are vital.

Butyl liner

Using butyl allows for the greatest flexibility, literally giving you the freedom to create as many different depths and outline variations as you wish. Although butyl liners are the most expensive option, their life expectancy is about 30 years, so they are a good value.

The water's weight will pull the liner in gradually.

Measuring for a liner

Butyl is expensive, so it is important to order the right quantity; the only way to do this is to do some math. Measure the greatest length (L) and greatest width (W). Then measure the deepest point and double it (call this 2D). You'll also need an extra 18 inches (45cm) on all sides for the overhang at the edge. Now grab a calculator. You'll need a sheet of butyl L + 2D + 36 in. long, and 2D + W + 36 in. wide.

Plastic or butyl?

Plastic flexible liners are readily available and considerably less expensive than butyl, but they are more prone to degrading in sunlight and rarely last more than five years.

Edging a pond

It is important to consider what you want the edge of your pond to look like, especially if you are installing a formal pool. Wildlife ponds are generally well-planted, so the appearance of the edge matters less.

Make sure of a perfect fit

Before laying your edging material, you will probably have to adjust the levels around the pond edges, especially if you are using a rigid preformed liner. These must fit snugly in to the hole—gaps increase the likelihood of damage because the weight of the water exerts considerable pressure. Dry sand or dry garden soil works well, and the drier it is, the easier it is to pack it tightly down the sides and beneath the outer lip of the liner.

Place stones at the edges

❀ Large, rounded stones at the edges of a pond are useful for small animals. (See page 150.) They are also a great way to hide the uppermost and outermost edges of the pond liner and will help to prevent soil from adjacent areas falling into the water.

❀ For a natural effect, use large stones on the outermost edge, gradually moving to smaller stones at the water's edge and into the water. Plenty of marginal plants will complete the look and be useful to wildlife.

A "beach" at the edge is better for wildlife.

Decks and jetties

Timber decking can be used up to the edge of a pond and even extend out over it, creating the illusion of a much larger pond under the deck. Supporting a wooden structure on piers over water is not simple, however, and you may want to get professional help.

Edging bricks

If using an edging of bricks for a formal pond, choose walkway bricks. These are very frost-resistant, and so less likely to disintegrate after a hard winter. Make sure that you avoid letting any cement fall into the water. If it does, fish it out or it can alter the water's pH and may poison wildlife.

Overhanging bricks or slabs are neat and formal.

Keeping stones in place

Make sure that an edging of stones can remain in place and look good by creating a depression for them around the edges of the pond. A slight flat shelf at the water line that's partly submerged, on which the smaller stones can lie, completes the effect.

Pond plants and planting

If you are after a formal pool or pond design, plants may not feature too highly on your list of priorities, but if chosen carefully they can certainly add a touch of drama and interest.

Hardy plants

Always check whether pond and marginal plants are hardy before you buy them. There is no need to rely totally on hardy plants, but if any are in the slightest bit tender, you will have to provide winter protection for them, bring them in to a frost-free temporary home each winter, or regard them as annuals and be prepared to replace them if they are damaged by adverse weather.

Buy healthy plants

Only buy plants that appear perfectly healthy and free from pest infestations. Once they are planted in the pond, problems are even harder to deal with than when things go wrong with plants in flower borders.

Check plant sizes carefully

Check each plant's ultimate height and spread, but if you are unsure after reading the comments on the label or in the garden center or nursery, check in a book. Some water plants might be invasive or prove too vigorous for any but the largest pond. Don't risk introducing something that could end up swamping out all your other plants.

Flag iris is attractive, but it is suitable only for large areas of water.

Invasive plants
(to be avoided)

Azolla caroliniana (Fairy moss)

Crassula helmsii (New Zealand pygmy weed)

Elodea canadensis (Canadian pondweed)

Hydrocotyle ranunculoides (Pennywort)

Iris pseudacorus (Yellow flag)

Juncus effusus (Rush)

Myriophyllum acquaticum (Diamond milfoil)

Myriophyllum proserpinacoides (Parrot feather)

Mesh baskets may be rigid or more flexible and bag-like.

Essential mesh

Pond baskets are a must. The mesh sides allow plenty of through-flow of water while keeping the soil and the plant in position. They are readily available from outlets selling pond and marginal plants.

Avoid burlap

If you cannot get a hold of pond baskets with fine mesh, keep trying. If you still cannot succeed, line a large-meshed basket with plastic mesh. It is best to avoid burlap.

Seal plants with gravel

Once the baskets are planted, cover the surface of the soil in each with a layer of good-size pebbles or gravel; this will help to keep the soil in place and reduce the risk of it falling into the water. If you intend to have fish in the pond, it will also help to prevent them stirring up the soil.

Still water

Waterlilies require still water, so will not be happy in moving water. Plant them in a still pond, pool, or rill, but avoid any with fountains or other pumped or circulated water, unless it is big enough for the plants to be sited well away from the movement.

Smaller, less vigorous waterlilies can be grown in a mini-pond.

Waterlilies need the right depth and several hours of full sun daily to flower well.

Plant at the correct depth

❀ Provided you put water plants into the pool at their correct final depth, there is no need to panic if the leaves are submerged when you first lower their planting basket into position. They will soon reorient themselves and grow so that they are at the surface.

❀ Waterlilies in particular often have very specific requirements when it comes to depth of water. They will either not thrive or simply fail to flower if planted at the incorrect depth. Check that those you like the look of will actually perform well in the pond you have—there is almost always an alternative waterlily if they won't.

Focus on wildlife

Wildlife really benefits if you install a pool, pond, or indeed most sorts of water features. The water provides a place to drink and bathe if it is easily accessible and created in a wildlife-friendly design. It can also be a suitable place to breed and live.

A beach area makes a pond safer and more accessible for wildlife in search of a drink.

Life on the edge

Plenty of marginal planting makes a pond appealing and ensures safe places for wildlife to hide from predators.

Fish are for fish ponds

If you want to encourage wildlife to your pond and to make it a safe place for it to stay, do not introduce carp or other fish because they prey upon wildlife species, their young, and their eggs.

Goldfish will eat tadpoles, newt eggs, and dragonfly larvae.

Beach attraction for wildlife

Straight-sided ponds are potentially lethal for wildlife that may tumble in and not be able to climb out. Make sure that your pond has at least one "beach" of progressively shallower water ending up on a pebble-covered area, perfect for less able swimmers.

When a pond turns bright green...

❀ Algae are the most common reason for this. If your new pond is green, don't be tempted to empty it and start again: be patient. The settling-in period invariably includes a few weeks of green water. This starts to clear as the pond gains its natural balance.

❀ Reducing the amount of light that hits the water's surface will generally help to decrease problems with algae. Using more surface-floating plants, including water lilies and oxygenators, will also help.

❀ Oxygenating plants include *Ceratophyllum demersum*, *Callitriche*, *Myriophyllum verticilliatum*, and *Ranunculus aquatilis*.

❀ Fish and their fecal matter raise nitrogen levels in the water, in turn increasing algae.

❀ Use barley straw. (See opposite.)

This problem is worse for ponds in sunny places.

Introduce pond snails

A good population of pond snails helps to keep algal levels down because they eat algae. Make sure you get either the ramshorn snail or the small round pond snail and that you avoid the giant pond snail—this one may also start to munch your pond plants!

Clear dead foliage regularly throughout autumn to limit sludge build-up.

Barley straw "soaks up" excess nitrogen in the water, starving algae.

Use barley straw to control algae

Barley straw really helps to control algae. Buy a pre-formed "pad" or simply put straw into a fine mesh bag kept submerged by the weight of a brick. Use about 2 ounces (50g) of barley straw for every 11 square feet (1m²) of the pond's surface. Put it in during early spring, and replace it every six months or so.

Autumn slowdown

You will need to do some maintenance throughout the year. (See pages 154–155.) But do any major work in early autumn when it will have the least impact on any wildlife in your pond. Make sure any creatures in the removed debris have a chance to get back into the pond.

Trapping giant pond snails

If you find you have the wrong sort of snail in your pond (the giant pond snail), then set a trap for them. Float good-size lettuce leaves on the pond's surface: the snails will be attracted onto the lettuce, and then you can scoop up the snail-infested lettuce with a pond net at regular intervals.

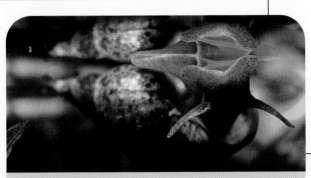

Giant pond snails find lettuce irresistible; use it as a lure to trap these pests.

General maintenance

Like any other part of your garden, ponds and water features benefit from some timely maintenance. Even wildlife ponds and wildflower meadows will work better if not left totally to their own devices.

Check carefully for duckweed

Numerous, tiny, green, floating leaves are duckweed (*Lemna*), which seems to appear from nowhere. Always check new plants for duckweed before planting them; a single leaf-like plant multiplies rapidly.

Duckweed soon builds up, and can spoil the appearance and functioning of a pond or water feature.

All about blanket weed

✿ Blanket weed is made up of filamentous algae, and is a serious and common problem, often clogging ponds. It will be encouraged by the same factors that encourage the pea-soup effect of algae: sunlight, high nutrient levels, and low oxygen levels. It can be discouraged in the same ways, including the use of barley straw. (See pages 150–151.)

✿ The easiest way to remove blanket weed is with a sturdy bamboo cane. Insert it into a mass of weed, swirl it around a few times, and you'll soon scoop up a lot of weed.

✿ Blanket weed can be composted in your compost bin or heap, but before you take it too far from the pond, give wildlife that may have been caught up when you removed it a chance to escape. Lay the weed on the ground in clumps, with a small amount trailing into the water, for a couple of days before composting it.

Ponds need to be promptly cleared of blanket and duckweed.

Feeding pond plants

Some pond plants may eventually need feeding, but as there is a serious risk of fertilizer contaminating the water, you should only do this when really necessary. Feed very carefully, applying a small amount of slow-release fertilizer directly into the pond basket. Don't attempt to feed surface-floating plants.

Don't feed an algae problem

Make sure that no fertilizers (including manure and artificial feeds) are applied in large quantities to flower beds or lawns that are close to a pond. Runoff can cause additional nutrients to flow into the water and so increase problems with algae.

Year-round pond care

Spring is a good time to remove, replant or divide, and then replant pond and marginal plants. To keep the pond at its best, make sure you only introduce healthy, clean stock and discard unhealthy looking divisions.

Feed fish after winter

If you have fish in your pond, take care when you start giving the fish food again in spring after a winter-break from feeding. Start with small quantities and then only apply every three days or so. Excess, uneaten food messes up the water.

Trim deteriorating foliage

Throughout the summer, even healthy pond plants will have the odd damaged or dead bit of growth. It is essential to cut this off and compost it before it gets a chance to rot in the water. Decaying foliage will raise nutrient levels and so increase algae.

Regular top-offs

Water levels are likely to drop in hot summer weather, so top them off occasionally. Doing this using a hose spray sprinkled onto the water's surface will also help to raise oxygen levels, which are inclined to fall during spells of hot weather.

Keep an eye out for dying leaves, and snip them off quickly.

Both fountains and top-offs applied from above the water surface keep a pool aerated.

Clear away the debris

Regular removal of larger quantities of faded pond and marginal plants is essential during autumn, when dieback is greater and more widespread. If you end up also thinning out a plant that has been growing a bit too rapidly, great, but make sure that any pond wildlife clinging to it is given the chance to escape back into the water before you compost it!

The more vegetation falls into your pond, the more often you will have to clean it out.

Catch the falling leaves

Net the surface of the pond to prevent leaves from nearby trees and shrubs falling into it. Make sure the net is in place by early autumn so you catch the maximum possible amount. Remove the net at regular intervals, before it becomes too laden down with leaves, and empty them into a leaf mold or compost heap.

Reduce fish food in autumn

In autumn, fish are starting to slow down considerably. If there are any in your pond, reduce the frequency and quantity of food.

Double netting

It can be difficult getting a net properly positioned over a large pond, and removing it regularly becomes a horrendous chore. The best solution is to get a relatively sturdy, easy-to-handle net in place and anchor it over the pond's surface for the whole of the autumn into early winter. You can then lay a relatively lightweight net over the top. The latter can easily be removed and replaced because the lower one helps to support it.

Melt ice gently: never smash it or pour boiling water onto it because you could shock or kill fish.

Creature comforts

If the pond freezes over in winter, the best way to create a hole without endangering creatures below is to hold a saucepan full of hot water on the ice until a circle melts beneath it—just don't let go of the handle!

Winter maintenance

In winter the only bit of real pond maintenance is attempting to keep the surface free from ice in at least one place. A total covering of ice prevents potentially toxic gases, such as methane, from escaping, and this can kill fish or small pond wildlife, such as newts. The age-old trick of floating a ball on the water's surface helps to slow the rate at which it freezes.

Structures & surfaces

Nearly every garden has a boundary, and to some extent every garden needs one so that it's clear to everyone precisely where your garden ends and theirs begins. This provides you with another planting surface and countless creative opportunities that you may not necessarily think of using. A fence or wall, or even a well-installed trellis, can look great when decorated with a well-chosen planting scheme.

Although some towns limit fence heights, you need not have a full-size boundary. In some situations quite a low-level fence or wall fits the bill. You could fill out adjacent beds with attractive plantings to cover the wall, or use containers.

As an added bonus, any vertical structure instantly provides support for some gorgeous plants, bringing height and variety to your planting schemes. With a bit of thought, even the most uninspiring of boundaries can be adequately disguised and concealed beneath a mass of foliage and flowers.

Creative design possibilities

With patios and decks, there is a huge range of styles and types from which to choose. And like your garden boundary, these too can really bring your own hallmark to a garden, whatever its size and style. Both boundaries and patios and decked areas play an important role in a garden, and at the same time may also affect the microclimate and the extent to which the garden can be used as an "outside room" or area for entertaining.

This chapter shows you how to

- ❀ Choose a boundary style—walls, fences, or trellises?
- ❀ Plan and build walls.
- ❀ Install paved, gravel, or decked areas.
- ❀ Maintain your patio or deck.
- ❀ Install and maintain arches and pergolas.
- ❀ Buy and care for garden furniture.

Setting boundaries

Before you decide on a new garden boundary, take a look at what your neighbors have used to assess its style and how it has fared in the local conditions. The strength and direction of prevailing winds may mean that flimsy options are best avoided.

Walls or fences?

Don't forget that although the cost of building a wall is much greater than the cost of a fence, even a well-made and beautifully erected fence will need more care and more regular replacement than a wall.

Trellis shapes and styles

Take a while to find out what is available before you take the plunge. Rounded trellis sections designed to be fitted on top of a fence come in convex or concave styles, which not only add extra planting space and a little more privacy but can look attractive in their own right before covered.

Curved trellis tops have a softer look.

Shop for quality

Fence panels can be a relatively low-cost and quick way to erect a fence, but it is worth buying from a reputable supplier and paying more for high quality, well-constructed panels. Don't buy any with loose parts: securing them is a splinter-ridden task, best avoided.

Sturdy panels are a good investment.

Use pressure-treated posts

Fence posts should always be made of pressure-treated lumber. If you need to cut fence posts to size, you may be exposing untreated areas of wood. If so, stand the cut post in a bucket of wood treatment for a day or two before erecting it. This will allow it to absorb some of the preservative before you use it.

Using trellis

Large, full-length trellis panels can be used to create either a garden boundary or divisions within your garden. You will need to like your neighbors or indulge in some very extensive planting if you use them for boundaries. But within the garden, they can provide a great support for lightweight climbers, partitioning off an area while still allowing you to see some of what lies on the other side.

Latticed panels imitate a trellis and bear more weight.

Brass fittings

Always use galvanized (zinc-coated) or brass fasteners and fittings when erecting a fence or trellis because these will be much slower to rust may not rust at all. The initial cost is a small price to pay for not having to re-do the job in a few years when ordinary fasteners and fittings will have rusted.

Matt, gray, galvanized nails resist corrosion.

Keep off the soil

The lower edge of a fence is most prone to rotting because it will regularly be damp. Fix a pressure-treated board rated for ground contact along the lower edge of the fence so that this is in contact with soil and plants. It's easier and cheaper to replace the board, and if you use the right board it may last longer than the fence!

Fine-tuning the fit

❀ Standard-sized fence panes are quick to install, but if a panel is too short for the space, insert a strip of wood between the post and the panel, and nail it in place.

❀ If the fence panel is just too wide to fit snugly in the space, use a plane to carefully remove a small amount of wood, but check the fit frequently so you don't remove too much.

Keep it safe

If a fence post shows signs of decay, do not attempt to repair it; it will not be strong enough for the job. Bite the bullet, and replace the entire post. But before you do, check other posts, too. It is likely that if one has started to go, others may need attention.

Blending in

If you replace a fence panel, there will be noticeable differences in color between old and new. Unless your planting is extremely dense and evergreen, this will show. Take the plunge and treat the whole fence, old and new, so that it all matches.

Preparation saves a lot of time later on.

Treating surfaces

❀ Avoid applying a wood treatment in very hot weather; sometimes it dries too fast. A warm or overcast day is best.

❀ Don't take shortcuts with dirty or algae- and moss-covered wood. If paint or stain doesn't stick well, it will quickly need reapplying. A stiff wire brush removes grime and roughens the surface, making applications adhere better.

❀ Repaint plant-clad fences in late autumn when the leaves have fallen.

All about walls

There is something permanent about a garden wall. Even one that has just been erected looks imposing and creates an air of stability—however flamboyant the adjacent planting.

Know your limits

Unless you are experienced at building walls, this is a job you should leave to the professionals. A poorly built wall looks awful and may be unsafe.

Save time and your back

If you are building a large wall and need a lot of concrete for the foundations, it really is worth renting or borrowing a concrete mixer—the amount of time and energy it will save you makes it a worthwhile expense. Ready-mixed mortar is a good buy unless you have a lot of mortar-making experience.

Mixing mortar takes a bit of practice.

Mixing mortar

To minimize waste as well as unpleasant and potentially harmful dust clouds when mixing mortar, dampen the surface of the mixing board slightly before slowly adding the mortar powder. Use a trowel to firm the powder gently and flatten the surface; then make a dip in the center. You can slowly pour the water into this and draw in the powder.

Brisk, dry, brushing is the only way to remove efflorescence.

Special treatments

If a wall is in a particularly damp area, it may be worth using a special treatment paint that minimizes the penetration of water. This reduces the formation of deposits and perhaps even extends the life of the wall.

Dealing with blooming walls

New bricks often produce a white, crystalline deposit called efflorescence. This looks bad, but it's only deposits of salts coming out of the brickwork. Don't wash it off because that will make the problem recur with a vengeance; instead, use a stiff wire brush to gently scrape off the efflorescence.

Feature walls

In a large garden, a freestanding wall incorporating an archway—separate from the boundary—makes a beautiful support for classic planting and will perfectly frame a view.

Is ivy destructive?

Self-clinging climbers, such as ivies (*Hedera*) and Virginia creeper (*Parthenocissus quinquefolia*), can damage a wall, but only if it is already not in the best condition. Flaking bricks or loose mortar may be made worse by a vigorous self-clinging climber, but neither is likely to be initiated by the climber.

Roots and pads on climbing stems are used to "stick" the climber to a support. They will not penetrate a solid surface.

Check for cracks

Walls need relatively little maintenance, but it is still worth checking them over from time to time. Any repairs are generally easier, quicker, and cheaper to make if carried out promptly.

Clean with care

If you use a pressure washer to clean off deposits of algae, moss, and lichen from a wall, take care not to use it on too aggressive a setting. The protective surface layer of the bricks can be loosened and damaged, especially on older walls.

Test settings on a hidden area of wall before letting loose.

Removing old mortar

❀ If the mortar or pointing is starting to fall from between the bricks of your wall, use a chisel or screwdriver to remove chunks that are loose, and then remove any sandy mix that lurks behind, using a soft brush.

❀ To do the job of repointing properly, you will need to remove the old mortar to about 1 inch (3cm) into the joint. This will ensure a longer lasting repair.

Prepare properly for repointing

If the bricks are left covered with dusty and sandy deposits after you have removed the loose mortar, the new mortar will not adhere properly. So make sure you clean these deposits off thoroughly before repointing. A damp sponge or sturdy rag should do the job.

Color-match mortar

Take the time to match the color of the mortar for the areas you are repointing. This may seem like an arduous process, but a wall with assorted colors of pointing looks awful. You will end up spending a fortune on climbers as you try to cover the mess, and it's still likely to show despite your efforts.

Let it dry

Once dry, mortar changes color quite noticeably. When you are trying to color-match, mix up tiny amounts of each mortar you make, allow them to dry, and then compare each of them with the existing mortar in the wall.

Ironed joints

If the mortar joints have this slightly concave profile, mimic it using a short length of garden hose pressed evenly but firmly along the length of the moist mortar.

Your joints may look terrible at first, but persevere—they will get better!

A special trowel can be bought, but is only worth it for large areas of pointing.

Weatherstruck joints

It is worth taking some time to match the profile of the mortar between each brick with that on the existing brickwork. A slanting, weatherstruck joint is best achieved using a bricklayer's trowel. The mortar is angled so that the upper end is slightly recessed into the space beneath the course of bricks above and the base of the mortar is very slightly protruding or level with the top of the bricks below.

Recoloring bricks

If some of the bricks have become discolored and are spoiling the look of the wall, take a spare brick of matching color; wet it thoroughly; and then rub it really firmly over the discolored or stained bricks, wetting the spare brick regularly as you go. Some color from the surface of the wetted brick should rub off and help to mask any staining on the wall.

Paving, gravel, and decking areas

If you want to be able to enjoy your garden as an "outside room," a level place for a few chairs or seats and a table is essential. Make your choice of surface with care as it will have a big impact.

A secluded seat is always enticing.

Where would you like to sit?

There are a number of factors to consider when deciding where best to construct a patio or terrace.

❧ A sheltered and preferably sunny spot is generally going to get the most use, particularly early and late in the year when a more exposed site is likely to be too cool.

❧ Although a nearby tree may be appealing because it will create some shade during hotter, sunnier weather, consider how much shade it will cast and at what time of day. Even if you want to create a shaded patio so that you can escape the sun, at least part of the area needs to be beyond the reach of the tree's branches because long after it has stopped raining, there will still be water dripping from the tree's canopy.

❧ If the site you have to use is rather exposed or it is overlooked by neighbors or passersby, incorporate enough space to plant a windbreak, erect a trellis, or use plants to create a little more privacy.

❧ A patio, especially one on which you are intending to enjoy food and drink, will benefit from being relatively close to the house. At the same time, consider the view that you will have when sitting out and eating, drinking, or simply relaxing.

What surface?

The surface you select is up to you, but factors such as the initial cost of material and installation (either your time or a landscaper's bill), and the amount of maintenance, will need to be considered.

A raised deck lets you enjoy greater views of the garden.

Matching the surroundings

If you have a wall or other hard surface nearby, make sure you consider this and its color and texture before deciding what materials to use. It is often best to restrict materials to a maximum of two types in any one area—for example, stone and brick or stone and gravel, rather than all three together.

Two materials are company, three would be a crowd.

Think long-term

Check that paving or slabs are all fully frost-proof, and if possible, that there will be an acceptable degree of color fastness over time—or at least that you like the color to which the slabs fade. You should also consider where natural stone materials come from and whether you are happy with this.

Get a firm footing

A properly leveled and firmed or compacted base layer is essential beneath surfaces of gravel or paving. If necessary, consider renting a machine to do the hard work of compacting the ground for you.

Never lay surfaces without a spirit level.

Planting holes

Think about the next step in the creation of your new patio or terrace, and when you make your paved, shingled, or decked area, ensure that you create a few planting opportunities, too. Plants generally prefer growing in open ground to growing in a container, and climbers in particular rarely thrive if kept in containers permanently.

Plants instantly soften a new deck or patio.

Make space for plants

If you are going to create planting holes or use planters, choose the location carefully. In particular, consider whether a plant grown there will become a trip hazard or be in the way of garden furniture. Any new planting opportunity should be in a good, out-of-the-way place. You should also make sure that you include areas of open ground for planting adjacent to any walls or fences that abut the surface you are creating.

Weeds are particularly problematic under gravel.

Clear the ground

Weed seeds or the roots of pernicious weeds beneath surfaces can cause constant problems that get worse with time. Always try to clear the area of weeds completely before starting to level or compact the surface ready for a new area of hardscaping.

The worst weeds

Weed-prevention fabrics can be a real help beneath gravel or shingle surfaces or under decks, preventing all but the most aggressive weeds from making an appearance. If you have problems with weeds such as brambles, horsetail, Japanese knotweed, or other notorious varieties, you should try to eliminate these as best you can before you lay the fabric.

165

Cut at the edges

Slabs may need to be cut to fit. Try to make sure that cut slabs are in out-of-the-way places, hopefully to be concealed by plants later on, and not in a position where they will be subjected to a lot of wear and tear.

Paving on a dry base

With paving slabs laid onto a bed of aggregate or rubble, there is often some initial movement for a few days after the slabs have been laid. Allow the newly laid paving to settle for a few days; then recheck the levels and adjust as necessary. Only add mortar between the slabs once you are certain everything has settled properly.

Substantial slabs can be laid on a dry foundation.

Safety first

When cutting a slab to create a new area or fit accurately into a gap, make sure that you wear goggles and tough gloves. The cut slab edges and fragments can be extremely sharp.

Cutting slabs

To cut a slab to fit a gap, you need to score both sides of the slab with a chisel, making sure each scored line is exactly lined up with the other. Each groove needs to be cut to a depth of about ⅛ inch (3mm). If in doubt, always cut the slab slightly too small, ideally about ¼ inch (5mm) all around. This will allow the slab section to fit into the gap despite any uneven edges. Once the grooves are complete, place a length of smooth, flat wood beneath the groove on the lower surface; then tap the upper surface of the slab with the hammer just to one side of the groove you have made. The slab should then break neatly along the scored line.

Use a broad bolster and a heavy hammer to cut.

The weakened line will break under pressure.

Be prepared to top off

With areas of shingle, pebble, or gravel, keep a note of the code number and name of the material you have used, plus the contact details for the supplier. I really do not know where it goes, but after a few years I always find that levels of these materials need topping off. It is also worth keeping a small, new sample of the material in a jar in the shed. If you cannot get hold of exactly the same material when the time comes, then at least you know what the original looked like when new, so you should be able to do some accurate matching.

Keep work areas clear

Always place a slab on a firm, flat and level surface before attempting to cut it. Any unevenness beneath means wobbly cuts.

Get even

If you find you have an uneven slab, you must deal with them, or they are likely to cause people to trip and fall. You may need to remove the layer of crushed stone underneath or add to it, or replace the slab.

Incorporate a slope

Where possible, introduce a slight slope or camber on the surface, especially those that will be impenetrable to rain (or virtually so). This camber should allow rain to be shed more easily and so prevent problems of standing water after heavy rain, and later growth of algae. You need a fall of about 1 inch (3cm) for every 6½ feet (2m) of patio or deck.

Don't skimp with mortar

Thin, light slabs should be laid on a mortar base. Lay a solid base, not "dabs"; if some mortar dabs settle differently, the slab will rock. Spaces under the slab also make it more likely to break under pressure, allow water accumulate and wash out soil, and make a lovely home for ants.

Spread the impact

To level slabs that are slightly uneven, get a block of wood or section of a plank; place it on the edge that is too high; then gently but firmly tap it with a rubber mallet until you achieve the desired level. The wood will dramatically reduce the possibility of your damaging the slab.

A rubber mallet can be used gently all over a slab to bed it down once level.

Abandon broken slabs

Instead of replacing broken, badly discolored, or missing slabs, why not remove them completely? Then replace the layer beneath with good soil mixed with compost, and make it into a low-level planter. If it is in the middle of the space, remove a slab from elsewhere to make a planting hole and replace the broken one.

Mortar edges

Even if laying slabs on a dry bed, it is worth mortaring at least under the last half slab along any "free" edge leading onto a lawn or gravel: this stops the slabs from slipping and is simpler than installing a retaining curb.

Maintaining your patio or deck

Maintaining patios and decking helps to keep them looking good and reduces the risk of excessive buildup of algae and moss. It might be a time-consuming job, but it rarely needs attention more than once a year.

Clear fallen leaves regularly in autumn.

Keep it clean

Any soil, compost, or even organic debris, such as fallen leaves and flowers, will create a potential seedbed for weeds if allowed to accumulate on a pebble or gravel surface, so always do your best to keep these surfaces free from materials like this.

Outdoor vacuuming

A good quality leaf-blower or garden vacuum can be a real help in trying to keep pebble or gravel surfaces clear of leaves and faded flowers. The materials you collect can always be added to the compost heap.

Easing in new slabs

If you have to replace broken slabs within an area of paving, it is often difficult to get them into place without damaging or scuffing the adjacent slabs. Lay a broom handle or spare piece of copper water pipe across the space that you need to fill. You can then place one end of the new slab into the space and the support will allow you to ease the slab down into position.

Check your deck

Decking may need regular treatment with a wood preservative, but the frequency and the best material to use will depend on exactly what the deck was made from and where it is, so check before you treat.

Opaque treatments provide the least UV protection.

Solving slippery decks

❀ Deck paint has gritty material in it, and should be slip-free in any weather.

❀ Galvanized chicken wire fixed over the wood with galvanized staples isn't pretty, but it is effective.

Clean and treat

Before treating wood decking, use a stiff wire brush to remove surface deposits of algae and moss, and repair or replace any seriously damaged or deteriorating boards.

Arches and pergolas

There is something really appealing about an arch or arbor. They help to give the feel of an established relaxed garden, and they add charm and often a touch of romance, too.

Keep pergolas wide for an open, welcoming feeling.

Using arches, arbors, and pergolas

❀ The style of any garden feature like this needs to fit in with your existing house and garden, or at least with the garden you are planning to create. A very modern-looking metal arch will look rather out of place in a cottage-style garden, and similarly an elaborate or rustic-style construction will not be best suited to a geometric, formal, or modern garden.

❀ If you want to keep maintenance to a minimum, consider coated metal structures. For me they do not have the initial appeal of a wooden structure, but if you plan your planting carefully, pretty soon you will be able to see very little of the underlying structure, and it will require minimal maintenance.

If buying a kit, you may need additional support for climbers.

Sizing arches and pergolas

❀ There is nothing worse than an arch or pergola that is not tall enough. When deciding on the dimensions of an arch, consider the tallest person likely to walk through it, and add on about 12 inches (30cm) for plant growth to hang down, ideally making it a total of 8 feet (2.5m) or more. And don't forget that the supporting posts or uprights will need to be buried in the ground.

❀ The width of an arch or pergola that spans a path needs some thought, too, and again, plant growth on the uprights needs to be considered or else you will end up with more of a tunnel than a pergola.

Buying and caring for garden furniture

Good quality, comfortable garden furniture makes your garden all the more appealing, even to the nongardening residents. So do your research, and take time and care to choose well.

Even if your table is on the lawn in summer, move it onto a deck or paving when damper weather sets in.

Keep off the grass

Wooden garden furniture will last a lot longer if you make sure that over the winter months it is kept on a surface where rain water does not accumulate. Avoid standing it on grass—it is likely to sink into the turf during wet weather, and the legs are then more likely to rot.

Undercover

Furniture of all types lasts longer if it's taken into a shed or other protected place over winter or, failing this, covered up. If like me, you enjoy sitting out in your garden on the odd wintry day, then just make sure you are vigilant about regular applications of wood treatments.

Leg treatment

Stand each leg of wooden garden furniture in its own pot of wood treatment for several hours to ensure that adequate amounts are absorbed to keep this high-risk area well protected. Re-treat at the recommended intervals.

Use the best material you can get for this job.

Caring for joints

Joints on wooden furniture are likely to hold moisture more than other areas, so check them more regularly, and use a medium-firm paintbrush to really press the wood treatment into those awkward corners.

Oil with teak

Teak oil makes a great annual treatment for hardwood furniture. Although hardwoods are much less inclined to rot than softwoods, teak oil will help to keep the wood in better condition for even longer and preserves the original color.

Plastic renewal

If your plastic or resin garden furniture is faded and nasty-looking but still perfectly sound, don't discard it, paint it. With a suitable paint, designed specifically for plastic, it can have a new lease on life.

Keep the shine

Plastic garden furniture benefits from a regular washing with water—not only to keep it clean, but also because any grit or grime that accumulates on it could cause scratching of the surface.

Hinges and fittings on folding chairs need regular attention.

Oil for protection

Metal furniture that is kept in the garden throughout the year will stay in better condition for longer if it is dried off thoroughly and then given an annual application of oil. If you do this right at the end of the main season, you can then leave the oil in place, only wiping off excess just before you need it again in the spring.

Lubricate moving parts

An aerosol of oil or water-displacing lubricant with a thin extension tube is perfect for hard-to-reach places on your furniture and for lubricating hinges and springs. It is so much easier than trying to reach these areas with an oily rag or a brush.

Dry before repairs

❀ If wooden furniture needs repairing, bring it under cover for a couple of weeks first. The wood must be completely dry before you tackle the repair or wood-replacement job; fillers and glues will not work on moist wood.

❀ Small areas of wood can be dried a little more speedily if you can get the furniture close to the house—a hair dryer works wonders.

Removing the rot

If you need to cut out rotted wood, make sure you remove adjacent discolored or suspect areas too, because these are likely to be in the early stages of decay. It is better to cut a bit more than you need to rather than not removing enough—wood filler will soon fall out if more wood starts to rot around it.

Sustainable wood

When buying wooden furniture, look for the logo of a certification organization, such as the Forest Stewardship Council (FSC), that ensures it comes from sustainable sources.

Caring for plants

No matter how much time and money you spend choosing and planting new plants for your garden, this can all be lost in a matter of days if you do not give the plants the TLC they deserve. As soon as they are home and in your care, there are things they will need, and without this initial aftercare, their chances of surviving, let alone thriving, are very poor. Basic needs such as adequate water, and later on some extra food, are essential to the plants, especially in that initial establishment period.

Even when the plants are established, most will not perform as they could unless you look after them. Most aftercare need not take more than a few minutes, but it can make all the difference between a miserable, poorly performing plant and one that is living up to and above any expectations you had of it.

Maintaining your plants
Taking time to care for your plants can be incredibly satisfying, and means you can

really observe what's going on and how things are progressing—and perhaps even catch and deal with an early infestation of a pest or pathogen attacking your plants.

The amount of time and effort you need to allow depends on your garden's size and style; formal gardens generally require much higher maintenance than more naturalistic ones. Just remember that plants and garden features need some input, but every second you spend will be well worth it.

This chapter shows you how to

❀ Care for your plants in the first few weeks after planting.

❀ Water your plants efficiently and economically.

❀ Feed and mulch your plants—plus organic and chemical fertilizer options.

❀ Weed your plants, and techniques for effective weeding.

Initial aftercare

The first few weeks or months after planting are generally the most critical. Once out of its pot, a new plant needs to get its roots into place quickly and get itself established, so if your time per plant is limited, make this initial aftercare period your top priority.

Beware of shocking your plants

If the conditions in the garden differ noticeably from the conditions in the nursery, garden center, or shop where the plants were before, make sure you give them the chance to acclimate, and try to avoid too dramatic a change.

Overnight protection can ease a plant into its new conditions, but remove it in the morning.

This mesh may not look like much, but it slows the wind enough to make a real difference.

Put up a windbreak

A temporary windbreak is a good idea: you can use fleece, or get special windbreak fabric for a larger planting. Whatever you use, the important thing is to get it in position as soon as (or preferably before) you plant.

Easy does it

Covering a new plant with fleece or even old sheer curtains for a few nights after planting should help it to acclimate to a less protected, cooler environment. This will also help to prevent wind damage, but it is important that you gradually allow the plant to get used to the harsher conditions—don't coddle it too much or too long.

Hardy plants aren't always totally hardy

Even a plant that is described as hardy may often prove to be slightly tender in its first winter, especially if you buy it relatively late in the year and it has been in the protected environment or a warm site. If there are any signs of fairly soft growth or you are even the slightest bit doubtful, you should take precautions because the plant may not have had sufficient chance for its growth to harden before the onset of winter in your garden.

Keep well watered

To encourage the roots to grow out into the soil and so allow the plant to become established, the soil needs to be kept really moist. If there is plenty of rain that is penetrating deeply enough into the soil, that will do, but if in any doubt, grab the watering can.

Unless there is a spell of wet weather, water to ensure the ground stays moist.

Water a wide area around a new plant to encourage the roots to grow outwards.

Drought tolerance takes time

Don't forget that even drought-tolerant plants, which should need little extra watering once established, will need watering if the soil is very dry in the first few weeks (for annuals) or months (for perennials and woody plants) after planting.

Sacrifice the first flowers

You may think it sounds crazy, but to get the best long-term performance from a new plant, it often helps to cut off all or at least some of the flowers when you plant it, or any that appear shortly afterward. These flowers may look appealing, but they will have a draining effect on the plant, drawing resources away from where the plant needs it most, in its roots and general structure.

Deadhead for good health

As soon as a new plant is in the ground—or earlier if you have a moment—grab scissors or pruners and do a thorough deadheading. This ensures that no resources are used on the formation of seeds and associated structures instead of on the vital early stages of establishment.

For best results, deadhead for the duration of the plant's flowering period.

Watering your plants

When it comes to watering, it is essential that you know the moisture requirements of your plants. Just as many plants may be killed by overwatering and excessive kindness as die through neglect and underwatering.

Watering when dry

Water is lost from the plant in especially large quantities during hot, dry weather, but windy weather often has an extremely dehydrating effect, too. Always check soil and compost moisture levels after windy periods, even if the weather has appeared quite cool and overcast.

Probe the soil to test how deeply water has penetrated.

Too little, too shallow

It is essential that any watering you do has a useful effect, and does not just moisten the soil on the surface or immediately below it. If only this area of the soil is moist, the plant's roots will tend to move toward this area, sometimes even growing upward. Once in the upper regions of the soil, they will be more prone to the effects of drought and heat than if they were in their usual place, lower down in the soil.

Winter drought

Unlike most deciduous trees, shrubs, and climbers, conifers and other evergreens are especially prone to drought during dry periods in the winter, late autumn, and very early spring because their foliage is still in place. During dry weather, make sure that they are watered adequately.

Wait and see

It can be very difficult to know just how far down into the soil the water you have applied has penetrated. On first inspection, if you dig into the soil, the water may not have gone very deep at all, but if you wait an hour or so before checking, you will tend to form a much more accurate picture of the moisture levels.

It is important to water conifers because they are always in leaf.

When to water

In the heat of the day, the soil surface temperature can become very high. This means that watering done then is more likely to allow a lot of moisture to be lost by evaporation, so whenever possible water in the evening or very early in the morning.

Keep the stakes long or the hose may slip over.

Avoiding hose damage

If you use a garden hose to water your garden, it is all too easy to drag the hose over or against precious garden plants as you move from one area to another, causing a lot of damage. To avoid this, drive sturdy wooden stakes into the soil on the bed edges and at intervals along the edges of very large beds. As you drag the hose it should always hit a stake rather than the plants in the border.

Soft and low

❀ Avoid strong jets of water. Plant top growth is easily damaged, and if you direct the jet at the ground, you are likely to displace the soil from around the roots.

❀ Many plant pathogens, such as powdery mildew and rust, thrive when the foliage is wet, so always try to avoid wetting the foliage when you water.

Reaching inaccessible parts

If there are areas in a bed, or perhaps within rows of vegetables, that become inaccessible later in the season, they can be difficult to water. When planting, lay a piece of plastic gutter with holes drilled at frequent intervals along its length, in the inaccessible place. Provided the gutter is kept level, you can simply pour water in at the accessible end of the pipe and the water should move along the gutter to reach the soil beneath it.

When jets can help

It helps to use jets of water when you have an infestation of red spider mites on the foliage of your plants. This pest really detests getting wet feet, so it pays to wet the foliage whenever you can, provided it is not during very bright sunlight.

Keep the water in

To encourage water to stay in the most useful place, create a slight ridge of soil in a circle around the base of the plant, large enough to encompass the feeding roots of the plant. You can then direct water into this "bowl" and it should all penetrate within the circle.

If all the water stays where it is needed, you can use less.

Once you have checked the flow is what you want, cover the hose.

Reducing watering loss

❀ A porous soaker hose allows very gentle and slow seepage of water into the soil. Perfect for watering newly installed plants, and less wasteful because the water does not run off.

❀ If you are using a soaker hose, make sure you cover it with mulch. This not only hides the hose from view but ensures that even less water is lost through evaporation.

Don't wet the petals

The petals of flowers are generally far more easily damaged than the leaves, so take extra care not to wet these when you are watering. This is especially important in sunny weather: the combination of water and hot, bright sunlight causes scorching of the petals or soft foliage.

Welcome rainwater

❀ Make sure you recycle water whenever possible. It makes such a lot of sense environmentally, and natural rainwater is generally the plants' first choice as well. (See pages 228–229).

❀ If you have hard water in your area, it will not be ideal for lime-hating or ericaceous plants, so wherever possible, water these plants with rainwater.

❀ Lime-hating or ericaceous plants may definitely do better when fed rainwater. But if there is no rainfall and your water barrels are empty, it is still essential to water these plants if their soil or compost becomes too dry, especially if they are growing in the confines of a pot. Hard water is better than no water.

❀ Small quantities of hard water can be made suitable for these plants by boiling it and allowing it to cool. Adding a few old tea bags or tea leaves to the water will help to acidify it slightly.

Watering in the shadows

Plants growing close to a wall, especially a house wall, are especially prone to dry soil conditions because the base and the foundations of the wall act like a sponge and absorb water from the soil. Plants on a house wall have the added problem of the roof overhang, which creates a very effective "rain shadow." Make plants in these areas a watering priority, and avoid planting drought-intolerant plants in this sort of position.

Whether sunny or shady, a bed by a wall is often dry.

To sprinkle or not to sprinkle?

It is tempting to use a sprinkler system to water the plants over the summer because it can be left to its own devices. Sprinklers also make light work of watering lawns and areas of dense planting. However, if they are left in one place for too long, they can be wasteful and can end up giving the leaves of the plants a light sprinkling, as opposed to delivering the water to where it is needed—at the roots. As restrictions are frequently enforced over the summer months, another watering method, such as a soaker hose or drip irrigation, may be a more environmentally sound option.

Feeding and mulching

There is no need to apply excessive quantities of fertilizer to your plants—indeed it may damage them—but the truth is that gardening creates some unnatural situations, and with plants packed in or cropping heavily, they benefit from feeding.

A balanced diet

Plants require nutrients as well as water and the energy they can create using sunlight. If you want your plants to perform to perfection, some supplementary feeding is generally a good idea, but don't forget that you can overfeed or feed incorrectly. Doing this is just as likely to result in problems as if you underfeed, so take care not to overdo it.

Keep on composting

Keep your soil in good health by regularly incorporating garden compost and well-rotted manure. This helps to ensure that soil micro-organisms are plentiful, as well as topping off many nutrient levels. It is cheap (or even free) and means you are less likely to need artificial fertilizers.

Organic matter is beneficial to the soil.

The power of potash

Sulphate of potash is used to promote flowering, ripening of stems, and toughening up of foliage. Potash is leached out of the soil readily, so this can be applied earlier in the year or later in the year, as well as during the classic feeding times. Because it does not promote soft growth, it is also perfectly safe to apply it during "off-season" times.

Sprinkle potash around the base of the plant; it will wash down to the roots.

Feeding: the basic rules

❀ Reduce the risk of soft growth being produced too late in the year by feeding only until midsummer. Applying feeds that stimulate growth in autumn would make the plant very vulnerable to frost.

❀ Feeding excessively, or too late in the season, may cause flowering shrubs or trees to bloom less well than they should because buds are more likely to fail or to drop.

❀ Never feed plants that are seriously stressed, especially if they are suffering from the effects of drought. They are unlikely to be able to make use of the fertilizer, and may even be damaged by it.

Don't starve seedlings

If seedlings or small plants waiting to be transplanted cannot be given the treatment they need immediately, apply a foliar feed to their leaves. This gives them a boost and at least partially makes up for the low nutrient levels in the potting mix. To avoid the risk of scorching, dilute the liquid so that it is half its normal strength.

Growth cycle

Plants generally grow more during the spring and summer, start to slow down in autumn, and pretty much come to a standstill during winter. This is in part a natural protection mechanism: any soft, new growth produced would be damaged by winter frosts. As a result, the best time to feed most garden plants with general or complete fertilizers is midspring to midsummer.

Fertilizer rules

Never use a fertilizer except in the way described by the manufacturers. A standard fertilizer, even if in liquid form, should not be used as a foliar feed. It has not been formulated for this, and so doing could mean that the plant does not benefit, or worse still may actually be damaged.

Always mix feeds as directed: a little bit more "for good measure" can be harmful.

Foliar feeds are the ultimate fast food for plants, giving an almost instant boost.

Quick feed

❀ If you are looking for a quick-fix feed with relatively fast results, choose a liquid feed. These are taken up and used very rapidly.

❀ Using a foliar feed—that is, one that is applied directly to the foliage—is generally regarded as being the quickest way to get nutrients into a plant. Make sure you apply this type of fertilizer on a cloudy day because using it during hot, bright sunlight may cause scorching on the leaves.

❀ Since foliar feeding seems to stimulate root growth, it is an excellent way to encourage initial plant establishment, reestablishment after transplanting, or replacement root growth after the roots have been injured.

❀ Because foliar feeds take effect relatively quickly, you can safely apply these to plants a little later in the season than when you are using root-applied feeds.

When to avoid lime

Avoid using lime if you have recently dug manure into your soil, have used it as a mulch, or are intending to do so soon. Lime will react with the nitrogen in the manure and release ammonia, which may damage the plants.

Feed and forget

Controlled-release fertilizer granules are useful in situations where you need to be sure that the plant will get food even if you forget to feed it. They have a resin coating that is permeable and allows more nutrients to be released when the soil or compost is moist and damp, less when it is very dry or cold. The result of this is that the plants get more food when they need it most, and less when they don't need it so much.

Granules may be loose or in "plugs" to push into pots.

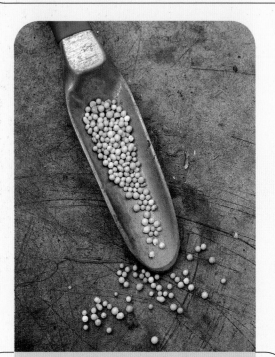

Fertilizers come in many shapes and forms, so check labels carefully.

Granular fertilizers

Granular fertilizers need to be dissolved into their liquid form if they are to be of use to the plant and not scorch it, so make sure that you feed plants either when the soil is already very moist or just before a heavy rainfall. If in doubt, or if neither of these options is possible, water the plant and the fertilized area thoroughly right after application.

Avoid touching the leaves

Always try to keep fertilizers (except foliar feeds) off the plant's foliage. They may cause scorching, especially if the plant is stressed or the weather is particularly hot and sunny. If the fertilizer has contaminated the foliage, try to brush it off right away; ideally you do not want to wet it. If this is not possible, then you could thoroughly drench all the affected plants with large quantities of water in an attempt to wash it off.

Concentrated fertilizer will scorch leaves: wash it off and down to the roots.

Avoid contact with roots

If you are incorporating a fertilizer into the soil before planting, make sure that it is mixed in thoroughly with the soil and that the roots of the plant will not come in direct contact with the concentrated fertilizer. If they do, root damage may occur.

Lack of balance

Sometimes the presence of large quantities of one nutrient may cause others to become less readily available to plants. For instance, if a lot of potash is used, perhaps to encourage fruiting of tomatoes or flowering of roses, then it is likely that the plant will start to show symptoms of magnesium deficiency.

Magnesium deficiency

❀ Magnesium deficiency affects the older, larger leaves first, showing as yellowing between the veins on the affected leaves. It may also show as browning or purple discolouration between the veins.

❀ Epsom salt is the most widely used treatment for magnesium deficiency. This can be watered into the soil or applied directly to the leaves for a much more rapid effect. Any solution that runs off is not wasted because it will also be taken up by the plant's roots.

Hose-end feeders can be adjusted to give a solution of the correct strength, saving time.

Magnesium deficiency can look alarming but is easily treated.

Quick feeding with a hose

Save time by using a hose-end fixture to get feed onto the plants. These are suitable for either a liquid feed or a granular or powdered one that has to be diluted with water before applying.

Phosphate for roots

Since phosphate helps to encourage root growth, it is particularly useful for new plants. Bonemeal is often used, but it can sometimes attract wildlife, such as foxes, that then excavate in the area looking for what appears to be a source of food.

Using ash safely

Wood ash contains useful amounts of potassium, but make sure that no unsuitable materials, such as wax firelighters, plastics, or painted or treated wood, have been burned on the fire. Only use the ash on the garden if it originates purely from plant materials. Ash from a garden bonfire will have lower levels of potassium if most of the wood burned was old and woody, and more if the materials included fresher, younger plant growth.

If you burn plant material that cannot be composted, it can still be useful.

Nitrogen-fixing plants

There are a number of plants, in particular the legumes – including beans, peas, lupins, and sweet peas—which have root nodules containing nitrogen-fixing bacteria in them. These are able to convert unavailable soil nitrogen into a form that is available to plants. Make sure you always include some peas and beans in a vegetable plot rotation system. (See page 119.) If possible, leave the roots of all these plants to die off and break down in the soil once their cropping or flowering period is over; this will allow them to continue to be useful for even longer.

Gloves for safety

It is always advisable to wear gloves when handling fertilizers. If you are using a dust formulation, wear a dust mask as well.

Always be careful when handling concentrated substances.

Make your own liquid feed

Make a very useful and totally free liquid feed for your plants by rotting down the top-growth of nettles and comfrey plants. You need about 2½ pounds (1kg) of nettles for every 2¼ gallons (10l) of water. Just mix the nettles with the water and ensure that they are completely covered with water. Keep the container tightly covered, and stir regularly; then, when the leaves have rotted down in a few weeks time, you can strain off the liquid. Dilute the concentrated fertilizer with about one part fertilizer to 10 parts water.

Top up the mulch, then pull it back from around the stems.

Replenish mulches

Top off all organic mulches regularly because the material will gradually become incorporated into the soil. Make sure that the mulch is not actually in contact with the stems or trunk of the plants; this can cause the stem to start to deteriorate.

Mulching for weeds

Mulching helps to smother small weeds or to create a barrier that prevents weed seeds from germinating. Keeping mulch levels topped off helps to reduce problems with weeds.

Small weeds will die under a light-excluding mulch.

Mulches for moisture

Help moist soil stay moist by applying a bulky organic mulch to the soil surface in spring. This prevents the surface from getting too hot and reduces moisture loss by evaporation.

Heavy-duty woven landscape fabric stops most weeds.

A barrier to weeds

It may not suit all areas of the garden, but if you use a covering of gravel or even large pebbles on the soil surface, this woven plastic sheet placed under the stones will allow water to reach the roots while providing a serious barrier to weeds trying to come up from the soil and to weed seed germination.

Depth of mulch

To be most effective, an organic mulch layer needs to be 2–3½ inches (5–8cm) deep. But if you run short, just put on what you can and then add to it as soon as you can. Some mulch is definitely better than none.

Weeding

Weeds compete for those basic needs of your garden plants—water, light, and nutrients. Everything from the smallest bedding plant to a young tree with the potential to be a giant one day can suffer, so don't underestimate weeds, either annual or perennial.

Make weeding a priority

Most weeds are extremely rapid growers that flower and set seed far more quickly than garden plants. Weeding needs to be a high-priority job because it is essential to remove weeds before they get a chance to set seed and multiply.

Which weeds make compost

❀ Weeds make an excellent addition to your compost heap—but avoid using any that have been treated with a weed killer, are just about to set seed, or have set seed. You should also leave out the roots of any that have pernicious root systems.

❀ Weeds with seeds and roots can form new weed plants in the compost heap. They are best left to rot in a large tub or barrel of water. Within a few weeks they will rot down, producing liquid feed. The liquid tends to be rather smelly, so keep the barrel in an out-of-the-way place!

❀ Perennial weeds often have seriously pernicious roots that are extremely difficult to remove in their entirety. Deal with them slowly, and try to ensure that you do get all of the root out. In many cases, each section of root left behind will have the potential to form a new plant.

A sharp hoe uproots weed top growth.

How to hoe

❀ A sharp hoe is a really good way to deal with annual weeds. Invest in a tiny hoe, usually sold as an onion hoe, which has the head only a few inches wide. This is perfect for weeding around small or closely packed plants with accuracy.

❀ Try to hoe weeds on a hot, sunny day, when they can be left on the soil surface and will dry to a crisp.

Digging out deep weeds

An old but sturdy table knife is a great tool for digging out longer-rooted perennial weeds, such as dandelions, because it can be inserted right down into the soil adjacent to the root.

Removing every bit of a tap root is tricky work.

Handle with care

Chemical weed killers can be used, but remember that they are, basically, plant killers; they have to be used with extreme care and precisely according to the manufacturer's instructions.

Avoid drifting weed killer

Herbicide drift is a serious risk, especially if you are using a sprayer, because tiny droplets are easily wafted around on air currents and thermals. Wherever possible use a watering can to apply weed killer.

Bruise the leaves

Some weeds are tough to control because they have a tough outer surface. To increase uptake of the herbicide, gently crush the foliage before applying.

Leave it late

Some weeds, such as nettles, benefit from a late-season spray, applied just before the foliage starts to die back. It seems that the weed killer is carried down into the base of the plant as the plant reabsorbs nutrients from its foliage.

A drip bar is ideal for targeting weeds accurately and efficiently.

Applying with care

❀ If you are applying herbicides using a sprayer, plant mister, or watering can, make sure that it is clearly and indelibly labeled and is only ever used for applying weed killers. Even extremely tiny traces of herbicide can cause a lot of damage.

❀ Always check that the product you have in mind is suitable for the job, and that it can be used on the type of weeds you are trying to control.

❀ A watering can fitted with a drip bar allows direct application of weed killer and little if any drift. If you are applying an herbicide in a bed that has other plants in it, make sure you protect these first, otherwise they may be damaged or even killed.

❀ Only apply weed killers during suitable weather conditions. The day must be calm, with no signs of excessive heat, wind, or rain.

❀ Cover or shield nearby plants with plastic bags, cardboard boxes, or sheets, or even disposable plastic dropcloths for larger plants. Remove these only when the herbicide has dried on the weed foliage.

❀ If you feel tempted not to bother with these precautions, just think how long it would take and how much it would cost to replace any plants killed by the weed killer!

Plants pull everything into their roots just before winter.

Simple propagation

Propagating your own plants need not be complicated or expensive. There are several ways you can build up your plant numbers with little effort, no well-honed skills, and, sometimes, no cash outlay.

You may be trying your hand at seed sowing, taking cuttings, or layering for the first time, or perhaps you have tried these techniques before. In either case, there are sure to be a few ways to make plant propagation easier and more successful.

The beauty of propagation

One of the great things about propagating your own plants is that you can raise exactly what you want. When you grow your own plants from seed, you can search the catalogs until you find what you want, or even collect and save the seed from one of your favorite plants.

For woody climbers, shrubs, and trees, if you can take cuttings or do simple layering using that perfect plant as your propagation material, you're guaranteed extra numbers.

Some plants are easier to propagate at home than others, and there is no doubt that in many cases a little bit of specialized equipment—perhaps just a heated propagator—will make it easier to successfully propagate a wide range of plants. That said, the outlay will not be huge and is nothing compared with the money you can save when you propagate your own plants and the satisfaction and pride you will feel when you see your little "fledglings" growing in the garden!

This chapter shows you how to

- ❀ Prepare and sow in trays and pots.
- ❀ Sow in a heated propagator.
- ❀ Manage without a greenhouse.
- ❀ Plant seedlings.
- ❀ Sow direct and collect seed.
- ❀ Take cuttings from a variety of plants.
- ❀ Divide plants and propagate by layering.

Starting with seed

Most of the plants that you might want in your flowerbeds or vegetable plots can be raised from seed, including some trees and shrubs. It is worth gathering a selection of seed catalogs, and buying or making some simple equipment to get started.

Choose easy seed

If you are new to seed sowing, it is worth starting with seeds that are relatively easy or at least avoiding those that are described as needing "some experience." There is plenty of time for those later. First, prove to yourself that you can do the basics.

Read the instructions

Seed packets will always tell you which months are suitable for sowing the seed. It's worth noting these because the weather conditions that follow will determine whether or not the plants you produce will do what they need to, and each plant has different needs.

Badges of merit

Some seed packets bear logos that show they have been assessed in trials and found to be plants of particular worth in the garden. All-American Selections (AAS) and the Pennsylvania Horticultural Society Gold Medal Plants indicate good buys.

You can start with just a few seed trays for most seeds. More equipment allows you to grow a wider range of plants.

Seasonal adjustments

There is a margin for common sense when it comes to sowing dates. If you are living in a particularly cold or especially mild part of the country, or have reason to believe that this will be a year with an Indian summer, adjust sowing dates by a week or two, so the plants are ready when the weather is right.

Tools of the trade

What you can sow depends on the equipment you have (some seed need a heat source, such as a heated propagator, to germinate) and also on the time of year. The right equipment lets you cheat a little on sowing dates, letting you sow seeds indoors (and with heat) either to make an early start or to catch up if you've left things go to the last minute.

Wait and sow

For seed that is to be sown directly in the garden, let your common sense prevail. (See pages 202–203.) If the ground is very wet and cold, don't sow, even if the seed packet says it is the right time. Wait until it gets a bit drier or milder.

Recycling at home

Using old food containers as seed trays is sensible because these are generally made from the sort of plastics that are not widely accepted for recycling.

Don't drown your seeds

There are all sorts of seed trays available, but make sure yours is equipped with drainage holes. I have seen a surprising number of seed sowing pots and trays provided in kits that are hole-free and will cause the seeds to rot or the seedlings to fail in days.

Drainage holes should be plentiful and not too small.

Don't skimp on drainage holes—it is hard to make too many. One every 1 in. (3cm) should be enough.

Make your own

If you want to recycle, create your own seed-sowing containers from thoroughly cleaned margarine tubs, ready-made salad pots, or fresh fruit containers and baskets. Use a sharp knife or a heated skewer to make plenty of drainage holes.

Save trays with lids

Some containers with potential for a second life as a seed tray are especially useful because they come complete with a clear plastic lid. This makes them perfect miniature propagators.

A lid keeps in heat and moisture, but take it off before the seedlings brush against it.

Preparing trays and pots

Getting pots and seed trays ready for sowing is rather like making up the spare bed for a very special guest—you need to get the conditions just right for them to do well and enjoy their stay. But, like guests, they will need moving on before too long!

Don't mix seeds

Full-size seed trays are great if you have a lot of one type of seed to sow, but you will usually want to sow less than this. It is possible to sow more than one type of seed in a single tray, but it is harder for you and for the emerging seedlings, which are likely to germinate at different rates or even require different conditions for optimum germination. Half- or quarter- trays are generally much better for smaller quantities.

The beauty of seed cells

I often use sowing cells—numerous tiny pots or cells together in one tray shape. The advantage is that you can dramatically reduce the amount of thinning out and transplanting you need to do. Because each has its own minipot for its own root system, you are less likely to disturb the roots of the seedlings when they are finally transplanted. The disadvantage is that the smaller individual volumes of compost are more inclined to dry out rapidly, so you will need to keep a closer eye on watering.

Sow seed in modules if it hates disruption.

Seed sowing mixes

For all but the most finicky seeds, you can get perfectly good results using a good-quality multipurpose potting soil. For the more difficult customers, choose a special blend sold specifically for seed sowing, or sometimes for seed and cuttings.

A compost sieve is handy for seed trays, and also for smaller potted plants that don't like lumpy compost.

Fine-tuning the soil

If your growing material is lumpy, the best solution is to invest in a compost sieve with medium-size mesh. Failing that, you can use an old kitchen colander or rigid vegetable steamer to sieve your soil ready for seed sowing. Avoid using a kitchen sieve: the mesh size is so small that virtually nothing comes through.

Avoid older potting mix

If you find some old soil in an open bag lurking around in the greenhouse, shed, or garden, use it as a mulch for the garden, or perhaps add it to fresh compost for a large plant. Use only fresh mix for sowing because older compost may harbor pathogens.

Using garden soil

You can sometimes successfully sow and germinate seed in garden soil, but the risks are high. Sowing in open ground is one thing, but in the confines of a pot or tray, problems such as damping off are more common, especially if extra warmth is provided.

Shake out the lumps

❀ If you are desperate to sow some seeds but have no sieve, you can remove the largest lumps fairly effectively by putting a quantity of potting mix in a large pot or bowl and repeatedly shaking it quite firmly and tapping the base of the bowl on the work surface. The lumps should come to the surface in much the same way as the lumps of butter come to the surface when you are making pastry or a crumble topping.

❀ Don't waste the larger lumps and twigs left after sieving. They can either be used in the very base of the seed tray or as part of the potting mix for larger plants.

Removing lumps by hand is not ideal, but most seeds clearly benefit.

Stand the potting mix in a sunny place or, ideally, a greenhouse.

Warm up cold soil

If you buy soil in cold weather, it too will be cold. So if time permits, put it somewhere relatively warm for a day or two before you sow the seed. Warming the soil will help to get things off to a quicker start, and if you are using a heated propagator, it will take little electricity to bring the mix up to the right temperature.

Sowing in trays and pots

Once the growing medium is in the trays or pots, the seed can go in and the process of growing your own plants from seed really begins. For the best results, take time over this seemingly simple process, and it'll pay dividends.

Filling the tray

Seeds need a decent depth of potting soil to develop their roots, but don't fill the tray to the brim. Doing this uses more material than you need and can make it difficult to water later. It is best to fill the tray to within about ¼–½ inch (0.5–1cm) of the rim.

A flat tamper will level compost better than your hands can.

Firming the surface

Potting soil needs firming, but not compacting, and the surface needs to be leveled. If you do a lot of seed sowing or intend to do so, then it is worth making your own tamper. Take a piece of wooden board the same dimensions as the surface of the tray minus ⅛ inch (3mm) all around, and add a small block of wood. You can then use the block as a handle to gently, but firmly, tamp the planting mix.

Tamp with a tray

As an alternative to a soil tamper, use the bottom of another seed tray the same size as the one full of soil. Hold the empty tray level on the surface; then press it down. The surface will be leveled, and in many cases it will also have some slight furrows in it (from the drainage grooves on the tray's base). These can be used as guides for sowing in straight lines.

Sowing at the correct depth

The depth that seed should be sown is stated clearly on the seed packet. Although seeds have an amazing determination to succeed in germinating, if you bury them too deeply, they need to use up a lot of energy to produce all that extra growth just to get to the surface.

Estimating depth

For seed saved from the garden or given by a friend, you may have to guess the correct depth. The general rule is that the smaller the seed, the smaller its reserves, and the closer to the light it should be. Scatter dust-like seed on the surface, and bury larger seeds to about their own depth.

Make sure you know what's what!

✿ Always label your seed trays as you sow them. It is easy to assume that you'll remember what you sowed and when, but this is not always the case, and seedlings often bear little resemblance to the mature plant, especially when very small.

✿ If there are children in the house, I recommend also writing labels on the pots and trays themselves, just in case small hands decide to collect the labels for you. I've had this happen to me!

Labels written with non-water-soluble pen or pencil are essential.

Sowing thinly means finding more space for seed trays but yields much better results.

Don't crowd seeds

Always sow seeds thinly in pots and trays. Sowing too thickly produces seedlings that are more likely to become etiolated, or "leggy," and be more prone to damping-off diseases. They will also be that much trickier to thin when the time comes.

Mix fine seed with sand

Very fine seed from plants such as lobelias is difficult to sow thinly. One way to make it easier is to mix the seed with several times its own volume of dry silver sand before sowing. Scattering this larger quantity of sand is much easier.

A pinch of dust-like seed is easier to sow if mixed into a teaspoon or two of sand.

With a little practice, you can sow very evenly from paper.

Small, finicky seeds

If you find small seeds sticking to your hands, take a piece of stiff paper or cardboard and fold it so that it has a crisp crease along the center. Tip some of the seed from the packet into it. You can then hold the paper in one hand and tap it sharply with the other hand to release a controlled stream of seeds onto the soil.

Covering seeds

If you sow in furrows at the correct sowing depth, you can simply flick the soil from the sides back over the seeds. For seeds that are randomly scattered or very small, it is easiest to use finely sieved soil, applied directly from the sieve and shaken over them.

How to sow seeds

Sowing seeds in straight lines rather than randomly scattering them makes it easier to prick the seedlings out later on. Large seeds can go into individual holes created with a dowel or pencil; for smaller ones, make a furrow of the appropriate depth using a plant label drawn over the surface.

A little time spent making furrows saves a lot of fiddling and frustration later.

A light covering

Some seeds need light to germinate but would not survive if left on the open soil surface. You can cover them with a thin layer of a material such as vermiculite, which will hold them in place, prevent them from becoming dehydrated too easily, and allow some light through. Alternatively, cover the tray with plastic wrap, a sealed clear plastic bag, or a sheet of glass.

Sowing deep-rooting seeds

It is best to use deeper containers for sowing some larger seeds, such as sweet peas (*Lathyrus*), that need to develop a good, sizable root system before planting. If you want to engage in a bit of recycling, roll newspaper into cylinders about 1½–2 inches (4–5cm) across to make individual pots. When the seedlings are ready to go into the garden you can even plant them without removing the pots; the roots will grow through the newspaper as it disintegrates in the moist soil.

Grouped in a tray, paper pots keep their shape.

Use warm water

Use tepid or warm water for watering seed trays. Cold water will chill the seed and lower the temperature of the soil, and you will have to raise it again for germination to be successful.

When to water

I prefer to sow seeds into dry soil rather than watering it first because I find the soil easier to work with, but if you do this, you will need to water thoroughly after sowing. If you water from above, the water hitting the surface will wash seeds, especially small seeds, around and into clumps. This will happen no matter how careful you are. Instead, I put the trays of sown seed into a container or sink with just a little tap water in it—not enough for the tray to float. After about ten minutes (the time depends on the type and quantity of soil in the tray) the soil will be thoroughly moistened, and the seeds will still be where you positioned them.

Let the compost pull up water gradually from below to avoid disturbing seed.

Dreaded damping-off

The most common reason for seedlings dying is an infection known as damping-off. It is caused by one or more microscopic fungi that kill off the plant roots or stem bases, making the seedlings flop and die. There are several ways you can easily reduce the risk of this.

❀ Only use municipal water on seedlings: water from a rain barrel is more likely to contain fungal spores.

❀ Use only fresh, proprietary soil for seed sowing.

❀ Avoid overwatering seeds and seedlings; they should be just moist.

❀ Sow seed thinly. Maintain the required air temperature. Temperatures that are significantly too high or low can cause problems.

❀ Consider watering the soil at the suggested intervals with a copper-based fungicide recommended for this purpose.

❀ To put on lush, soft growth, make sure the seedlings have plenty of natural light, and don't leave them in the propagator for too long.

Top-dressing seed trays

If trays or pots are going to be standing outside, a layer of grit can protect the seeds from pests and colonization by weed seeds. Indoors, a layer of vermiculite is ideal for covering small seeds, retaining moisture, and ensuring a well-drained surface around young seedling stems, but it is far from essential for most seeds.

Sowing with heat

The range of plants that you can raise from seed is greatly increased if you have access to a heated propagator. These are really useful and simple to use, and worth the investment—even a small, inexpensive propagator will increase your options.

Plan your seeding

If you want to germinate several different types of seed at the same time, you may be faced with a problem: some seeds require lower temperatures than others to achieve a good germination rate. Try sowing your seeds in batches, grouping the seeds so that those requiring similar temperatures are sown together; there is room for a degree of compromise. You can also place pots of seeds requiring slightly lower temperatures on the base of upturned pots or trays within the propagator: introducing a little space between the soil and the heat source in the base of the propagator results in slightly lower temperatures.

Uneven heating

Quite often the heating element in a propagator seems to supply heat unevenly. Take advantage of this by noting which areas are the warmest and which are the coolest, and you can position trays and pots of different seeds accordingly.

Capillary matting

Most propagators come with a piece of capillary matting that fits snugly onto the base. This allows the water you put in the base of the propagator tray to be drawn up to the seeds but without the risk of them becoming waterlogged. For this effective watering system to work, you need to keep the matting just moist at all times. Wash it really well before each use, just in case it is harboring any fungal pathogens.

Ordinary detergent and hot water are great for cleaning.

Clean every time

After each use, thoroughly clean the tray and lid of the propagator. This will help to reduce the potential for disease problems, and it cuts down on the buildup of algae on the lid, which would otherwise reduce the amount of light reaching the seedlings. Make sure you do not wet the electrical apparatus when you clean it.

Don't bake seedlings

Most propagators have vents in their lids, allowing some air circulation. It is essential to keep these open on hot, sunny days because even in a thermostatically controlled propagator, temperatures can build up to potentially fatal levels, and seeds or seedlings will literally bake to death. It is best to keep seeds and seedlings out of direct, very hot sunlight, even with the vents open.

Managing without a greenhouse

If you don't have a greenhouse and need to raise seeds in a warm environment, you can generally get reasonable results on a sunny windowsill during the summer months. If the windowsill faces south or west, you may even need some shade on hotter days.

A cut down, foil-lined box maximizes light.

Limited light

Plants on windowsills generally only get sunlight from one direction, and they have a tendency to become etiolated (leggy, pale, and rather weak) and to grow toward that light source and so become lop-sided. You can take steps to avoid this.

✿ Stand your pots or seed trays on a sheet of aluminium foil, or even better, stand a foil-covered card on the room side of the sill. The foil reflects the daylight back onto the plants.

✿ Rotate your pots and trays at least once a day, preferably more frequently, so that the effect of one-sided light is reduced.

Stroke your seedlings

Research shows that seedlings develop sturdier stems and are less inclined to become lanky if they are stroked regularly! Gently brush over the tops of the seedlings with a piece of paper or card, back and forth, several times a day. It may sound funny, but it works, and the more you do it the better the results. This technique also works really well for seedlings in greenhouses, probably because it mimicks the effects of a gentle breeze.

Cheap insulation

Covering pots of seedlings with a clean, clear plastic bag or a miniature plastic cloche allows them to receive maximum light while dramatically reducing problems associated with fluctuating temperatures or the soil drying out. Make sure you don't let them get too hot.

Into the frame

If you need a place to grow seedlings after they have left the confines of a seed tray or propagator, a cold frame should work well. It must be well insulated and adjustable enough to keep temperatures at a suitable level.

Homemade propagator

Make your own miniature unheated propagator to fit over a single flower pot: cut the base off a clear plastic soda or water bottle, and use the upper half to pop over the pot like a cloche. You can even remove or replace the lid to regulate the temperature.

Less stylish than Victorian glass cloches, but just as effective.

Pricking out and planting

When you need to move small seedlings to a larger home—known as pricking out—or plant them in the garden, make sure they are well watered before you move them. Dry growing medium clinging tightly to fine roots is likely to cause them to tear.

Before pricking out

Prepare the new pots before you start to prick out seedlings. That way you can pop the delicate roots straight into the growing medium and reduce the risk of them drying out or becoming damaged.

Watering

Watering seedlings right after they are transplanted is worthwhile, even if the soil was already quite moist. The extra water helps to settle the soil around the plants' roots and ensures that they establish in the new position quite quickly.

Water from below

If water pours onto the compost surface too rapidly, it may dislodge the compost from around the base of the seedling. If in doubt, stand the pots of newly transplanted seedlings in a tray of water until the surface of the compost starts to glisten, indicating it has taken up plenty of water.

A brief soaking ensures good contact between roots and soil.

Hardening off

Even hardy plants need hardening off before they can safely be planted outside. This just means toughening the plants gradually before permanently moving them from a windowsill, propagator, greenhouse, or frame. Nights are often much cooler than days, so for the first few days bring plants in at night.

Prime time for damping-off

If you are dealing with seedlings that are particularly prone to damping-off, try using a copper fungicide for the first watering after pricking out.

Handle with care

Holding a seedling by the stem is potentially lethal for it. Only pick up or maneuver seedlings by the "seed leaves," which are much tougher.

Making a frame

If you have a lot of seedlings and small plants, it may be worth constructing an inexpensive cold frame. It can be as simple as bricks or paver blocks topped with an old window frame or several layers of fleece.

Sowing direct

Many seeds can be sown straight into the garden without the need for any potting mix, trays, or special equipment. Some, such as poppies (*Papaver*) and candytuft (*Iberis*), invariably perform significantly better if direct sown.

Remove stones

Before you sow, make sure the soil surface is well leveled. Raking will bring some larger stones to the surface. Remove these because each blocks an area of soil surface, preventing you from sowing there.

Which seeds?

Not all flower or vegetable seeds can be sown direct, so always check the seed packet. For flower seeds, look for the words "hardy annual" (often abbreviated to HA on the packets), and on vegetables, look for a mention of "sowing direct."

Concentrated fertilizers may harm seedlings, but a little manure is ideal.

Sowing early

❀ Soil conditions may be a bit too cold if you sow early in the season. Covering the soil with a sheet of black plastic for a week before you intend to sow will help to increase the soil's temperature and may also shelter it from excess rain. Make sure the sheet is well anchored with large stones or bricks.

❀ You can use black trash bags, but these can be quite thin. Compost bags are generally made from much thicker plastic—just cut the bag open to create a flat sheet; then anchor it to the soil with the printed side down and the black side up.

Prime conditions

For best results, make sure that the spot you have in mind is sunny and adequately fertile. Digging in some well-rotted manure or garden compost before you sow will help to improve texture as well as fertility. At the same time, it also improves the soil's ability to retain moisture, so it really is worth the effort.

Judging the conditions

Sowing times are important, but always take local conditions into account. If the soil is wet and cold, many seeds are likely to rot before they get a chance to germinate, so it is worth waiting.

A black sheet will warm the soil and dry out a wet surface.

Top ten hardy annuals for sowing direct

Bright poppies are easy sown direct.

Calendula officinalis
(Marigold)

Centaurea cyanus
(Cornflower)

Eschscholtzia californica
(California poppy)

Gypsophila elegans
(Baby's breath)

Iberis (Candytuft)

Linum grandiflorum
(Flowering flax)

Malcolmia maritima
(Virginia Stock)

Nemophila menziesii
(Baby blue-eyes)

Nigella damascena
(Devil-in-a-bush)

Phacelia campanularia
(California bluebell)

Nigella has masses of jewel-like flowers.

Aim for a natural look

Mark out different areas with horticultural sand. This soon disappears but shows where to sow each type of seed. Avoid using builder's sand; it may contain contaminants. The sand sold as "play sand" is perfectly good, and if you have children and a sandbox they won't miss a little.

Areas with irregular outlines look more natural.

Protecting the seeds

If cats or seed-hungry birds visit your garden, it may be worthwhile putting up a temporary scaring device on the seedbed or using randomly spaced canes and taut strings to keep them off. If you use strings, it is absolutely essential that they are kept taut because loose strings may entangle birds.

Check the heights

When you are planning your annual summer flower display, consider not only flower color but also the plant's expected height. It is easy to be misled by the pretty picture on the seed packet, and you need to make sure none of the flowers tower over their neighbors.

Gauzy, tall plants can come to the front, but generally taller plants are best kept to the back of a bed.

Sow annuals in rows

It may be tempting to simply scatter the seed within each sowing area, but if you sow annual flowers in rows it is much easier for you to tell which are seedlings and which are "weedlings" when the growth appears. Once the plants have started to put on growth, the fact that they started off in straight lines will be completely masked, so you won't end up with regimented rows.

Sow thinly

I like to sow hardy annual seeds thinly, ideally aiming for a distance of only about one-third of the suggested final spacing distance between each seed. This allows for a bit of waste through failure or pest attack and dramatically reduces the amount of thinning out you have to do later.

Labeling rows

Once you have covered the seed over with soil to the suggested depth, make sure you label each area clearly. This means you know what you are expecting and can spot complete failure before it is too late to re-sow. I find that pens sold as laundry markers or good-quality permanent marker pens are generally better for writing on plant labels than those sold in garden centers.

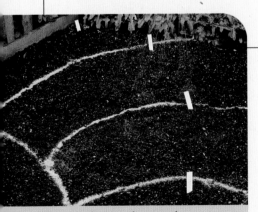

You can forget what you have sown surprisingly quickly.

Make your furrows

A piece of bamboo cane or a sturdy stick from the garden makes a perfect tool to draw across the soil surface to create the furrows into which you can sow the seeds.

Weeding

❀ However well you prepare the ground, some weeds will always appear. Most weeds germinate and grow more rapidly than garden flowers, so hand weed carefully and regularly.

❀ A small-headed onion hoe can be used with care on weeds that appear between the rows.

❀ After removing weeds, always water the area thoroughly, even if the soil is moist. This will help to resettle the disturbed soil.

Use thinnings

You can reuse thinned seedlings or plants in other areas of the garden. To minimize root damage, water the soil before thinning. Thin in the evening or early morning when the temperature is relatively low, and pop the thinned seedlings into a plastic bag to reduce moisture loss before replanting them.

Shallow furrows are all you need.

Don't thin all at once

Thin over a period of time. If you thin plants out to the suggested final distance the first time you thin, some disaster in the form of a pest or a pathogen may leave you with a rather sparse display.

Water thoroughly

Always water the area thoroughly after thinning so that the soil settles back closely around the roots of the remaining plants. You need to do this even if the soil appears quite moist.

Collecting seeds

One way to make plant propagation even more economical is to collect your own seed. You can build up large numbers of your favorite plants, and you already know that they will thrive in the conditions you have to offer.

Most poppies will self-seed with abandon.

Self-seeding plants

Take advantage of natural self-seeders. When you remove faded hardy annual seedheads, give them a few sharp shakes over the areas where you would like some plants next year.

Natural fallout

Many plants shed seed that then germinates and thrives, so take advantage of self-sown seedlings of plants such as hellebores, aquilegias, forget-me-nots (*Myosotis*), and hollyhocks (*Alcea*). They often do very well in the spot they have "chosen," but they may need transplanting to fit in with your plans or prevent paths being blocked or other plants overshadowed.

Collecting and saving seeds

Although saving seeds produced by plants growing in your garden may seem like a great idea, remember that many will not come "true." That is to say, the seedlings may look good, but they will not necessarily be the same as the plants from which you collected them.

Self-sown plants have done half the job for you, so keep an eye out for them.

Picky seeds

Some seeds have quite specific requirements for germination—periods of cold and warmth, the heat of fire, even chemicals in smoke. With the trickiest, purchased seed is more reliable, but you might be lucky with your own.

F1 seeds

Of all the plants in the garden, those sold as F1 hybrids are least likely to come true. These are vigorous hybrids of two distinct parents. Their offspring may be worthwhile, but can be quite different from the parent plants.

Bide your time

If you have your eye on seed from a plant in your garden, avoid the temptation to collect seedheads or seeds before they are ripe. Generally there is little if any more development once the seeds are removed from the plant, and they will remain immature and nonviable if removed too early.

Seed catcher

A paper bag attached loosely around the nearly ripe seedhead will catch seeds as they ripen. This prevents them being shed and falling to the ground and, provided the bag is paper, they should be fine in there for a day or two. Plastic bags would cause condensation to build up, and the seeds would be more likely to be damaged.

Keeping dry

A small amount of silica gel helps to keep the air inside a container adequately dry. I reuse the little sachets that sometimes come with electrical equipment.

Don't be greedy

Plants generally succeed better when sown with care than when self-seeding—you won't need masses of seed.

Collect on a dry day

Always try to collect seed on a dry day and when the plants themselves are not rain-soaked or damp from dew. The drier the seed is when gathered, the more likely it is to store successfully.

Most seeds can be rubbed from seedheads with your fingers.

Clean seeds for storage

If you save your own seed, clean it up by removing attached bits of seedhead, which may harbor moisture and possibly even pests or pathogens. Label it, and store in a cool, dry place until it can be sown.

Berry seeds

To remove seed from berries, squash the berries gently by hand and remove the flesh as thoroughly as you can. Then place all that remains in a bowl of warm water, and rub gently until the flesh floats off.

Chemicals in the flesh of fruits can prevent germination.

Simple softwood cuttings

Most softwood cuttings need to be taken in the spring. At this stage, the new shoot growth is still very flexible or soft and will be in a perfect state to root quickly, often in the simplest of setups.

Morning cuttings

The best time to collect material for softwood cuttings is early in the morning when the stems have not yet lost any moisture in the heat of the day. If weather conditions have been dry, it also helps if you can water the plants the night before.

Cutting practice

❀ Use really sharp pruners to minimize damage to the material and the plant.

❀ Use clean, clear plastic bags. Put each type of cutting in a separate bag immediately: this will really help to prevent the cuttings from flopping.

Taking cuttings does not harm the plant.

Short-term storage

Ideally, you should root the cuttings immediately after taking them. If for some reason there is an unavoidable delay, fold the top of the bag of cuttings over, and put the bag in the vegetable compartment of your refrigerator.

Cuttings will keep for a few hours in a fridge.

Healthy sideshoots

Always choose the best-looking, healthiest sideshoots for softwood cuttings. Avoid any that are damaged or looking miserable, and try to avoid any sideshoots that are bearing flowers or buds.

Pinch out the buds

If all of the sideshoots are bearing small buds, then you will have to use some of them. Carefully pinch out each bud, taking it right back to the point where it joins the stem.

Pinching out buds avoids energy being wasted on the flowers.

Leaf nodes contain plant hormones that help rooting.

Rooting preparation

Before rooting, trim each cutting so that it is 2½–5 inches (7–12cm) long, and remove the lowermost leaves to leave a bare stem. Then use a very sharp knife to make a straight cut just below a leaf node—this is the junction on the stem where the leaves were attached.

Rooting in compost

Softwood cuttings can be rooted in well-drained cuttings soil. Rooting in soil means that it is particularly easy to pot them once rooted. If you use this method, it is worth dipping the ends of each cutting in hormone rooting powder to assist rooting.

Rooting in water or gel

Softwood cuttings can be rooted in a jar of tap water or in a proprietary rooting gel. If you are using water, make sure the jar is really clean. Support the cuttings so that their leaves do not flop into the water. Fixing a piece of chicken wire or some aluminium foil over the top of the jar creates a good support system, but if using foil, you will need to make holes in it with a pencil before inserting the cuttings.

Supported by foil, the cutting hangs with its end in the water.

You can watch the roots form on the cutting.

Protection for cuttings

Enclose each jar or pot of rooting cuttings in a clean, clear plastic bag fixed around the rim so that it is not in direct contact with any part of the cuttings. This will help to prevent them from losing too much moisture from their leaves, and protect them from extremes of temperature.

Top plants for softwood cuttings

Abelia
Abutilon
   (Flowering
   maple)
Caryopteris
Ceanothus
   (California
   lilac)
Cotoneaster
Cytisus (Broom)
Enkianthus

Erica
Forsythia
Fuchsia
Hydrangea
Kolkwitzia
   (Beauty bush)
Lavatera
   (Mallow)
Perovskia
Philadelphus
   (Mock orange)

Fuchsias are the easiest plants to grow from cuttings.

Semiripe and hardwood cuttings

Semiripe cuttings are cut just below a node and ideally have a soft or flexible tip and a slightly hardened or woody base, known as a heel. Hardwood cuttings are taken from fully ripened, woody stems. Both are cut from the current season's growth.

Heeled cuttings

Rooting can be stimulated by paring away a sliver of bark about 1 inch (3cm) long on one side of the base of a semiripe cutting. Then trim off any sideshoots, the lowermost leaves, and the soft tip.

This heeled cutting is a good starting point.

Top plants for semiripe cuttings

*Aucuba**	*Escallonia**
*Azara**	*Garrya**
Berberis (Barberry)	*Ilex* (Holly)
Buxus (Box)	*Lavandula*
*Callistemon** (Bottlebrush)	*Mahonia*
Camellia	*Olearia* (Daisy bush)
*Carpenteria**	*Photinia**
*Ceanothus** (California lilac)	*Pieris**
	Pyracantha (Firethorn)
Choisya	*Rhododendron**
*Cotoneaster**	*Skimmia**
Daphne	*Viburnum*
Deutzia	*Weigela*
*Elaeagnus**	*Needs to be taken with a heel.

Penstemons are easy to propagate this way.

Trim large leaves

Cuttings taken from shrubs with large leaves can fail because they lose too much moisture. Cut across each leaf, half-way down, using sharp scissors before rooting the cuttings.

Rooting powder

Dipping the base of the cutting into hormone rooting powder will help stimulate root growth. Excessive hormones can damage the cutting's base, so make sure that not too much powder adheres to the cutting by tapping it sharply before inserting it into the rooting medium.

Scrape the surface to promote rooting.

Use fresh hormone rooting powder.

Crowd control

Semiripe cuttings should root well in good quality cuttings soil. You can put several in one pot, but the foliage from one must not touch that of its neighbor because this may encourage fungal problems.

When to take different cuttings

❀ Choosing the right moment for the best semiripe cuttings can be difficult. If you can, take a few every two weeks or so—at least some of them are bound to hit the perfect date for best rooting.

❀ Hardwood cuttings are generally taken in late autumn or early to midwinter. They are simple, but take the longest of all cuttings to produce roots.

Cut at the very base of this year's growth.

Hardwood cuttings

Hardwood cuttings are best cut 10–15 inches (25–38cm) long from the area where this year's growth meets last year's, on stems about as thick as a pencil. Most hardwood cuttings can be rooted either in pots kept in a cold-frame or simply in a trench in open ground. Once watered in, cuttings can be placed in a propagator for faster results. Or if you do not have one, use a clear plastic bag, making sure that the bag does not touch any foliage left on the cuttings.

These cuttings can be set quite close.

Preparing a trench

If you decide to root hardwood cuttings in a trench, prepare this before you take the cuttings. Weed the ground, then dig out a trench about 6 inches (15cm) deep. Just before you are ready to use it, add a layer of coarse horticultural sand about 2 inches (5cm) deep in the base. This will ensure adequate drainage during wetter weather.

Into the trench

Use sharp pruners to remove the very tip of the cutting, taking it back to just above a bud or a pair of buds. Insert the cuttings into the trench so that each one is about 5–6 inches (12–15cm) deep into the soil and has 6–12 inches (15–30cm) of stem protruding.

Planting out

Hardwood cuttings rooted in pots in a cold frame have usually formed sufficient roots by the spring to allow them to be planted. Cuttings rooted in open ground are generally a little slower to root, so transplant these to their permanent homes the following autumn.

Top plants for hardwood cuttings

Buddleja (Butterfly bush)

Cornus alba (Red-barked dogwood)

Forsythia

Ligustrum ovalifolium (Privet)

Philadelphus (Mock orange)

Ribes (Flowering currant)

Rosa (Rose)

Rubus

Salix (Willow)

Spiraea (Snowberry)

Tamarix (Tamarisk)

Weigela

Easy divisions and layers

Many herbaceous plants benefit from being divided. After a few years, the older, central part of a clump becomes less vigorous. Lift the plant; remove decrepit parts; and replant smaller, vigorous sections. Layering is good for shrubs that are tricky to grow from cuttings.

Spring divisions

If you garden in heavy clay soil, divide perennials in the early spring. At this time they are less likely to suffer the serious setback that winter wet could cause.

Dividing with forks

The age-old idea of using two forks, inserted back-to-back into the clump to be divided, really does work. Make sure you drive each fork in firmly and to an equal extent before you start to ease them apart, dividing the plant into clumps. There is no need to use full-size forks on a tiny but well-established clump that needs dividing—use a pair of hand forks instead.

Sturdy forks divide the toughest clumps.

Dividing perennials

Generally speaking, herbaceous perennials are best divided in either autumn or spring. If the plant gets too dry or flops in the heat when lifted, the new divisions are less likely to thrive. Divide plants only when they are not suffering from drought stress, and ideally do it in the cooler early evening. They can then have the evening and night to recover before facing the tougher daytime conditions.

Top plants for propagating by division

Achillea (Yarrow)
Bergenia
  (Elephant's ears)
Campanula (Bellflower)
Doronicum
  (Leopard's bane)
Geranium (Cranesbill)
Heuchera
  (Coral flower)
Hosta
  (Plantain lily)
Liatris (Blazing
  star)
Lychnis
  (Campion)
Nepeta
  (Catmint)

Paeonia (Peony)
Polemonium
  (Jacob's ladder)
Rudbeckia
  (Coneflower)
Thalictrum
  (Meadow rue)

Check the roots

Check plant roots carefully for weeds.

If there is a problem with pernicious weeds, such as couch grass, nettles, oxalis, or docks, in your garden or the garden from which the division came, check the root system over carefully. Remove even the tiniest bits of weed root.

Anemone hupehensis and similar autumn-flowering types divide well.

Pin down runners

On plants that naturally produce runners, you can pin a runner down with a U-shaped piece of galvanized wire. Once the runner has rooted, simply sever it from the parent plant.

Layering is natural

A number of shrubs naturally propagate themselves by simple layering: you may find well-rooted branches around existing shrubs. They can be severed from the parent; grown to form a better root system; then planted.

Peg the stem down; then cover it with more soil. You may want to label the spot.

Anchoring the layer

Use galvanized, sturdy wire to form a U-shape with which you can anchor the stem into the prepared soil. If you have wounded the stem, and this area is kept open and in contact with the soil, rooting will be further encouraged.

Encouraging roots

❀ Strip leaves from the section you anchor down, except at the shoot tip.

❀ Wound the lower surface of the stem at the point where you want the roots to form, about 10–12 inches (25–30cm) from the shoot tip.

❀ Dust the cut with hormone rooting powder to stimulate more root growth.

Cut shallowly to leave a tongue.

Encourage low growth

Encourage vigorously growing shoots low down on the shrub because these root best. About one year before you want to try layering, prune stems low on the plant so that plenty of new, vigorous shoots are produced. These can then be used for layering.

Shrubs for easy layering

Aucuba

Carpenteria

Chaenomeles
   (Flowering quince)

Corylopsis

Erica (Heath)

Gaultheria

Laurus

Magnolia

Rhododendron

Skimmia

Syringa (Lilac)

Layering is by far the easiest way to propagate lilac (Syringa).

Friends & foes

Every garden teems with creatures—from the large to the microscopic. Some of these are pests that can spoil your plants, while others should be encouraged. Many are neither friend nor foe, simply an integral part of your garden.

It is essential to get to know which to make welcome and which to reject—and this isn't always straightforward. All too often, people assume that because they don't recognize an insect on their plant, it is the one responsible for the holes on nearby leaves.

Not all pests are equally easy to track down or spot in the garden. Identifying which pests are significant and which can be left to their own devices is key to successful gardening, especially if you want to avoid using pesticides.

Combating pests
Pests can be a problem for any gardener, whatever their level of experience or size of plot. There are all sorts of ways that you can try to tackle pest infestations when they do get a grip,

but the idea of getting something else to control them for you may tempt you more. Your garden is full of potential allies, creatures that won't attack your plants but will prey upon or parasitize pests. It makes sense to identify the creatures in your natural pest-control team, and learn how to encourage them to breed and live in your plot. If your gardening is restricted to a tiny yard, or even a window box, there are still some creatures waiting to help you perfect low-maintenance, chemical-free pest control.

This chapter shows you how to

❀ Provide for natural allies—which creatures to encourage and how.

❀ Garden for natural allies—entice the natural pest-control team onto your plot.

❀ Identify common pests and diseases.

❀ Deal with slugs, snails, and vine weevils—three pests that will challenge your green convictions.

Providing for natural allies

Most birds are welcome in a garden, and in my view we should encourage them all—even finches that nip off fruit-tree buds and pigeons that shred cabbages, although you may want to protect your plants! Don't forget to provide for your smaller allies, too.

Invitation to dine

Hanging up bird feeders encourages birds to regard your garden as part of their potential territory. Not only will you enjoy seeing them on the feeders, but when pests are in your garden, the birds will help you to keep them under control.

Buy a protected feeder if you have squirrels in your garden.

Fresh water helps to keep thirsty birds off summer fruit.

Bath time

A supply of easily accessible clean water provides a welcome spot for birds to drink and bathe. Make sure it is in a position where they are not at risk from the neighborhood cats.

Bed and breakfast

Use roosting pouches and encourage thick, dense hedge growth so that birds can have a relatively safe, warm spot to roost at night.

Pecking order

Suspending a peanut feeder on a tree branch is a sure way to bring in small and very useful garden birds. I've often seen titmice form a line on a branch, and those waiting their turn on the nut dispenser invariably peck away at cracks and crevices on the tree bark and stems, removing aphids, insect eggs, and caterpillars.

A range of birds, including many finches, eat rose hips.

Fruitful harvest

Grow plenty of seed- and berry-bearing plants, like *Viburnum* and *Amelanchier*, that can supply a natural food source for birds.

Nesting instinct

Put up some nesting boxes to encourage birds to take up residence and breed in your garden. Make sure you choose those that have been properly designed and constructed so that the birds will be safe in them: look for logos of national bird protection organizations. Site boxes in a sheltered place out of direct sunlight so that they aren't too cold or too hot.

Stripes are stars

Bees in all shapes and sizes are an integral part of a garden, and many are wonderful pollinators, too, helping ensure that your vegetable and fruit crops are prolific. Similarly, striped hoverflies are also great pollinators and one of the best aphid predators; they can look like wasps, but with a thicker waist, so don't swat them.

Flowers in your garden are pollinated by a huge range of insects, from large bees to tiny flies.

Indiscriminate pesticides kill the creatures you enjoy seeing, as well as the pests.

Don't harm visitors

Avoiding using any pesticides will go a long way toward encouraging good populations of all sorts of insects, including butterflies, moths, and bees, as well as potential predators and parasites of pests.

Home comforts

There is now a wide range of "hotels" and "feeding stations" that you can place in your garden. These will instantly provide hideouts for birds, butterflies, bees, and other creatures that are great to have in the garden.

A string of birch bark makes an attractive insect habitat.

Natural enemies

I love cats, but it has to be said that they are generally considered to be one of the worst enemies of garden birds.

Gardening for natural allies

There are lots of pretty plants that both look good and bring in those beneficial insects. On the whole, the simple, non-double flowers are the most insect friendly, so make sure that you include some. Small changes in your gardening habits make a big difference.

Fancy hybrids offer less

Make sure that you grow plenty of "natural" flowers, and not just wall-to-wall hybrids. Many of these are sterile, so they do not produce pollen or nectar to feed insects.

Recycle plant stems

Some of the chunkier herbaceous plants, such as hollyhocks (*Alcea*), have hollow stems. Come the winter, the dead stems provide a perfect overwintering site for ladybugs and lacewings. If the foliage is diseased, save a few stems, having first cleared them of the old, dead leaves.

Flat flower heads offer more

A plant that produces a sizable flower head composed of lots of tiny flowers is often a particularly good and safe nectar source. Some of the tinier beneficial insects are likely to drown as they attempt to feed in very large flowers. Nectar in very deep flowers may also be inaccessible, especially to some parasitic wasps and predatory insects that have particularly short mouthparts. So grow some plants such as fennel, dill, or elder (*Sambucus*).

Sedums are superb nectar plants.

Time of their lives

Many potential garden allies, such as lacewings and hoverflies, have more than one distinct life stage, and it is only the larval stage that preys upon pests. Of course, you need adults to get larvae, so it is important to treat all life stages with respect. Make sure you know how to identify the adults, larvae, and if possible, the eggs of any potentially beneficial insects.

Leave stems in place or use them as part of a "hotel."

Adults have their own needs

Do all you can to encourage the adults of hoverflies and lacewings to visit and breed in your garden so that they can then produce pest-eating larvae. The adults feed on protein- and sugar-rich pollen and nectar. By growing suitable flowers, ideally the non-double, open-centerd kind, with easily accessible nectar, you should increase the appeal of your flower beds.

Delay the tidy up until spring

Even if your beds and borders need a tidy up after summer, try to avoid being too hasty. By leaving some areas of the garden unkempt over the autumn and winter, you will be providing hiding places and safer, warmer overwintering sites for some of the beneficial creatures you need to encourage. Try to leave most of the tidy-up until spring.

Top flowers for attracting beneficial insects

✿ **Californian poppy** Thriving in sunny, well-drained sites, pretty *Eschscholtzia* with yellow, orange, or cream flowers can be direct sown.

✿ **Candytuft** With readily available pollen and nectar, perfect for beneficial insects, *Iberis* is of the easiest hardy annuals.

✿ **Coriander** An annual herb producing masses of tiny white flowers that is perfect for direct sowing.

✿ **Fennel** The flower heads of both the green and bronze forms of this hardy perennial are great for beneficial insects.

✿ **Goldenrod** A really tough herbaceous perennial, *Solidago* can be direct sown and has showy, golden flowers.

✿ **Poached-egg plant** The yellow-and-white flowered *Limnanthes douglasii* is a hardy annual loved by hoverflies.

✿ **Pot marigolds** Gorgeous, bright gold *Calendula officinalis* can be direct sown and keeps on flowering until hit by frosts.

✿ **Scorpion Weed** A hardy annual with bluish, scented flowers, *Phacelia* is perfect for direct sowing.

Useful allies in pest control

✿ **Ladybugs** are very attractive, and both the soft-bodied larvae and the adults consume huge numbers of aphids.

✿ **Lacewing** young or larvae are efficient predators, eating mainly aphids, but also other pests such as thrips and the eggs of moths.

Lacewings are easy to recognize.

✿ **Hoverflies** have soft-bodied, yellow-gray larvae that are great aphid eaters—a single one eating up to 50 in a day, nearing 1,000 in its lifetime.

✿ **Ground beetles** are often seen quickly scuttling off when you move pots, low-growing plants, or loose slabs. They are mostly black and often shiny, and are excellent predators of many pests including slugs, vine weevils, and some insect eggs.

✿ **Some solitary wasps** feed their larvae on aphids, weevils, and other insects.

✿ **Fast-moving centipedes** eat a lot of soil-dwelling creatures and their eggs.

✿ **Flower bugs** feed on aphids, mites, thrips, and a range of small insects with their sharp mouths.

Leaf litter and logs protect centipedes.

✿ **Devil's coach horse beetles** are predators of soil pests including slugs, cutworms, and leatherjackets.

Common pests and diseases

It would take far too much time to get the know all the potential pests and pathogens of every plant that you might possibly want to grow, but there are some that just seem to crop up everywhere, so get to know them first.

Keeping perspective

Before you sink into misery because there is a sizable range of pests and problems in your garden, remember that there are also plenty of plants in your garden that are healthy and performing just fine.

Timing counts

Just how much an infestation of pests or an outbreak of a pathogen really matters depends on many things, including the plants that are under attack and the time of year. With some problems, such as an attack of rust or powdery mildew on a shrub, do not worry too much if the problem arises toward the end of the summer or into early autumn on a deciduous plant. Whatever the effect, the foliage would soon be about to deteriorate anyway.

Autumn cleanup

A thorough cleanup of infected material after the leaves have fallen, possibly combined with some pruning to remove stem infections, may often be all that's needed after a problem.

Check it out

It is worth taking the time to quickly check over plants on a regular basis. This means you will be able to spot problems before they get out of hand and, in turn, you will be more likely to succeed in controlling them quickly and efficiently.

Getting into the habit of regular health checks also lets you appreciate your plants close up.

Select chemicals carefully

If you do decide to use a chemical spray against a pest or pathogen, make sure that you choose something that mentions the particular problem and the specific plant on the label. An unsuitable chemical will have little if any useful effect, and in the process you may endanger other organisms that are susceptible to the chemical.

Understanding aphid pests

Commonly known as greenfly and blackfly, aphids in reality come in numerous shades of green, brown, gray, yellow, pink, and black. They damage the plants on which they feed, and they may also transmit viral infections that do more serious damage. Aphids often cause leaf curling and yellowing, and their sugary excreta is called honeydew. When splattered on plants or other surfaces, honeydew may attract harmless but unsightly gray-black sooty mould fungi.

Aphids love luscious, sappy growth, so they are very fond of well-fed garden plants.

Dealing with aphids

There are several useful and naturally occurring predators and parasites of aphids. They include hoverfly, ladybug, and lacewing larvae, parasitic wasps, predatory midge larva, and several bird species. There are also several proprietary sprays available that should control aphids. Some of these are systemic in action, moving through the plant, so they could be useful for infestations that are difficult to reach.

Ladybugs eat aphids at any life stage.

Treating ants

Proprietary ant killers or boiling hot water are the most widely used methods of controlling ants, but you are most likely to have success if you first disturb their nests using a garden fork.

Hungry caterpillars

Caterpillar pests are common. For crops, it is best to try to prevent the adult butterfly or moth from getting access to the plants in the first place—fleece or very fine netting should do the trick. If you pick caterpillars off an infested plant, remember that they make a welcome snack for garden birds on the bird table.

Finding ants' nests

Ants can be a real nuisance, especially in a hot, dry summer, and their ant hills and the soil loosening activities can do some indirect damage to garden plants. If you find ants but don't know where the nest is, the best thing to do is to put down something with serious ant-appeal, like a dollop of jam, and trace the line of ants back to the source—that way you will quickly find the location of the nest.

Ants will find a sweet bait like this and carry it off surprisingly fast.

Red spider mites

Red spider mites thrive in hot, dry conditions, so anything you can do to raise humidity in a greenhouse will help to decrease their numbers. Regular misting with plain water works well because these mites hate wet feet! A very thorough cleanup and scrub-down of all the interior glass and staging at the end of the season will help to reduce numbers considerably the following year.

You don't need to wash the mites off, just wet the plants.

Hungry for red spider mites

There is a useful predatory mite that will eat red spider mites, their young, and their eggs. Called *Phytoseiulus persimilis*, it works well but is best used in protected environments, such as greenhouses and conservatories.

Biocontrols can be ordered for delivery at the ideal time.

Greener sprays

There is no resistance to sprays based on fatty acids, plant oils, or starches. These smother insects rather than poison them and are generally considered greener than toxins.

Sprays for mites

There are several proprietary mite sprays available if you choose to use the chemical route, but some greenhouse red spider mites are showing resistance to many of them, so you may have to try a few.

Preventing mildew

Damp foliage or humid air both encourage powdery mildew growth, so try to improve air circulation around your plants, and avoid wetting the foliage if at all possible.

Dairy solution

Proprietary fungicides for use against powdery mildews work well, but if you prefer to go for a greener option, many gardeners report finding that a 10 percent solution of milk in water is an effective treatment.

Making mildew worse

There is a definite correlation between dry soil conditions and the extent and severity of powdery mildews. If the soil is dry, mildews are generally much more of a problem, so keep the soil moist and well mulched. (See page 185.)

Larger fungi

If you see larger fungi, such as toadstools or bracket fungi, appearing on or around a large tree in your garden, it is essential you find out exactly what the fungus is. Some are of no consequence, but others can indicate that the tree is potentially in danger. Always get the precise identity checked out, and take prompt action if necessary. Removing a fungal growth from a tree does not remove the problem; it may help to limit spore production, but the damage is likely to continue within the tree.

Even in a moist soil some plants, such as *Aster novi-belgii*, are prone to mildew.

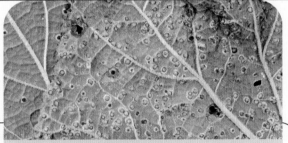

Gather rust-spotted leaves and discard or burn them, rather than composting.

Powdery mildews

Fungal powdery mildews are very common and show as powdery white fungal growth. This is generally most extensive on the upper surfaces of leaves but can appear on the lower leaf surfaces, stems, and even petals and prickles.

Rust spots

Fungal rusts are almost always much more problematic during damp years or if conditions on the foliage are wet. Rust fungi need a film of moisture (albeit minute) on the leaf surface if they are to spread and infect. Try to avoid wetting the foliage unnecessarily, and improve air circulation.

Resisting rust

Using a dressing of sulphate of potash and avoiding excessive use of high-nitrogen feeds will help to increase a plant's resistance to rust by keeping the leaf growth a little bit tougher.

Leaf spots

Most fungal leaf spots, with the notable exception of blackspot on roses, are generally fairly weak pathogens and only likely to cause significant damage on a plant that is already in trouble. Improving growing conditions and cultivation techniques should reduce the risk of pathogens causing a problem.

Fungal leaf spots are usually dark, often grayish, and may bear minute, fungal-fruiting bodies.

Slugs, snails, and vine weevils

In any gardening pest survey, these "big three" always rank highly due to the frequency with which they terrorize our gardens. They are loathed by gardeners. What can you do?

Larger black slugs feed mainly on decaying organic matter.

Does size matter?

Most of the damage done to garden plants is from the smaller slugs, especially the grayish-black keeled slugs, and from the pinky-gray field slugs. The larger slugs generally feed primarily on dead or decaying organic matter.

No place to hide

Keeled slugs spend most of their time belowground, venturing aboveground to feed but returning again quite promptly. Using a soil-applied and soil-acting treatment, such as the nematode bio-control for slugs, therefore makes a lot of sense.

Barrier methods

Barriers work quite well against slugs and snails, but nearby plant material must not form a bridge over them. They also need to be put right up against the plant stem, otherwise slugs may come up from below within the confines of a barrier even if they cannot get over it.

Where they hang out

In the late summer and autumn, take time to look for colonies of hibernating snails. They often accumulate in huge numbers behind dense climber growth, under loose slabs, piles of pots, or even under loose tree bark.

Snails hibernate in clusters, so hunting can be efficient.

An array of defences

The barriers that work best seem to vary from garden to garden; some of the favorites are copper (copper rings, copper tape, and copper-impregnated fabric), cocoa shells, pine needles, and crushed shells.

Taste for alcohol

Beer is the traditional lure, but interestingly slugs and snails seem to show little appetite for most alcohol-free drinks—perhaps they just do not have the same smell!

Setting traps

Trapping slugs is an age-old technique and well worth trying. Make sure that the beaker in which you put the lure is plunged into the soil, but that the rim protrudes ½–¾ inches (1–2cm) above the soil surface. This should prevent useful creatures, such as ground beetles, from ending up in the trap.

Empty and top off your traps regularly—they soon fill up!

Cereal killer

Stale milk works well as a slug bait, and if you sprinkle a small quantity of oats or muesli into the liquid you choose, it appears to make it even more appealing.

Parasites

Biological control for slugs works very well, especially against keeled slugs, but the soil needs to be kept moist so that the nematodes can move around freely. Since snails live above the soil level, they are not affected by the biocontrol.

Adult weevils attack leaves, while larvae feed on roots.

Vine weevils

Chemicals are available to control vine weevil. There is also an effective biological control in the form of a nematode, which generally proves most effective when used as a drench in mid-spring or from late summer to early autumn. The soil needs to be fairly warm and moist.

Competent climbers

Vine weevils cannot fly, but they are extremely good climbers and can scale all but a totally smooth surface. A sticky barrier of non-setting glue or petroleum jelly often proves to be a great defence. To protect plants on greenhouse staging, try standing the legs of the staging in bowls kept topped off with water—vine weevils don't like to swim either.

After dark

Most vine weevil activity happens at night, so if you want to check that these really are the pests that are responsible for the leaf notching on your plants, go on an evening walk around the garden with a flashlight.

Do not disturb?

Vine weevils are extremely good at "playing dead" when disturbed—do not be fooled by this.

Greener gardening

There are few gardening fashions and trends that I would recommend following. I'm a great believer that your garden is your free-from-constraints space, and that you need to do what you want to do, not what someone else tells you to do. However, the issue of caring for our environment sweeps aside this rule.

Love your garden, and there is a good chance you will also have more than a passing concern for the planet and everything that lives on it. But that is not to say that you want to be a fully fledged organic gardener who sticks to a strict code of conduct. You may simply want to be a bit greener and enjoy what I call common-sense gardening. Either way you will be reducing your adverse impact on the garden and the environment as a whole, while continuing to enjoy gardening.

Going green

With the current interest in greener gardening, it is so easy to go green. If you have ever wanted

to use environmentally friendly methods in the garden, don't be put off by the thought that you'll be turning your pleasurable hobby into a weighty milestone. Greener gardening really is no harder than conventional gardening. Perhaps it requires a little more thought, but to an extent the more organically maintained garden may be better equipped to look after itself. And then, of course, you'll also be able to enjoy the knowledge that you have done your part for a worthwhile cause.

This chapter shows you how to

❀ Save water in the garden.

❀ Recycle household water outside.

❀ Use water sparingly.

❀ Adopt greener methods.

❀ Master organic techniques.

❀ Use biological controls and traps.

❀ Create a composting system for your kitchen and garden waste.

Creating a water-wise garden

Whether you are subject to seasonal watering restrictions, have a water meter and are worried about the cost of watering, or simply want to irrigate your plants less, water is a resource that we should all conserve, whatever the weather.

All soils are helped by organic matter.

Dig in organic matter

Bulky organic matter, such as well-rotted manure, garden compost, leaf mold, or used proprietary compost from seasonal containers, will always help to reduce water use by increasing the soil's ability to retain moisture. This is especially useful in light, sandy soils because these tend to drain very rapidly and contain little organic matter.

Clay soils

If you have a heavy soil that gets too wet when it rains, it will still suffer if water is not readily available. During very dry weather, clay soil will shrink and form cracks, often damaging plant roots in the process. The cracks are often quite deep and can increase moisture loss from deeper levels in the soil.

Dense clay hardens in dry weather.

Improving soil texture

As well as improving the soil in a whole bed or border, it is worth incorporating extra organic matter into individual planting holes and pits. Make these as large as possible.

Weed regularly

Weeds take a significant quantity of moisture from the soil, so regular weeding is a good idea. If the soil has developed a slight cap or crust (this is especially likely on heavier soils), this helps to keep moisture in to some extent, so try to keep the surface of the soil intact when weeding if at all possible. Light hoeing or hand-pulling generally creates a lot less disturbance than forking.

The ideal time to weed is after rain when the ground is soft.

Dealing with large weeds in dry conditions

If conditions are really dry and some larger weeds have appeared, then try cutting the weeds off at the base, leaving just a stump without disturbing the soil. It takes a bit of extra time, but you can then remove the weeds properly later when conditions are a bit better.

Weed waste

When weeding in hot weather, always allow the severed bits of annual weeds that have not set seed to remain on the soil surface. They soon decompose in the heat and form a lightweight mulch that helps to conserve the moisture in the soil.

Mulching magic

Mulching is one of the best ways to reduce moisture loss from the soil surface by evaporation. To have the most effect, only apply mulch to a soil that has been thoroughly wetted. To be really effective, an organic mulch should be 2–3 inches (5–5.7cm) deep, kept clear of the plants' stems, and applied so that it covers the plants' roots.

Water does not evaporate easily through loose mulch.

Using black plastic

Black plastic can be used as a mulch that seals in moisture effectively, but is not something I would recommend. It also prevents water from getting into the soil from above and reduces the ability of oxygen to get into the soil or carbon dioxide to leave. As a result, it often adversely effects the populations of the various soil organisms.

The diversity of mulch

All too often mulching is associated with flower beds and borders, but it is also a really useful way to reduce moisture loss from vegetable plots, fruit and bushes, and even containers.

Lightweight hurdles are quickly installed and filter the wind well.

Create shelter

Both sun and wind have a dehydrating effect on plants and also directly on the soil. Creating a bit more shade and erecting some form of windbreak will have a significant effect on water usage, especially on a particularly sunny or very windy site.

Plant adaptation

Research suggests that you can succeed in training a plant to survive on less water. Water only one-half of the root system at a time, with the minimum amount necessary to prevent wilting. Many plants seem able to adapt to surviving on less water—try it out.

Recycling water

If you do not already have a water barrel, go out and buy one. If you already have one or two, consider getting a third. Apart from rain, each day a phenomenal amount of "gray water" is produced from a house, much of which could safely be used on plants.

Stands or legs are essential for barrels.

Setting up

A full water barrel is extremely heavy, so make sure that a new water barrel is put on a very firm, level base and that it is not leaning against anything it shouldn't. Check the height of its stand carefully when you set it up. You need to be able to easily place and remove a watering can beneath the tap on the barrel. Ideally, you need a level area on which you stand the can so that you can leave it to fill while you turn your back and do another quick job.

Filling your can

If it is not possible to position the barrel adequately high off the ground for easy watering can filling; then use a short piece of garden hose attached to the end of the tap to allow you to fill the can a short distance from the barrel.

Use a flexible hose for filling a watering can.

Stretching the pipe

Getting a piece of hose properly and firmly fixed to the tap can be a tricky job. Take a mug of boiling water out to the water barrel, and plunge one end of the hose into the water for about 30 seconds—but take care not to scald yourself. This softens the pipe and makes it much easier to stretch it over the tap. It then rapidly contracts to make a watertight fit.

Very hot water is needed for a tight fit.

Install a pump

If you have water barrels quite far from the main areas needing the water, it is really useful to have a pump. This gives enough pressure for you to use a garden hose directly from the water barrel. You can also siphon water into a container closer to the area that needs water.

Collect gray water

Water barrels connected to roofs will only fill up when it rains, and that may well mean they are empty when it has not rained for a while, just when you need water most. Make sure you have at least one barrel connected to the downspout from the house so you can collect suitable "gray" water from the bath, hand basins, and the shower. The final rinse water from a washing machine may also be used, but water from earlier rinses, dishwashers, or any chemically softened source may contain contaminants.

Water with bath water

Try siphoning or pumping water directly out of the bath through a window and onto your garden if you do not have a suitable water barrel connection.

Keeping the water in the barrel clear

Fixing a piece of medium-gauge mesh over the end of the downsprout from a roof will help to dramatically reduce the quantity of larger contaminants, such as leaves, insects, and twigs, getting into the barrel. Make sure you remove the mesh regularly because it will soon clog, especially during autumn and winter.

Use oil to avoid mosquitoes

If mosquito larvae start to appear in the water barrel during warm weather, make sure the lid of the barrel is firmly in position; this should help to reduce the number of eggs that can be laid in the water. A tiny quantity of plant oil, such as sunflower or olive oil, poured onto the surface of the water will form a very thin oily layer and should kill off the larvae before they hatch. Use as little as possible, and make sure you do not bail water out of the barrel or else you will take the oil too. When the time comes to drain the barrel, tip out the last bit (containing the oil) rather than letting it get into the tap.

Oil is a safe way to kill mosquito larvae, effectively by smothering.

Annual cleanup

From time to time you will need to empty out and thoroughly clean a water barrel, otherwise algae will build up to such a level that you will be watering them onto your plants. Use a broom and some soapy water to reach the deeper areas at the base of the barrel.

Water quality

Water collected in a barrel may have picked up some bacterial or fungal contaminants on its journey from the roof to the watering can. Just in case, it is best to use stored water on more mature plants and those growing in open ground, not pots.

Fit more barrels than downspouts

Fitting a good-size water barrel to a downspout from the guttering on a house, garage, conservatory, or greenhouse will give a great supply of water after rain. The amount collected after a heavy downpour can be considerable, so a single barrel is likely to be filled to capacity quickly. Use connector pipes to link the first barrel to an additional barrel, and you can double the amount you collect.

Using water carefully

Whatever the size or style of your garden, you will need some water to maintain it, but water is a precious resource, so you should try to avoid wasting it. Careful use of water does not mean your garden will suffer.

It's all about timing

Water evaporates rapidly if it hits a warm surface or is applied during hot, sunny weather. In the warmer months, water your garden either in early evening once the soil has cooled so that plant roots can take up the moisture before the conditions heat up the following day or water very early in the morning before the soil warms up, allowing the water to reach the roots before temperatures rise again.

How often?

It's better to water thoroughly but less frequently than to apply a little water more often. A good drenching soaks down to the plant roots, where it is needed, but a light sprinkling may only moisten the soil surface, not reaching roots and evaporating before the plant can benefit. If the upper soil is repeatedly soaked while the soil around the roots stays dry, the plant may start to produce roots near the surface, which are much more easily damaged.

Create a basin

If you create a slight dip or basin in the soil around the base of a plant, when you apply water it will run toward the plant and not away from it. Ideally, do this at planting. Provided you take care not to damage the roots or risk them growing too close to the soil surface, you can create a shallow yet efficient basin around an established plant.

Water the plant base

Plants may be damaged by water on their leaves or petals, especially during hot weather, and many infections thrive on wet surfaces; wetting leaves also wastes water. Aim the end of the watering can or the hose directly at the base of the plants, beneath the foliage: you will avoid all the problems and the plants will enjoy all the benefits.

Water the roots, not the foliage, for best results.

A pipe or even a deep pot helps you to get water to the roots.

Watering roots efficiently

A length of pipe close to the roots of a plant, with one end protruding above the surface, allows you to pour water directly down to the roots. After watering, cover the hole so that it cannot act as an escape route for soil moisture.

Avoiding runoff

If the soil has become very dry, there is a tendency for the water to run off the soil surface when it is finally wetted by rain or by you. It is then lost to an area of the garden where is it not needed or, worse still, to a paved or similar area. You can prevent a lot of this runoff by simply wetting the soil surface slightly before soaking it thoroughly. Whether rain looks imminent after a dry spell, or you plan to do some watering, half an hour or so beforehand, gently wet the soil and far more water will then get through to where it is needed.

Efficient hosing

If your hose doesn't have a nozzle—perhaps when drawing water from a barrel—make a few sharp kinks in the hose if you have to do something else briefly while watering. Bending the hose double near the end and poking the kink into the mesh of chicken wire usually stops the flow—not as efficient as turning off the tap, but far better than wasting water.

Hose nozzles

Invest in a nozzle or gun for the end of your hose, rather than watering with your thumb over the end. Make sure it produces a range of sizes of droplet and will cut off the water supply when not in use so that if you have to leave it for a moment it won't keep using water.

Sprinklers

Sprinklers may be an extremely easy way to water your garden, but they can also be extremely wasteful. If you are going to use one, either set an alarm to remind you to move it around frequently, or fit a timing device to the tap.

A lawn with longish grass survives dry spells better than a fine, close one.

Lawns and watering

❀ Don't panic if your lawn turns brown because most lawns are more tolerant of drought than it might appear. They usually recover completely under all but extreme conditions.

❀ The tougher the lawn grasses, the better they are at surviving drought, so try to avoid very fine lawns.

❀ If a very dry lawn is suddenly watered or rained on, it is inclined to shed most of the water and little will reach the roots. Spike the surface with a garden fork before watering and a lot more water will get into the soil.

❀ If you allow your lawn to grow a little longer when there is a drought, the world won't fall apart. Far from it, the lawn will actually resist the adverse effects of drought better when not cut too short or too frequently.

❀ Letting the clippings remain on the surface of the lawn after mowing (provided they are not too long) will help during a drought because they will act like a mulch and help to retain soil moisture.

Greener gardening methods

Greener gardening is not just about you altering some of your gardening methods and habits, but also about helping the garden to look after itself and, at the same time, make life easier for you.

Use native plants

It makes sense to shop locally as far as possible. Buying plants that have been grown locally, rather than imported from the other side of the world, is often not as difficult as you might think. Increasingly, nurseries and garden centers are making it easier to tell which plants are at least grown in this country.

Help plants to help themselves

Keeping your soil in good health, with plenty of natural nutrients from organic sources and a fair helping of naturally occurring soil microorganisms, helps to keep plants robust. This makes them better able to cope with pests or infections, and if they do get damaged, plants that are basically healthy and vigorous are better equipped to produce plenty of replacement growth.

Work with nature

Try to resist the temptation to grow plants that will always struggle in the conditions you have to offer. They will be more prone to pest and pathogen attack and hard to keep healthy.

Make room

Check your planting distances and stick to them. Plants that are crowded are likely to suffer competition, and many infections and pests thrive in overcrowded schemes.

This border will have looked sparse at first.

Move fast

Regular checks on plants allow you to catch problems early and to do what it takes to stop them from spreading. Often there is not a need for any sort of remedy. If you find a problem, act promptly.

If you act fast you will beat pests more easily.

Green pruning

Pruning shears can be a useful tool for green gardening. If you promptly prune any problems such as cankers, they are easier to control, and if you routinely prune woody plants to keep them open-centerd, they enjoy better air circulation and are less prone to problems.

Plant debris in your garden

Some advocates of greener gardening say that it is good to leave plenty of plant material around the garden to act as refuges for beneficial insects, while others say that these refuges will attract problems; I say use common sense. Only leave seemingly healthy twigs or foliage around the garden, and don't be too tidy. But if there is too much debris, yes, it can act as a perfect slug and snail hotel.

Fallen leaves can mulch earth, but may kill grass.

Recycle plant pots

Always save, clean, and then reuse plant pots and trays that you get from the garden center. Cleaned out properly, there is no reason why they cannot be used again and again. If you find you build up an excessive quantity of them, then offer them to local fund-raising groups or schools who may need lots of pots for raising large numbers of plants.

Use recycled materials

Wherever possible, try to use recycled materials in your garden – food containers for raising seedlings, plastic bottles as compost scoops or mini-cloches, clear plastic fruit containers as miniature propagator tops, etc. Try to repair or refurbish garden furniture to keep it going that little bit longer.

Choosing pots and planters

Try to go for non-plastic materials or pots and planters made from recycled plastic. There is an increasing number of good-looking wooden, ceramic, and woven-stem planters available.

Larger pots can be expensive: be creative and try re-using other containers.

Environmentally friendly wood

If you are buying wooden furniture or fences, make sure that the wood is environmentally acceptable. Various certification organizations exist, such as the Forest Stewardship Council, which means you can have wood and a clear conscience.

A plant isn't fussy about the origins of its pot: all it needs are drainage holes and a decent depth.

Organic techniques

Whether you decide to become, or indeed already are, an organic gardener, there are plenty of techniques that are well worth using. And if the idea of being an organic gardener does not appeal to you, read on as you will still find the tips useful.

Rotate plants

Crop rotation makes great sense in the vegetable garden or plot. See page 119. Generally, ornamental plants are grown for more than one year, and some are pretty well permanent and cannot be rotated, but most of us grow at least some bulbs and corms, such as tulips or gladioli, that we lift, or use seasonal bedding plants. Try to make sure you put any one type of plant in a different spot each year. This makes it less likely that pests and pathogens, especially those that live in or on the soil, will build up to damaging levels. It also helps to reduce any nutrient imbalances that could occur if the same or closely related plants were grown on the same spot for many years in succession.

Grow resistant varieties

It is becoming increasingly easy to track down varieties of your favorite plants that show good resistance to certain problems. Check seed and plant catalogs each year because availability varies, and try to choose at least some of your plants on the basis of pest or disease resistance. Vegetable seed suppliers are especially helpful when it comes to making it clear which varieties are resistant to what, and are particularly useful for organic or green gardeners.

Planting and sowing times

Sometimes you can avoid a problem by taking care when you sow or plant. For example, early potatoes are much less likely to succumb to slugs, wire worm, or blight because they are generally out of the ground before these become most damaging. Similarly, later sowings of carrots rarely succumb to carrot fly.

Creating barriers

One of the best ways to prevent pest attack is to create a barrier to that pest, perhaps of netting, fleece, or very fine mesh, so it simply cannot get to the plant to lay eggs on it or eat it.

Barriers are excellent protection against certain insects, but some crops need insect pollination.

Position barriers early

If you are using barriers, they may not need to be in place at all times, but it is always best to get them in position a bit early. Seasonal variations can mean that pests or pathogens appear earlier than you expect them, or than the books suggest.

To spray or not to spray

I prefer to avoid using any garden chemicals but some, such as those based on derris and copper, are regarded as acceptable for use by organic gardeners.

Repeat applications

Many organic sprays are less inclined to remain active for long once applied—this is obviously part of their appeal. Remember that this may mean that more frequent applications are necessary than if you were using a chemical spray.

Although some of the sprays allowed by organic standards are highly toxic, they biodegrade quickly.

Many garden insecticide sprays will damage all insects; this includes the organic sprays.

Spraying time

Nonselective sprays can damage beneficial insects, including bees and other pollinators. Always apply the treatment as directly as you can, and make sure that you spray at dusk or later, once most of the pollinating insects are no longer on the flowers.

Timing your pest control

The timing of any control measure is important, so make sure you are doing what is necessary at the right time. A spray may be organic, but it may have little if any effect if applied too early or too late and in some instances may even cause harm.

Minimize damage

Green or organic gardening should mean that you have little need to use any sort of pest-control agent. If you do, those such as the sprays based on fatty acids or plant oils have a much lower impact both on harmless creatures and on the environment as a whole.

Biological controls and traps

These are perfect for the green gardener. Buying packets of mites or insects to release into your greenhouse might seem crazy, but these are predators or parasites of the pests that trouble you, and they act like guided missiles. Traps are also useful in the garden.

Check the instructions before applying.

Follow the instructions

When using biological controls, it is just as important that you read and carefully follow the instructions as it is when using chemicals. They may be green solutions, but they won't perform as they should if used incorrectly.

Timing of controls

If you decide to use biological controls, bear in mind that being living creatures they need to be purchased and used promptly, so order them as soon as you see the first signs of the pest infestation starting. Order them too early and before the pest arrives, and they will not survive; order them when the pest has already done a lot of damage and is in huge numbers, and you are giving them too much of an uphill battle.

Sticky traps

Sticky traps can catch flying pests in large numbers. The color yellow attracts insects, and some traps also carry a pheromone attractant.

Sticky traps help to control whitefly and thrips.

Controls in the greenhouse

Most biological controls available are for use against greenhouse pests. The protected greenhouse or conservatory environment means problems are quick to spiral out of control, but also allows you to use predators or parasites that need protected, warm conditions to thrive and destroy out your pests.

Don't combine with pesticides

Biological-control predators and parasites are likely to be damaged by most pesticides. You should not use chemical controls at the same time, or for at least the last few weeks before introducing the biological controls. Some chemical pesticides have a much longer residual effect than others, so check with your biological control supplier.

Keep an eye on the overnight temperature.

Ideal temperatures

Most biological controls are temperature sensitive and need a minimum temperature of about 68°F (20°C) to perform well. Generally, this is not too hard to achieve because the pests they control tend to become a problem only when temperatures are fairly warm.

Controls don't need control

Biological controls available to gardeners are very specific in their action. This means that there is no need to worry about, say, the parasitic wasp that has been introduced to control a pest such as whitefly. The wasp is only interested in whitefly: it will not attack anything else.

Range of controls

There is an ever-increasing range of biological controls available. They include controls for glasshouse whitefly, red spider mite, mealybug, aphids, some scale insects, thrips, vine weevil, slugs, chafers, and leatherjackets.

Preventing escape

Biological controls are generally pretty well-behaved and stay around the pest-infested area. There's therefore no need to worry about them walking off or flying out through the greenhouse vents. The one exception is the mealybug predator, *Cryptolaemus*, the adult beetle stage of which can fly away. Simply cover the plants onto which you have released it with fleece for a few days to get it used to its new home.

An Australian ladybird (here the larvae) controls mealybugs.

The biological control mite used to control red spider mite is orange-red.

Sticky barriers

Grease bands are traditionally used around the trunks of fruit trees to prevent gypsy moth caterpillars climbing them. They can also be put around pots to protect the plants; this will stop ants from moving aphids onto the plants.

Composting your kitchen and garden waste

Compost bins or piles are invaluable. By all means recycle some of your green waste via your local refuse collection service or tip, but if you want to do the best thing for your garden and the wider world, avoid transporting it, and compost at home.

Compost bin setup

❀ Two or more separate bins means that one can be emptied while the other is being filled. It is much simpler and easier to make good compost this way.

❀ The bigger the bin the better: a capacity of 1 cubic yard (1m³) is ideal.

Add animal manure

Compost activators help to add extra nitrogen to the composting material, so increasing the rate and extent to which it is broken down. Adding some fairly fresh animal manure (such as horse, cow, pig, or sheep) will have the desired effect.

Use a good mix of soft and woody matter.

Bacteria, fungi, and soil organisms cause decay.

This may take months to achieve, but it is worth it.

Use organic manure

If you want to be truly green, consider the origins of the manure you use in your garden, and avoid anything that is not from organic farms. You can of course cut back on transport of this too, and use material from a pet rabbit's hutch or from local chickens or geese.

Keep adding, keep turning

Add fresh plant matter, dry woody materials, and torn up paper in roughly even quantities regularly. Turn the compost pile often with a pitch fork, and add water if it looks dry.

Composting grass clippings

If you have a lot of grass clippings from your lawn, it is generally impossible to add them all to the compost one time (unless of course you have a huge composting system). Add what you can and save a bag or two for later, or consider making a separate bin for grass clippings. You can help this to compost down with the use of an activator formulated especially for use on grass clippings—ordinary activators are not suitable.

Too much grass added to a mixed compost pile at once can turn slimy.

Pile maintenance

Organic matter will not break down readily if the pile becomes either too wet or too dry. Aim to keep it just moist, and if possible use a bit of old carpet or a blanket to keep the heap a bit warmer during the winter and between turning it.

The bacteria that start the composting process like to be warm and moist, but not too wet.

Layer compost material

It is best to add material to the pile in layers. Never use too much of any one type of material at once and, ideally, alternate layers of drier material with moister, greener ingredients. You may get away without turning!

What to compost, what not

If you want to include old sweaters, fabric, or carpet in your composting system, make sure that they contain no artificial fibers—just cotton, linen, other plant-based materials, and wool. Chop up this type of material thoroughly before adding it to the pile, and ensure that you have plenty of fresh, moist garden ingredients at hand. Avoid using meat scraps in your compost pile. They will attract vermin.

Lighting & design

You may not have thought about using lighting in your garden, but it can make a real difference. There are four main reasons why you might want to consider adding light to a garden: security, practicality, safety, and decoration.

If you have bright security lights that switch on when the sensor detects movement, always make sure that there is an override that allows you to switch them off when you want to sit out in the garden after dark and use other, more subtle lighting methods.

Lighting your garden
The range of garden lighting is far greater today than ever before, with everything from small solar-powered lights to elaborate systems that require professional installation. Generally, softer lighting is perfect for that outdoor room effect, and stronger, more directional lighting works better for producing dramatic, artistic effects. It is worth looking at catalogs from a few garden lighting specialists and checking out some night-lit gardens before you start.

Design inspiration

You can also enhance your garden by modifying its design. You may have had the same garden design for years or you may be working with a new garden. Whatever your raw materials, you do not have to completely overhaul the design. Whether you want to build a new arch to make use of the verticals or install a few new plants to make your beds look bigger, in this chapter you will find small tweaks you can apply that will make a world of difference.

This chapter shows you how to

❀ Light your garden in an attractive yet practical way.

❀ Get inspiration and ideas for changing your garden's design and layout.

❀ Change the look of your garden by working on the vertical with arches, supported climbers, and trees.

❀ Transform your plot with optical illusions and tricks of the eye.

Lighting the garden

Not every garden or gardener benefits from, or aspires to, garden lighting, but it is worth considering. When used skilfully, it can do great things for gardens from the tiniest backyard to the most elaborate country estate.

Small fittings with LED bulbs are ideal for lighting decks and are widely available in kit form.

Low glow

To make steps safer you can either install specially designed lights into the tread of the steps when they are constructed, or position attractive low-level, low-voltage lights on either side of the flight of steps.

Practical lighting

Use lighting to make it easier and safer to get access to the far end of your garden or to illuminate your terrace or patio for that late-evening glass of wine or barbecue.

Simple solutions

If you want a very quick and low-cost lighting solution in your garden, simply suspend a light from a sturdy tree branch, from which it can cast delicate shadows on the ground or plants beneath. Your light could be as simple as a tea-light in a clear glass container, a storm lantern, or a self-contained solar-powered light.

Special effects

Lighting can create beautiful and dramatic effects that you can enjoy both when outside and from inside the house. Try out different lighting positions with a powerful flashlight to cast shadows, highlight the textured bark of an old tree, or make the most of a wonderful branch system.

Ground-level lights behind the trees throw them into silhouette against the textured wall.

For maximum impact, spotlight only one or two objects.

Highlight textures

A beam of light positioned close to the ground so that it shines up the trunk of a tree or wall will illuminate the textures. The effect this produces looks particularly good on trees with peeling, patchy, or patterned bark, such as many of the gum (*Eucalyptus*) or cherry (*Prunus*) trees, or snake-bark maples (*Acer capillipes*).

Think theatrically

A spotlight or two will make a great statement lighting up a favorite planter, urn, statue, or plant. Position the light at the side or from the base of the feature, and you should create some really dramatic shadows. Be careful with brighter lights—several carefully positioned lights always produce a more attractive effect than just one or two extremely bright ones.

Ambient lighting

On a terrace, patio, or barbecue area, provide subtle lighting using globe lights. Or perhaps add a few strings of outdoor white fairy lights draped around a nearby wall, arbor, arch, or pergola, or through the branches of an adjacent tree. You'll be able to see what you're doing or what you're eating, and it'll be a lot safer too.

Low voltage is safest

There are many attractive low-voltage and easy-to-install kits available that you can set up and position yourself. It goes without saying that when dealing with electricity you need to take great care: only use equipment sold specifically for outdoor use and follow any installation and safety advice closely. For a more elaborate lighting system, it is best to employ a specialized garden lighting firm to install it.

Underwater lighting provides glow without glare.

Lighting water

Lights can produce fantastic effects in ponds, fountains, or other water features, adding a truly magical air to your evenings in the garden. You will need special underwater lights, but that extra expense is well worthwhile.

There are many solar light designs, but low-level path lights are perhaps the most useful.

Eternal sunshine

The range of solar-powered garden lights is constantly increasing and there are several different types available. Some float in a pond, others are suspended or simply pushed into the ground close to paths and steps or among your plants, and some have larger, separate solar collectors for more power. All of them absorb energy from the sunlight during the day and then illuminate your garden at night—not the brightest of lights, but good for subtle effects.

Solar lights stand alone

Solar-powered garden lighting is well worth considering. It has particular appeal because the lights need no specialized installation work and there are effectively no running costs.

Charging up

Most solar lights last longer and perform better if you run them down completely and then allow them to receive a full charge from the sun (or even artificial light), usually for 16 hours or so, but check the instructions for precise details. If you do this before the first use, and occasionally after, the life of the battery is greater.

Switch to the professionals

For installation of any lighting other than a complete low-voltage kit, you will need to employ a registered contractor or notify the building authorities.

Be a good neighbour

❀ Don't fill your garden with bright lights that blind your neighbors and the wildlife: only switch the lights on when you need them, or use motion sensors or dimmer switches.

❀ To avoid light pollution, choose lights that shine down, and don't leave dramatic uplighting on all night.

❀ If you want dusk-to-dawn security lights, use low-energy bulbs or low-voltage systems and aim the lights down. Save brighter lights for motion sensors.

Catching the rays

Most solar garden lights have obvious solar panels on them. Ensure that they are able to produce as much light as possible. Always position the light so that the panel is in full sun for as much of the day as possible.

Antique charm

If you want temporary, delicate lighting and are prepared to watch it closely, candles in storm lanterns or other wind-resistant displays on tables or other level surfaces are delightful.

Design inspiration

The garden of your dreams is very much a personal thing, and the way you want it to look is up to you, especially if you're starting from scratch. Here are some design ideas and effects that are well worth considering.

Plan your priorities

Whether you are faced with the totally blank canvas of a completely unplanted patch of soil, or you just want to make a few changes and improvements, it is worth sitting down with a bit of paper—ideally larger rather than smaller—and making a list of exactly what you are trying to achieve or improve. On the rest of the paper, sketch out the rough shape of the garden, and do some designing. Use smaller pieces of marked paper to represent any movable features.

Small change, big effect

You can make a garden appear quite different by simply altering the size or shape (or both) of the lawn. If you remove an area of sod carefully, it is quite possible to reuse it in another part of the lawn, and this also means you will not need to go to the trouble of trying to match in newly bought sod with the old lawn.

Not set in stone

Altering the size or shape of a terrace or patio also dramatically alters a garden. The slabs can always be re-used, perhaps to turn a boring, static square into a more interesting shape. You can even move a patio entirely.

Enclosing your garden

If some parts of your garden are unappealing because of an ugly view or because a neighbor's windows overlook them—leaving no privacy—try altering your boundaries.

❀ Consider installing a higher boundary fence or growing a taller hedge. There may be restrictions that limit the height of the boundary, so it is advisable to check with your local planning department, just in case.

❀ If you already have a perfectly good boundary but it is simply too low, it is worth considering adding trellis panels to the top of it. They are relatively inexpensive and are easily added on top of an existing fence.

Trellis panels taller than your fence refresh the design while adding height.

If a shed is on a boundary, perhaps a little negotiation could see it wreathed in climbers.

Hiding small eyesores

If there is an unsightly view that is only visible from one area or an object that is relatively small, such as a neighbor's garage, shed, or climbing frame, then you may be able to block it out using some additional planting. You can use trees to either totally block out an eyesore or to break up the view of the eyesore so that it feels less intrusive.

Disguising necessary evils

Arches, pergolas, and screens planted with attractive climbers will add interest to your garden and can be used to obscure eyesores beyond or within your own plot.

Use visual aids

When planning where to put up any fence, trellis, arbor, or pergola, find a post or even a bamboo cane that's the same height as the proposed installation, and position it in the intended place. This will make it much easier to get an accurate picture of whether your idea will actually work.

Look from all angles

Always check that what you do or don't want to see in the garden is visible or hidden from all the necessary angles and heights. Stand and look from different positions in the garden and from several windows in your house, even the upstairs if necessary.

Train plants over items like compost bins—as long as you still get access.

Research problem gardens

If your garden is one of those so-called "problem" types, perhaps suffering the effects of being coastal, windy, dry, or very damp, go and look at gardens open to the public that have similar problems to see how they solve them. It is worth taking a look over neighboring gardens too, and always remember to take a notebook and pen.

Coastal gardens suffer wind and salt, but their mild climate gives new opportunities.

List the pros and cons

When overhauling a garden, methodically list all the things you like about it and everything that's less appealing. You may find all you want to keep is one fantastic tree—or that really all your problems are caused by one overgrown tree that is casting excess shade and taking all the goodness from the soil. Remember that the appearance and impact of some features will change with the seasons.

Consider sun and shade

Plot the areas of sun and shade and of light shade and deep shade at key times of day throughout the year, not just at noon, or your seating area may be dark and cool when you want an evening drink. Remember, if you go out to work, you can spend seven evenings in the garden each week, but only two lunchtimes.

Don't rush in

In a new garden, you should ideally wait at least a full year before overhauling it so that you can see what comes up—many great secrets are often revealed. Just clear obvious weeds to ensure that those potentially wonderful hidden plants are able to appear in their full glory.

Get the style right

Look at your house and any other existing, immovable features when thinking about your design. Classic lawns and flower beds look good with most styles, but a strongly Mediterranean style with lots of mosaics inspired by a holiday visit may look really strange around a mellow stone cottage.

Do some climate research

Really research your local climate if you are in a new area or thinking of a totally new planting. Find a local weather station on the Web and look at the seasonal averages of temperature, sunshine, and rainfall to find out just how hardy the plants need to be. These are much better than zone maps in books, which usually don't have that level of detail.

Reaching new heights

A garden that is just on one level may seem a bit flat and unexciting, so it is always worth trying to add some height to your plot. The site may be level, but you can create interesting effects by introducing vertical structures and plantings.

A structure's appeal increases as plants grow over it.

Instant height

Erecting an arch or arbor can totally transform a garden, especially once it is planted. It need not be huge if space is short; anything will help.

Trees increase the volume of plant material and are valuable to wildlife.

A quick and inexpensive way to raise your sights.

Simple supports

In a tiny plot, a tepee of canes clothed in annual climbers, such as sweet pea (*Lathyrus*), can produce the desired effect and need not cost much—just a handful of canes and some sweet pea seeds.

Living structure

A specimen tree can have a huge effect, acting as a focal point while adding height at the same time. Choose something with real impact and ideally with more than one season of interest—offering, say, autumn color and good-looking bark, or spring blossom followed by fruits later in the year.

Tricks to transform your plot

The garden you have in front of you may seem to have certain unavoidable—and perhaps some unappealing—features, but with thought, planning, and some careful planting, you can often make it look quite different.

Trick the eye

If the garden is not as long as you'd like it to be, you can transform how long it seems with some careful planning. Create a path that tapers, gradually becoming narrower as it gets further from the house. You can then exaggerate the effect even further by planting the sides of the path with shrubs or trees that are progressively shorter the further they are from the house. Add the final deceptive touch by adding two containers, each of the same design and with the same types of plants in it, but one much smaller than the other. By installing the smaller one in the distance, and the larger one in foreground, the illusion is complete.

Creative cutting

If your short garden already has a hedge in it, try creating a clear but gentle slope on top of it, trimming the hedge so that you take more off the height at the far end, and less off the end close to the house.

Stealing beauty

A small garden can be made to seem larger if you allow it to make use of any views that surround it. If you are lucky enough to have a garden that overlooks fields, hills, or woodland, for example, then make sure that you can see these wonderful views from within the garden itself, not just from the upstairs windows.

Distant glimpses or vistas can blur your boundaries.

Window on the world

A frame emphasizes any view.

If you feel you need higher fences for wind protection, you can still enjoy distant views. Create a circular aperture, often known as a moongate, in a hedge or a wall, or simply make sure that part of your fence overlooking the view is quite low.

Reflected glory

A carefully installed mirror positioned at the end of a walkway or alcove will reflect back a view of your garden, making it appear as if the garden extends much further into the distance. To make the mirror most effective, allow plants growing near or next to it to encroach over the edges slightly.

Dividing the view

Sometimes dividing a garden into separate "rooms" or areas, ideally each with a different feel or atmosphere, will help to make a garden seem larger. This works especially well if you ensure that you cannot see all areas of the garden from any single location.

Blurring the boundaries

Rather than making solid screens within a garden, use living boundaries, such as loosely planted hedging or a line of bamboos. You can see through them to some extent, but you cannot get a complete or clear view of the other "rooms."

Bamboo makes an excellent semitransparent screen.

Sweet peas provide an eye-catching and beautifully scented divider.

Pale but significant

By including plenty of plants with pale or pastel-colored foliage or flowers, you help to increase the apparent size of a bed or border.

An elegant combination of foxgloves and daisies.

Climbing coverage

Trellis panels planted with climbers make good internal dividers. Use lightweight climbers such as jasmine and sweet pea.

Repeating plants or featuring striking colors at the front makes a bed feel bigger.

Plants with big impact

If a flower bed or border is smaller than you would like, try growing plants that have particularly striking foliage colors or shapes toward the front of the border—the back will then seem to recede.

Index

Acknowledgments

The publishers would like to thank to all who have contributed to this book.

Special thanks to Pippa Greenwood for her time, energy, and enthusiasm.

All photographs have been taken by Torie Chugg for Octopus Publishing Group with the exception of the following.

Key: b bottom, c centre, l left, r right, t top

Alamy: Angela Jordan 47t, blickwinkel 237cr, Brian Hoffman 56b, Carole Hewer 237t, Garden World Images Ltd 4 cl, 60b, 144bc, 220r, Holmes Garden Photos 148, Natural Visions 99c, Nordicphotos 231, WoodyStock 215cr

Andrew Lawson: 46tl, 251cl, Chilcombe House, Dorset 110, Design: Carol Klein/Glebe Cottage 28, Design: Rosemary Verey/Barnsley House 87, Manoir aux Quat' Saisons 25t, Torie Chugg 216b

Clive Nichols: 83b, Denmans, Sussex 249cr, Design: Cartier/RHS Chelsea Flower Show 1998 247b, Design: Claire Mee 242b, Design: Claire Warnock & Rachel Watts 233tr, Design: Jacquie Gordon/RHS Chelsea Flower Show 1999 249cl, Design: Joe Swift 240, Design: R Golby/RHS Chelsea Flower Show 1995 232r, Design: Ruth Chivers 55, Garden & Security Lighting 242t, Greenhurst Garden, Sussex 76t, Launa Slatter, Oxon 52cr, Pettifers, Oxon 15cr, The Nichols Garden, Reading 243t, The Old School House, Essex 53b

Construction Photography: 168r

Derek St Romaine: 63b, 97, Mr & Mrs Hickman, Thames Ditton, UK 106l

DK Images: Dave King 236r, Mark Winwood 48cr, Peter Anderson 146cr, Steve Hamilton 143b,188, 199t

FLPA: A & L Detrick 19cl, Angela Hampton 227t, J van Arkel/Foto Natura 151b, Nigel Cattlin 99l, 135t, 217 b, 223c, 237bl, Wayne Hutchinson 236l

Gap Photos: Amanda Darcy 62b, 112b, Andrea Jones 31tl, Brian North 222l, Clive Nichols 142t, Clive Nichols/Pettifers, Oxon 64, Elke Borkowski 37cr, 38tl, 243b, FhF Greenmedia 86bl, 93t,105bl, 129b, 137l, Friedrich Strauss 51b, 52t, 66bl, 76c, Geoff Kidd 221cl, Howard Rice 81b, 88l, J S Sira/Design: Conran 131cl, Janet Johnson 89t, 127r, 186b, Jerry Harpur 161, Jerry Harpur/Design: Stephen Anderton 44, John Glover 33c, 37cl, 83t, 149cr, 226r, 245, John Glover/Design: Barbara Hunt 30l, John Glover/Design: Marnie Hall 227b, Jonathan Buckley 41r, 203b, Jonathan Buckley/Design: Carol & Malcolm Skinner 92l, Jonathan Buckley/Design: Simon Hopkinson, Hollington Herb Nursery 249bc, Juliette Wade 136l, 144tl, 144cr, Leigh Clapp 113c, Leigh Clapp/Spurfold Garden, Surrey 147cr, M Howes 89b, 160r, 175cl, 187b, 195c, 230r, Mark Bolton 24t, 75t, 145t, Mark Bolton/Design: Kate Frey/RHS Chelsea Flower Show 2005 150br, Mark Bolton/Sir Michael & Lady Angus 127l, Paul Debois 58b, Rice/Buckland 40tl, 54c, 138r, 204l, Richard Bloom 88cr, Richard Bloom/Keith Lewis's Garden, Surrey 224, Richard Bloom/The Elisabeth C. Miller Botanical Garden, Seattle 176r, Sarah Cuttle 147b, Suzie Gibbons/Design: Kathy Taylor 246, Visions 235l, Zara Napier 108b, 239r

Photolibrary/Garden Picture Library: Alec Scaresbrook 49, 149tl, Anne Green Armytage 16cl, Bill Beatty 217t, Botanica 84bl, 113t, Christopher Gallager 114l, David Cavagnaro 118l, Eric Crichton/RHS Chelsea Flower Show 1994 17cl, Flora Press 48bl, Francois de Heel 129t, 151tr, Friedrich Strauss 41l, 48br, 60t, Georgia Glynn Smith 180t, Howard Rice 54bl, 115b, 139r, 143t, Jacqui Hurst 136r, James Guilliam 126r, Jane Legate 96l, 155cl, John Beedle 77r, John Glover/Design: Sarah Raven/RHS Chelsea Flower Show 1998 140, John Swithinbank 211cl, Juliette Wade 95b, 239l, Linda Burgess 49br, Lynne Brotchie 78, Mike

Howes 125, 131tr, Marie O'Hara 101b, 150t, Mark Bolton 164l, 248, Mark Bolton/Design: Stephen Hall/RHS Chelsea Flower Show 2005 156, Mark Winwood 165tr, 167, 178t, Mayer Le Scanff 115t, Rice/Buckland 210bl, Ron Evans 33t, Rosalind Wickham 61br, Steve Hamilton 105br, Susie Mccaffrey 137r, Zara McCalmont 39cl

Garden World Images: 7t, 22bl, A Graham 109r, Botanic Images Inc. 82bl, C Fairweather 166l, D Bevan 56t, 68t, F Davis 59l, 151cl, J Dracup 96c, 128r, 185tl, J Swithinbank 40b, 46bl, 82t, 124, L Cole 126l, 222r, M Fry 166cr, N Astley 114b, N Bell 145b, P Smith 146cl, T McGlinchey 47r, 49tr, 57b, 93b, 95cr, 142bl, 154l, 159l, 159b, 160l, 162r, 163l, 163r, 166tr, 170c, T Cooper 155t, T Sims 76b, 100r

istockphoto.com: Stacey McRae 82br

Mel Watson: 85

Modeste Herwig: 61t

Neil Soderstrom: 31cr, 43br, 73tr, 73cr, 77cl, 181r, 205t, 210t

Octopus Publishing Group Limited: Lee Beel 185bl & cr

Photoshot/Photos Horticultural: 61bl, 80t, 81t, 84cr, 119r, 134t, 179, 181b, M Howes 200

Science Photo Library: Brian Gadsby 184cl

Shutterstock: 75b, 202cl, 14, A & S Aakjaer 100l, Alan Egginton 175tr, Aleksandar-Pal Sakala 51t, Anna Dickie 52cl, Brandon Blinkenberg 182l, Chrislofoto 22br, 27t, Christina Richards 74r, 117tr, deetone 9, Eugene Bochkarev 54t, Fotosav 117b, Graca Victoria 22t, Ilya D Gridnev 66r, Jeff Banke 73l, Jeff Gynane 19tr, Jerry Horbert 250l, Joanna Zopoth-Liliejko 219tr, Kanwarjit Singh Boparai 202tl, Lars Magnin 2, Malle 15cl, 42l, Mark Bolton 63t, N Joy Neish 62t, Niserin 104l, Norma Cornes 34, Phil Morley 219cl, ppl 162l, Richard a McGuirk 105tr, rossco 10, Sally Wallis 120, Sharon D 17br, Sharon Kennedy 150bl, Sony Ho 26bl, Stephen Finn 101tl, Steve Lovegrove 112t, Steve Simzer 101tr, The Supe87 244, Thomas & Amelia Takacs 23cl, V J Matthew 32tr, Vasyl Helevachuk 211b, Vera Bogaerts 50l, 107, Zaporozhchenko Yury 74l

The Garden Collection: Andrew Lawson 251cr, Derek Harris 106r, Derek St Romaine 172, Gary Rogers/Design: Alex Daley & Alice Devaney. RHS Tatton Park 2005 165c, Jane Sebire 165b, Jonathan Buckley/Design: Alison Hoghton & David Chase 90, Jonathan Buckley/Design: Anthony Goff, Spencer Road, London 164cr, Jonathan Buckley/Design: C Lloyd, Great Dixter 33bl, Jonathan Buckley/Design: Roger Oates 212, Jonathan Buckley/Design: Stephen Firth & Brinsbury Students 26tl, Liz Eddison 19br, 96br, 158r, Liz Eddison/Design: C Beardshaw/RHS Chelsea Flower Show 2002 153, Liz Eddison/Design: Kate Rayner, RHS Tatton Park 2001 12, Liz Eddison/Design: Kay Yamada/RHS Chelsea Flower Show 2003 247t, Liz Eddison/Design: Luc Larmor/International Festival of Gardens, Chaumont-Sur-Loire 2005 251tr, Liz Eddison/Design: Thomas Hoblyn/RHS Tatton Park Show 2006 170t, Marie O'Hara 154cr, 174cl, Nicola Stocken Tomkins 35, 119b, 178b, 250r, 251bl, Torie Chugg/Design: Sue Hitchens 59r

Thompson & Morgan: 135br

Torie Chugg: 86r, 174r, 176l, 182br, 183l, 184r, 186t

Author acknowledgments:

Pippa Greenwood would like to thank Chris and his staff at Hilliers Garden Centre, Liss, where many of the photographs were taken, all at Mitchell Beazley for their wide-ranging input, and her family and friends for their inspiration, patience, and props borrowed.